DIE WEHRMACHT IM KAMPF

ARCTIC FRONT

The Advance of Mountain Corps Norway on Murmansk, 1941

WILHELM HESS

Translated by
LINDEN LYONS

Series editor:
MATTHIAS STROHN

CASEMATE
Pennsylvania & Yorkshire

AN AUSA BOOK
Association of the United States Army
2425 Wilson Boulevard, Arlington, Virginia, 22201, USA

This edition first published in the United States of America and Great Britain in 2021
Reprinted as a paperback in 2025 by
CASEMATE PUBLISHERS
1950 Lawrence Road, Havertown, PA 19083, USA
and
47 Church Street, Barnsley, S70 2AS, UK

Originally published as Die Wehrmacht im Kampf 9: Wilhelm Hess, *Eismeerfront 1941: Aufmarsch und Kämpfe des Gebirgskorps Norwegen in den Tundren vor Murmansk* (Heidelberg, 1956: Scharnhorst Buchkameradschaft)

Paperback Edition: ISBN 978-1-63624-529-4
Digital Edition: ISBN 978-1-61200-973-5

A CIP record for this book is available from the British Library

Printed and bound in the United Kingdom by CPI Group (UK) Ltd, Croydon, CR0 4YY
Typeset by Versatile PreMedia Service (P) Ltd

For a complete list of Casemate titles, please contact:

CASEMATE PUBLISHERS (US)
Telephone (610) 853-9131
Fax (610) 853-9146
Email: casemate@casematepublishers.com
www.casematepublishers.com

CASEMATE PUBLISHERS (UK)
Telephone (0)1226 734350
Email: casemate@casemateuk.com
www.casemateuk.com

Front cover: German soldiers in winter camouflage suits with sub-machine guns, 1943. (Bundesarchiv, Bild_101I-103-0943-13)

The Publisher's authorised representative in the EU for product safety is Authorised Rep Compliance Ltd., Ground Floor, 71 Lower Baggot Street, Dublin D02 P593, Ireland.
http://www.arccompliance.com

Contents

Foreword

The common view of the German invasion of the Soviet Union in the summer of 1941 is based on the operations of mechanised units and formations which cut through the Soviet forces and occupied vast areas of territory, inflicting heavy casualties on the enemy. And yet, this is not the whole story of Operation *Barbarossa*. German troops had occupied Norway in 1940 and Finland had had to cede territories to the Soviet Union as a consequence of the 'Winter War' of 1939/40. Naturally, the Finns were eager to reclaim the lost territories and decided to join the Germans in the war against the Soviet Union. This opened the northern flank for operations against Soviet troops. From a German perspective, the main aim of the operation was to seize the harbour of Murmansk, which remained ice-free even in winter. From the start, the invasion ran into problems: difficult terrain, logistical issues and fierce Soviet resistance meant that the offensive stalled and that the operational objective, Murmansk, could not be seized by the attacking forces. This would have consequences for the rest of the war, as the western allies were able to send material and equipment to the Soviets via this port, which, arguably, kept the Soviet Union in the war. Despite the strategic importance that the failed offensive had, this part of Operation *Barbarossa* is often overlooked and it is good that we now have the translation of an account of this operation.

Wilhelm Hess was particularly well suited to write this account, which was originally published in German in 1956. As a Bavarian and a member of the German mountain troops it was logical that he would get posted to Norway, and he spent the majority of World War II fighting in Norway and on the northern part of the Eastern Front. He was the quartermaster of Mountain Corps Norway in 1941 and the senior quartermaster of the Twentieth Mountain Army in Lapland from 1942 until 1944. He spent the years 1945 to 1948 as a British prisoner of war and joined the new West-German Army, the Bundeswehr, in 1956. He retired with the rank of major-general in 1968. His background in logistics means that his account deals in detail with the essential, but little loved, issues of supply and equipment. His writing clearly conveys the logistical issues that the troops were facing in the northern sector, and Hess thus re-emphasises the general perception of the Wehrmacht, which might have been tactically brilliant, but whose operations were constantly being hampered by insufficient re-supply. The book is, naturally, a product of its time, but it is interesting to read how frank and open Hess is in his assessment of the problems that the German troops were facing, and throughout the book Hess pays respect to the fighting spirit of the Soviet soldier.

Hess produced a highly readable and insightful account of the fighting at the northern flank of the cataclysmic struggle between Nazi Germany and the Soviet Union in 1941, and it sheds light on an often overlooked episode of Operation *Barbarossa*.

Prof. Matthias Strohn, M.St., FRHistS
Head of Historical Analysis,
Centre for Historical Analysis and Conflict Research, Camberley
Visiting Professor of Military Studies,
University of Buckingham

Introduction

For a period of five years, German troops from all branches of the Wehrmacht fought side by side with the Finnish border guard units on the Arctic Front. It was the first time in history that military operations were conducted by large formations along the northern coast of Scandinavia. A modern army suddenly swept into an isolated and by nature inhospitable region that did not yet possess the level of importance it would assume in present-day polar strategy.

The high point of the war on the Arctic Front was the assembly and advance of Mountain Corps Norway in the summer and autumn of 1941. Commanded by General of Mountain Troops Eduard Dietl, this formation would later become the XIX Mountain Corps. It did not reach its objective. It is intended that this book will be of value from the point of view of military science by describing and analysing the environment, the sequence of events, and the reasons for certain decisions that were made. The account here is based on the available documents, personal records, and currently available literature. The author was the quartermaster of Mountain Corps Norway in 1941 and the senior quartermaster of the Twentieth Mountain Army from 1942 until 1944 and is therefore able to draw upon his personal experience of the conditions and actions on the Arctic Front. Special thanks must be given to Captain (ret.) Alfred Schulze-Hinrichs for his account of the operations of the 6th Destroyer Flotilla.

Wilhelm Hess
Munich, 1956

Translation of Place Names

Included in this list are only those place names where the German and English differ considerably.

German	*English*
Eismeerstraße	Arctic Ocean Highway
Fischerhalbinsel	Rybachy Peninsula
Herzsee	Heart Lake
Kap Pikschujew	Cape Pikshuyev
Knyrk-Järvi	Knyrk Lake
Knyrk-Järvi-Lubol	Knyrk-Lubol Lake
Kolafjord	Kola Bay
Landebucht	Landing Bay
Langer See	Long Lake
Lopatkinapfad	Lopatkina Trail
Neuer Weg	New Road
Runder See	Round Lake
Simnaja Motowka	Zimnyaya Motovka
Stromschnellenhöhe	White Water Hill
der Syväri	Svir River
Tschaprsee	Lake Chapr
Uraweg	Ura Road
Vuollejärvi	Vuolle Lake

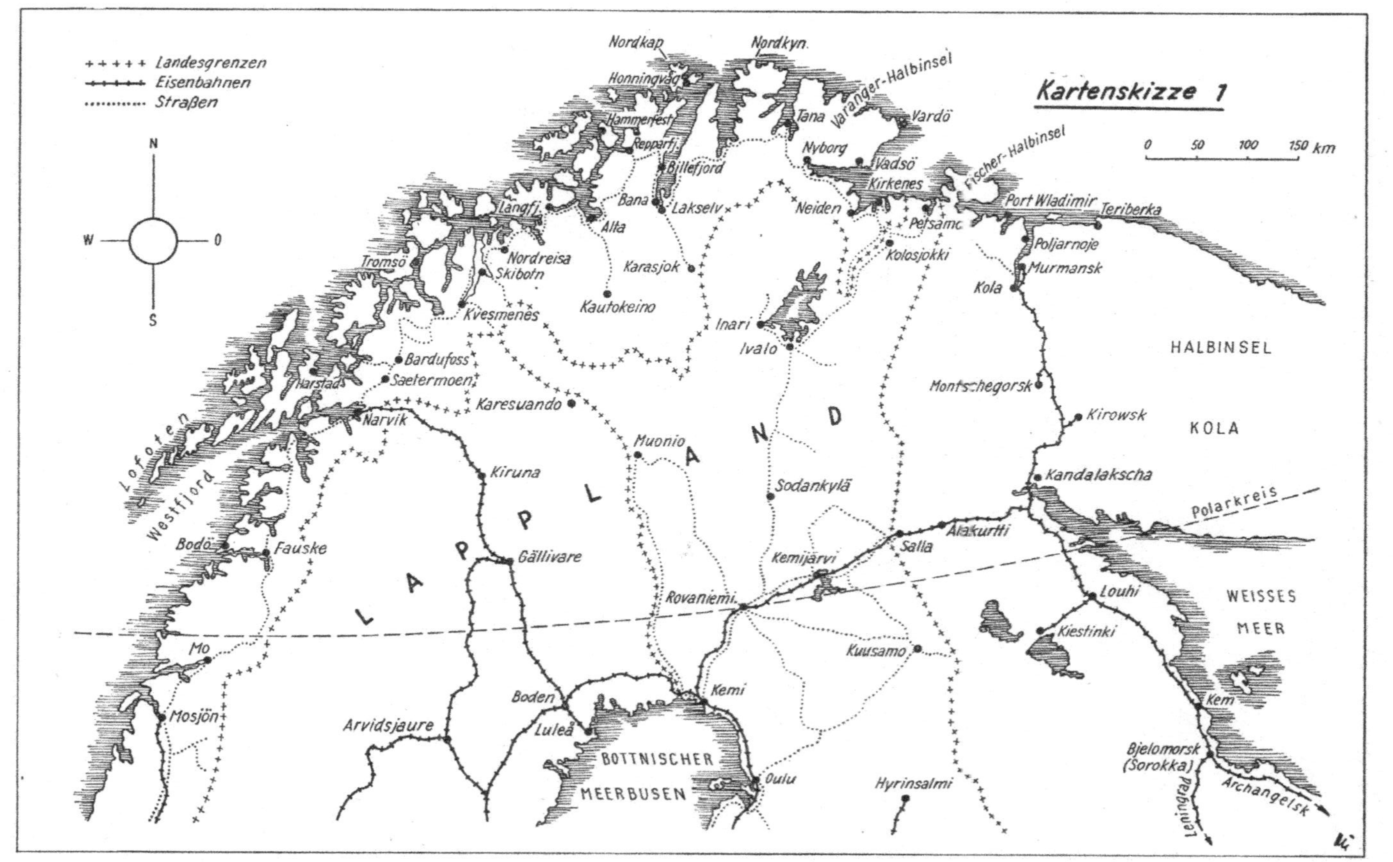

Map 1: Northern Fennoscandia

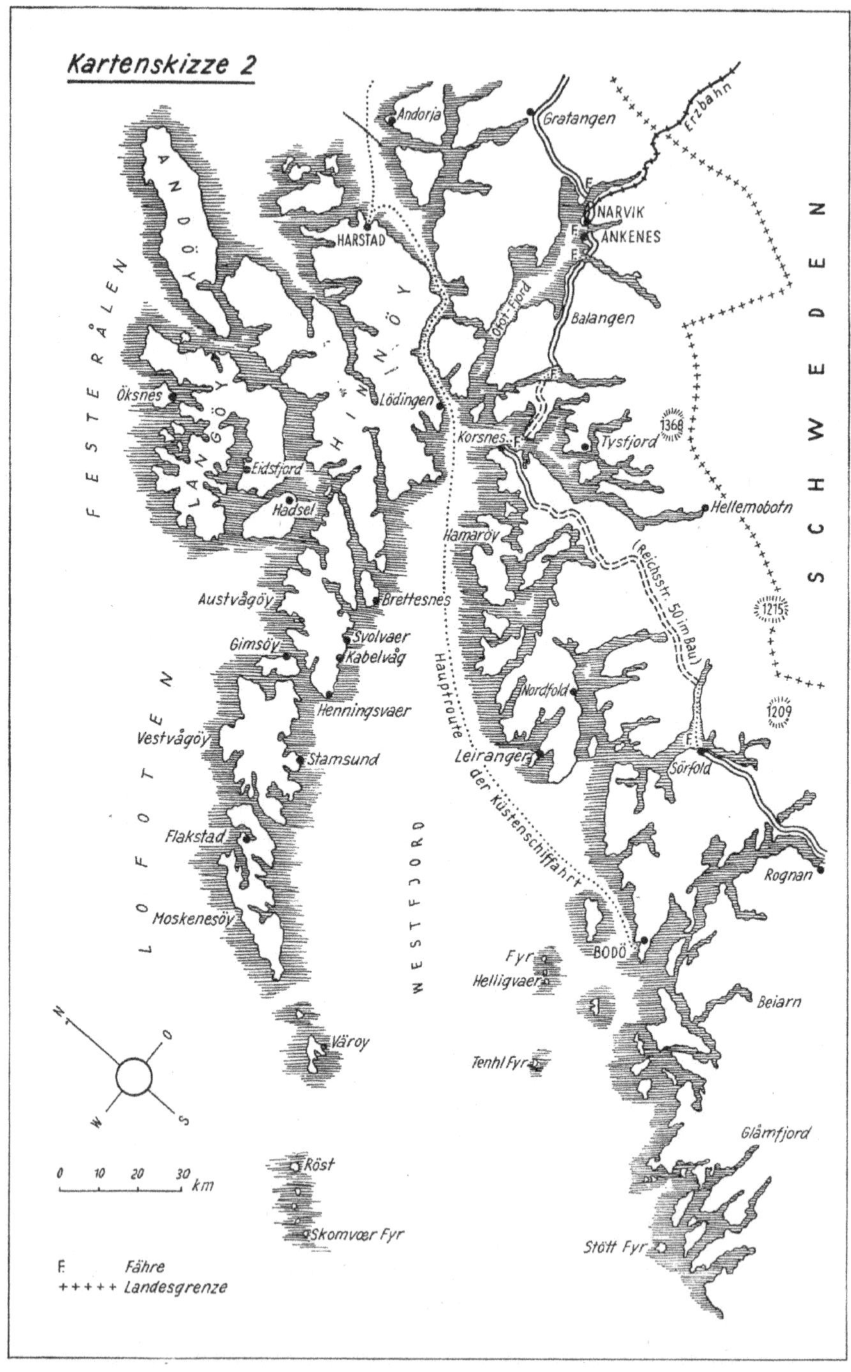

Map 2: The Norwegian coast near and to the south of Narvik

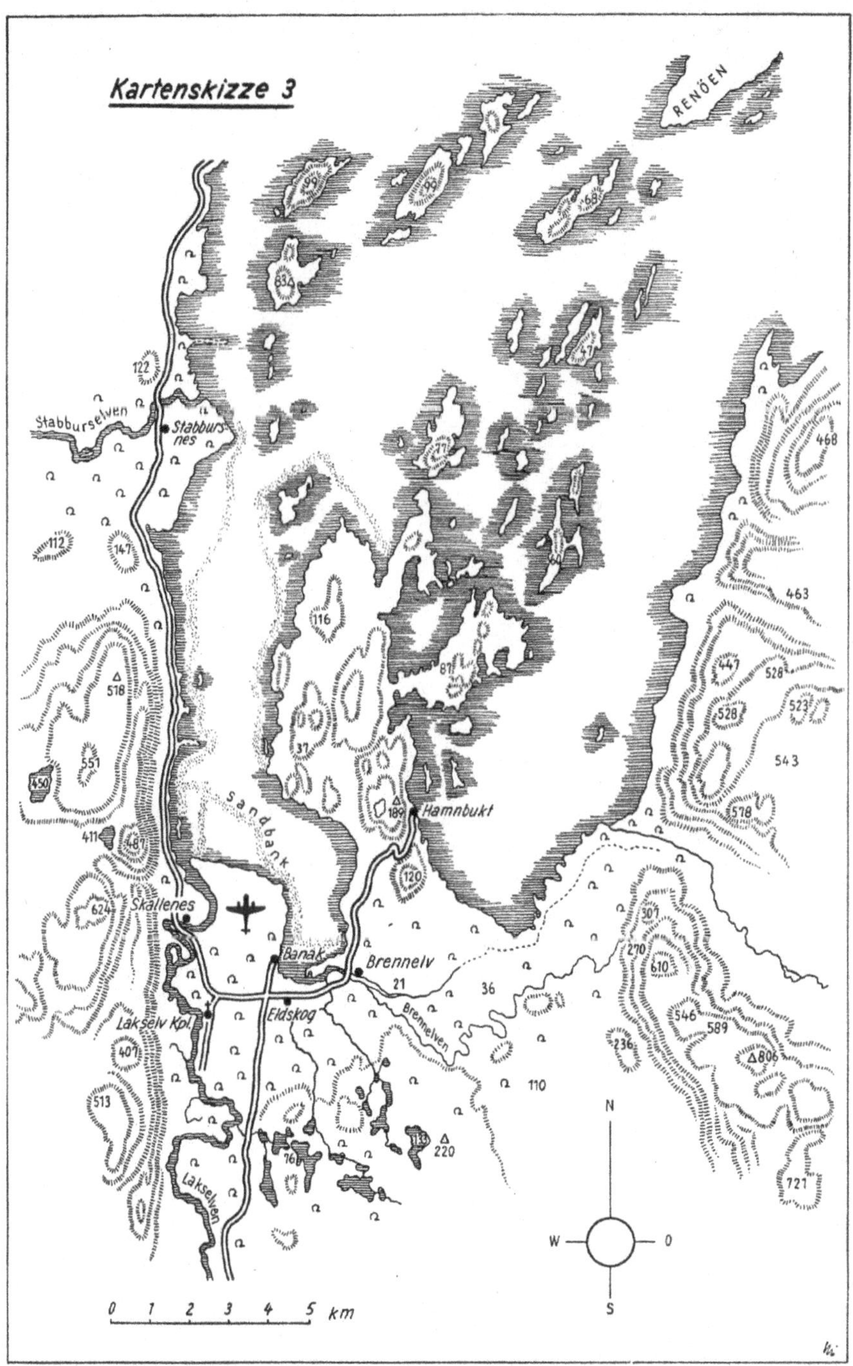

Map 3: Banak Airfield and the surrounding terrain

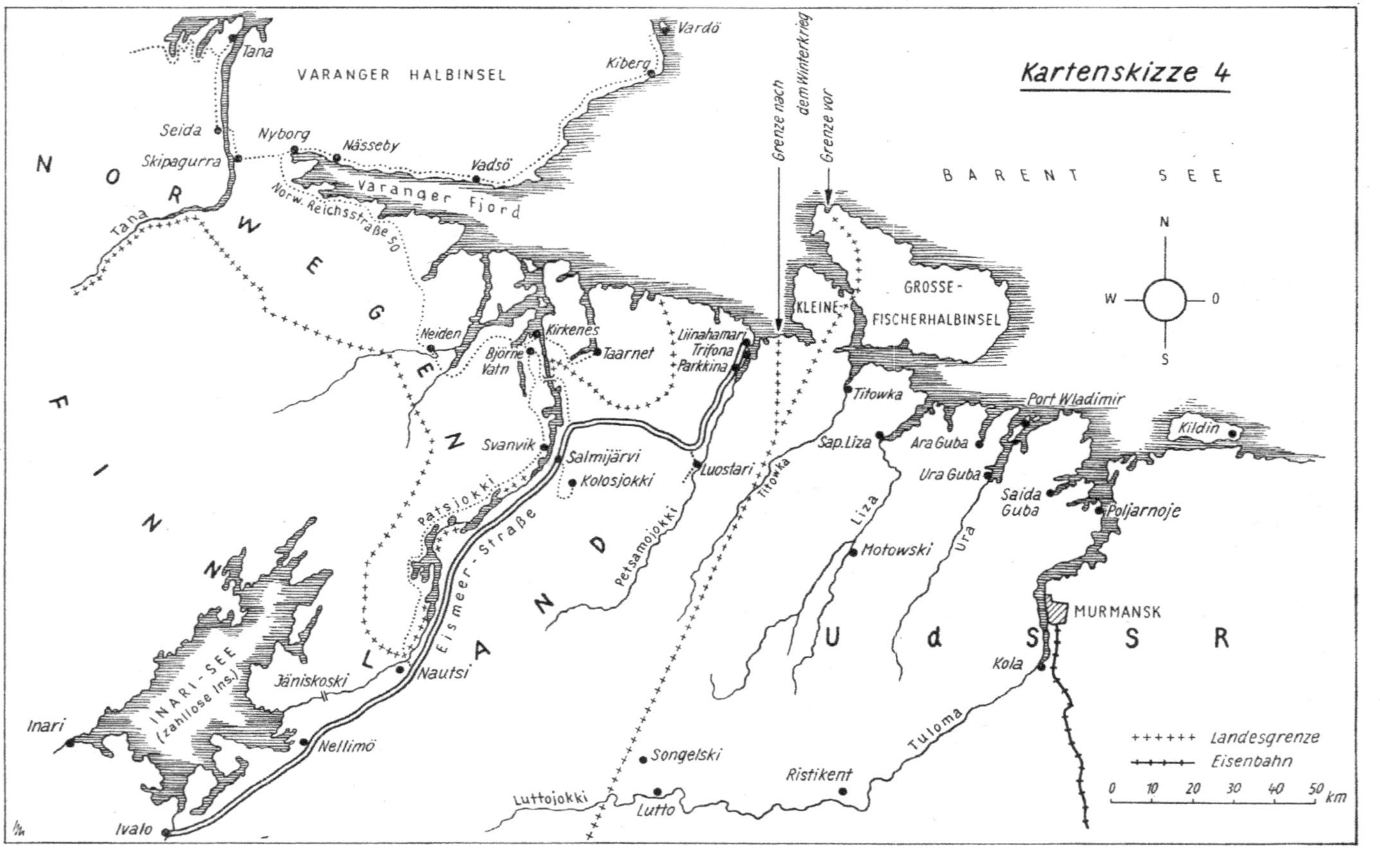

Map 4: The area of operations of Mountain Corps Norway

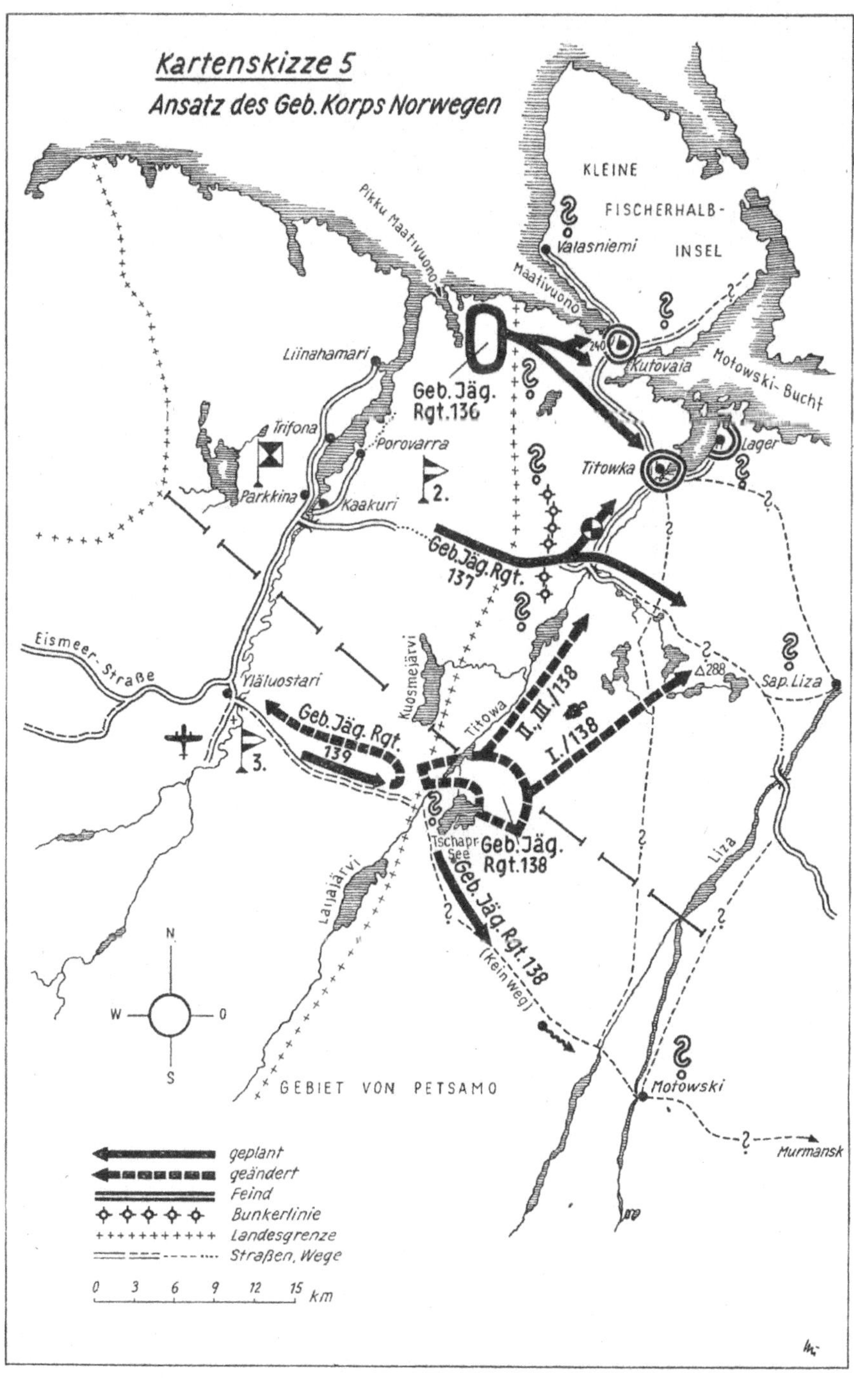

Map 5: The planned and actual advance of Mountain Corps Norway

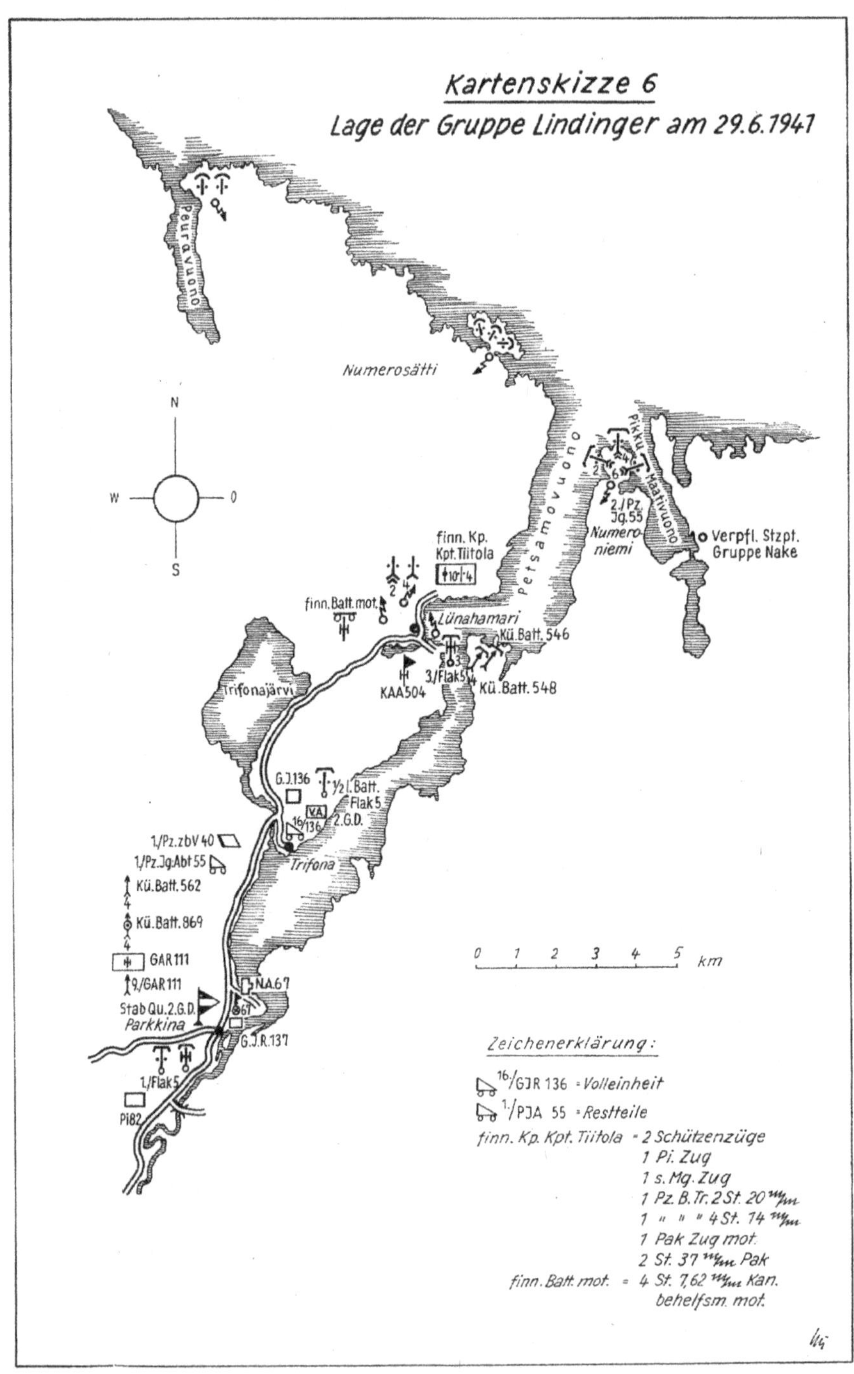

Map 6: Positions of Group Lindinger on 29 June 1941

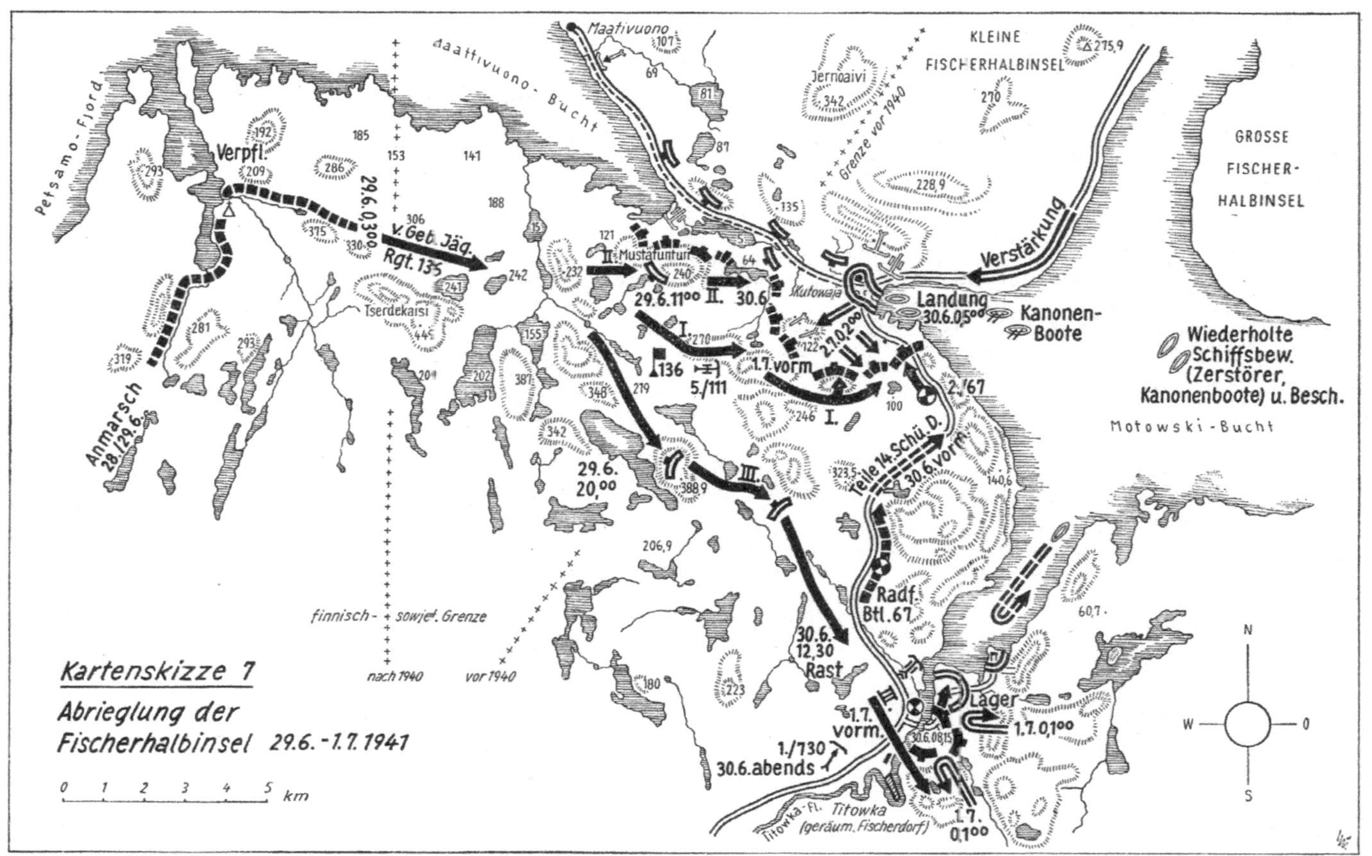

Map 7: The isolation of Rybachy Peninsula, 29 June–1 July 1941

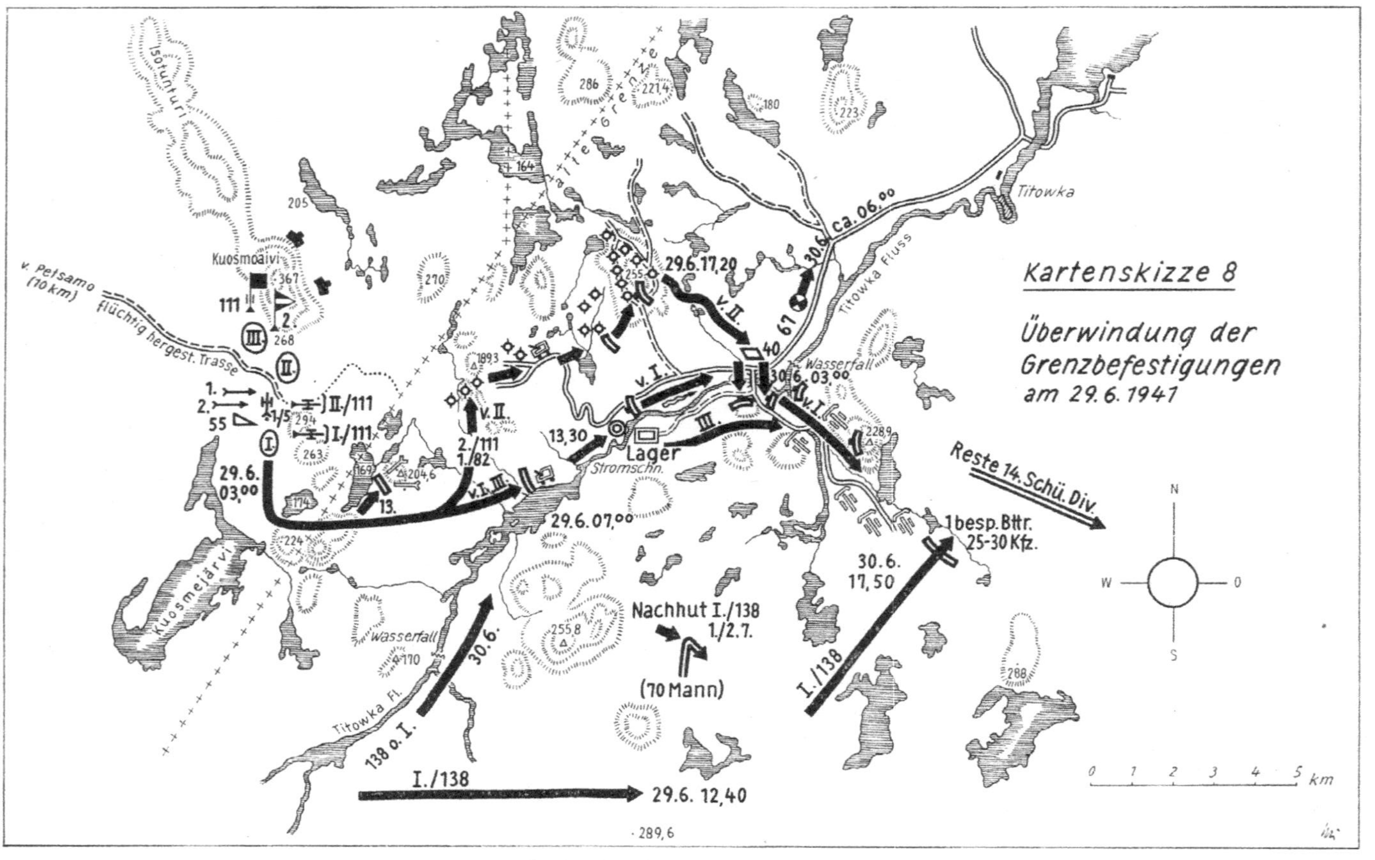

Map 8: Overcoming the border fortifications on 29 June 1941

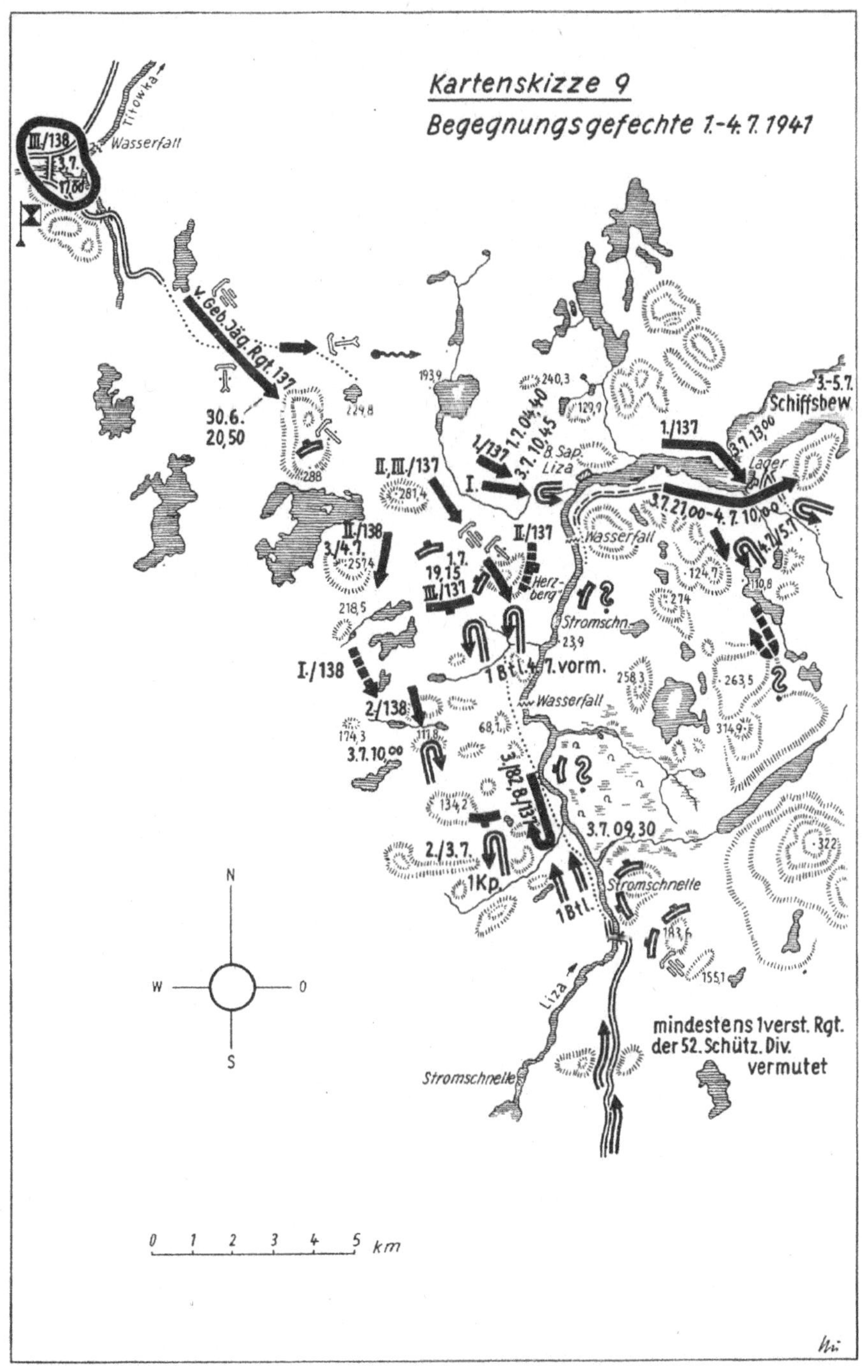

Map 9: Meeting engagements, 1–4 July 1941

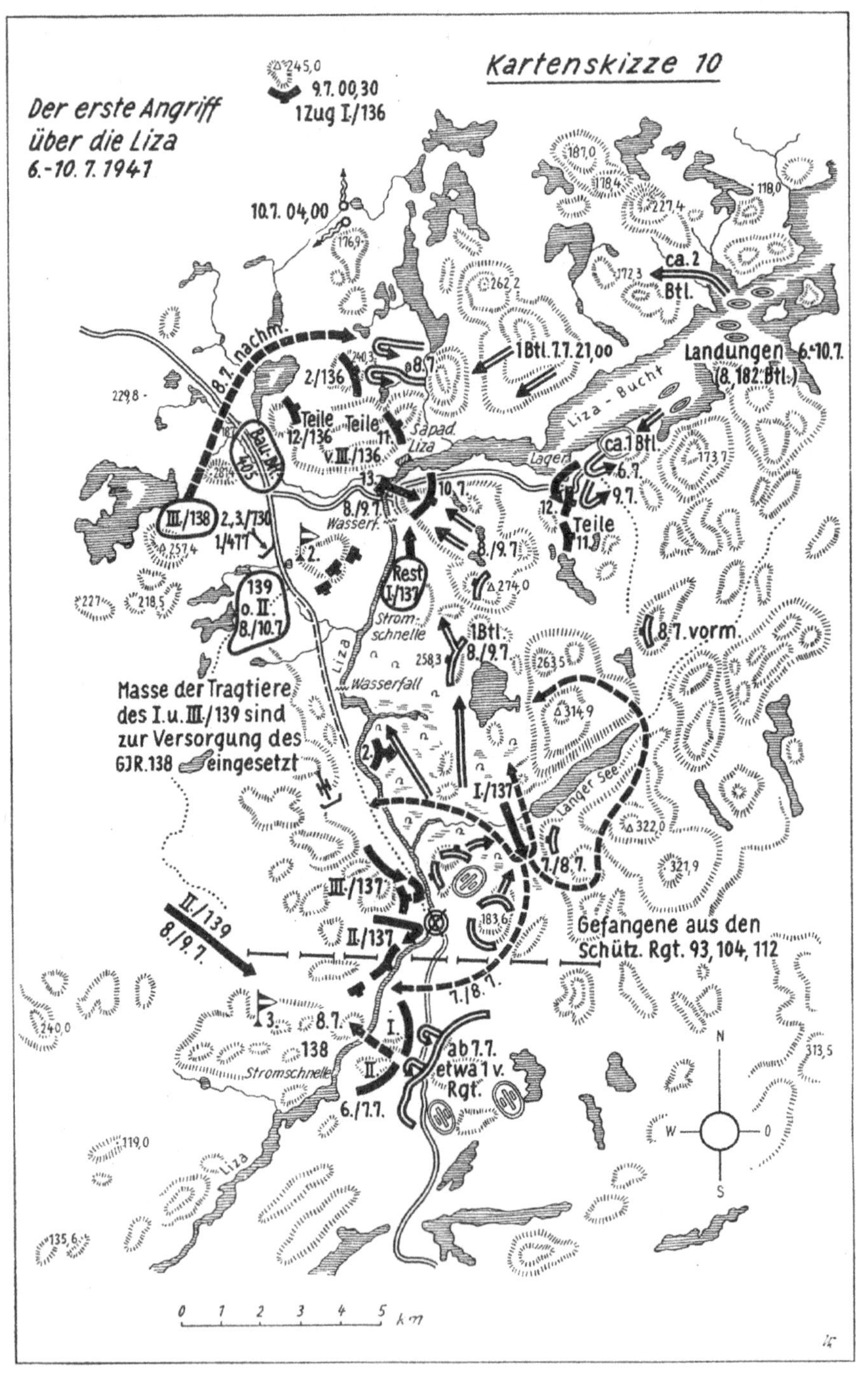

Map 10: The first attack across the Litsa, 6–10 July 1941

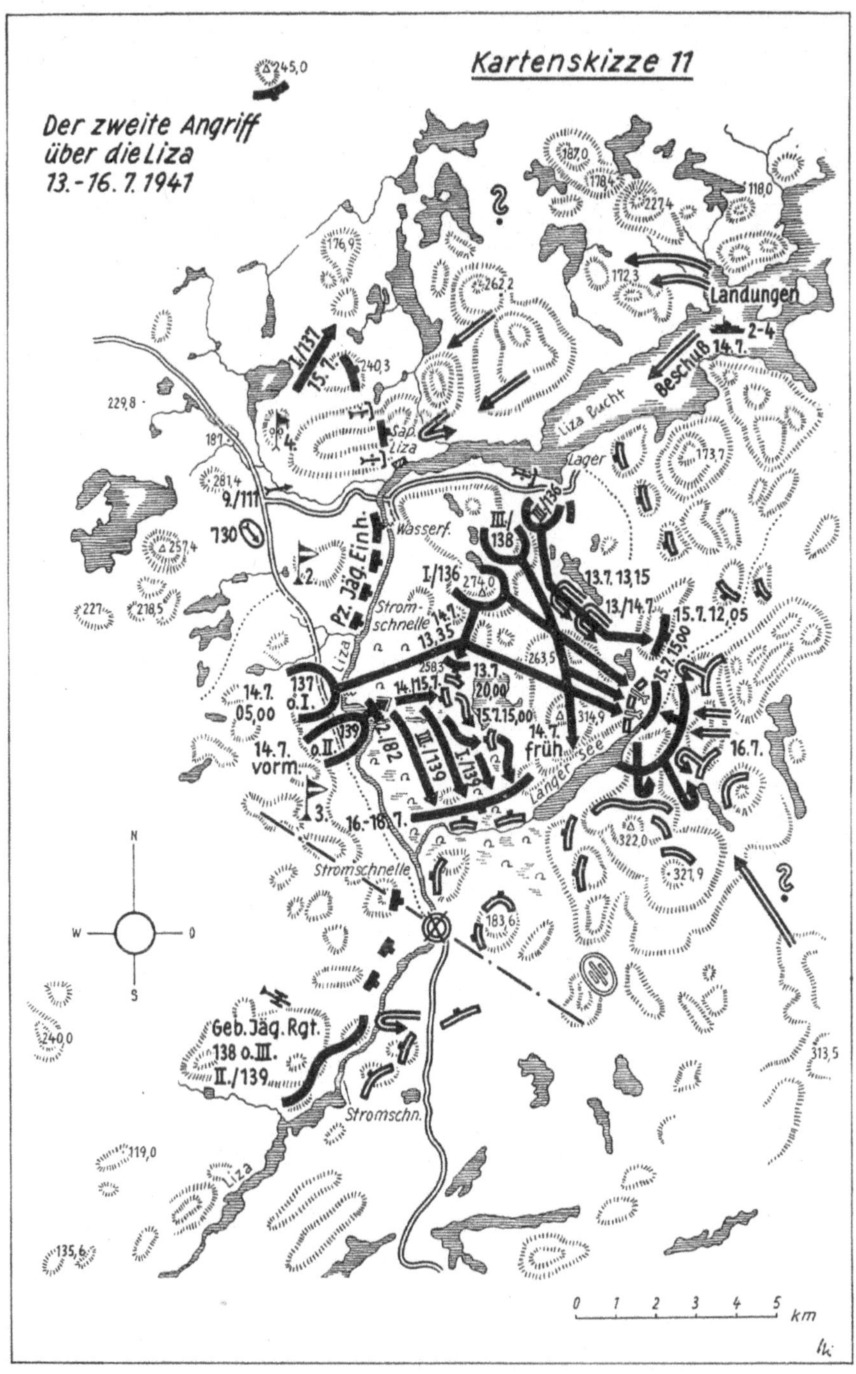

Map 11: The second attack across the Litsa, 13–16 July 1941

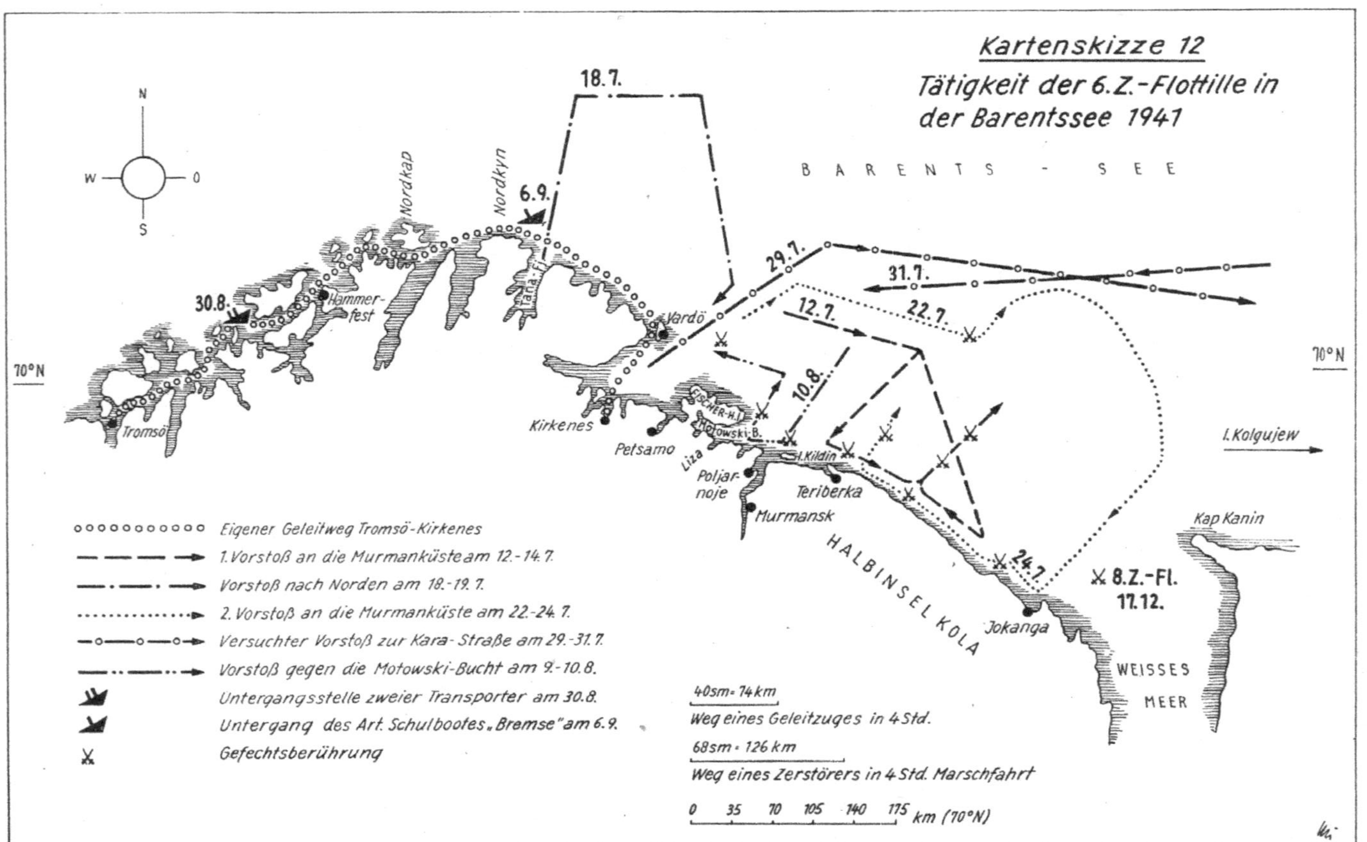

Map 12: Operations of the 6th Destroyer Flotilla in the Barents Sea, 1941

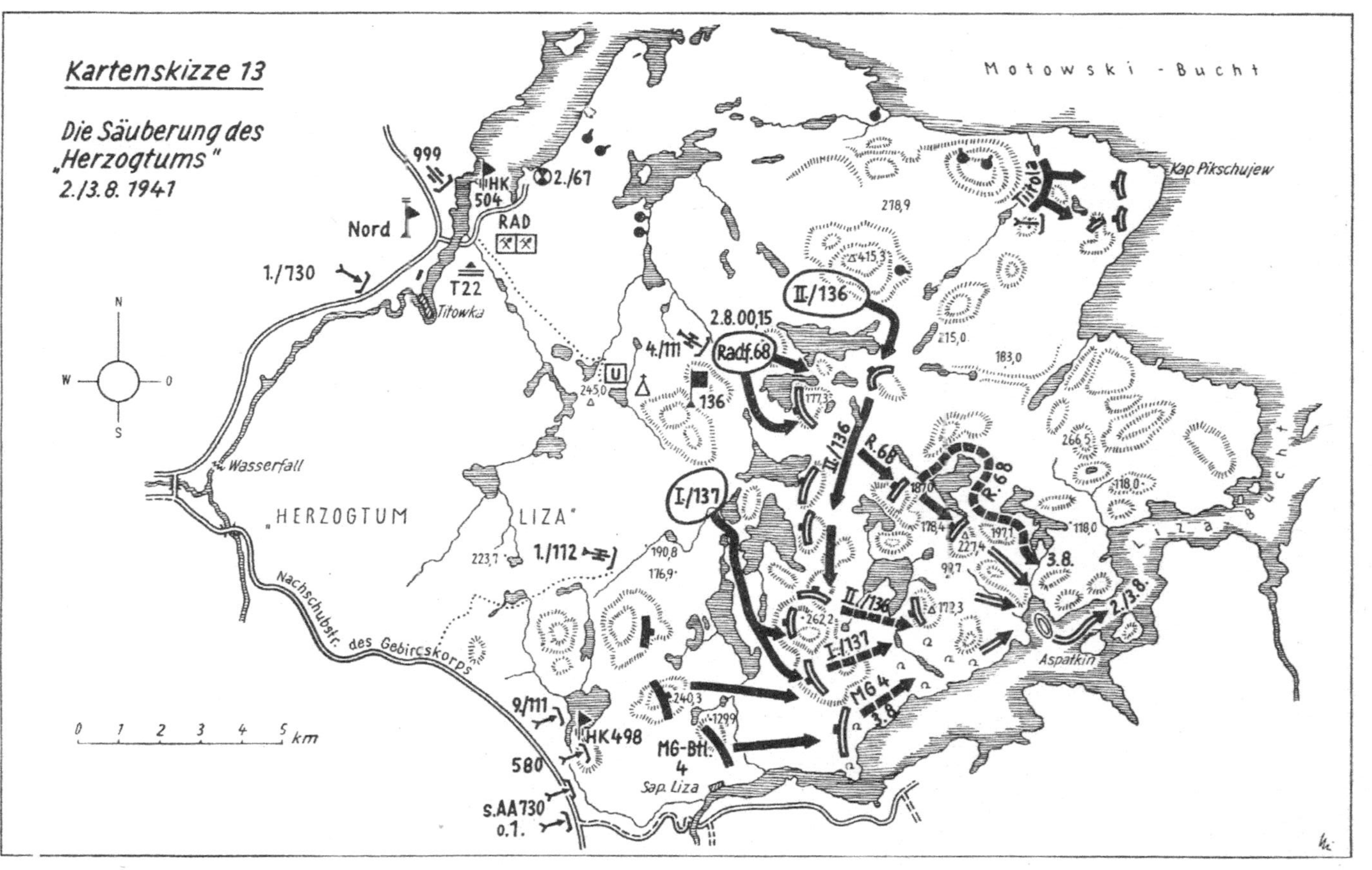

Map 13: Mopping up the 'Duchy of Litsa', 2–3 August 1941

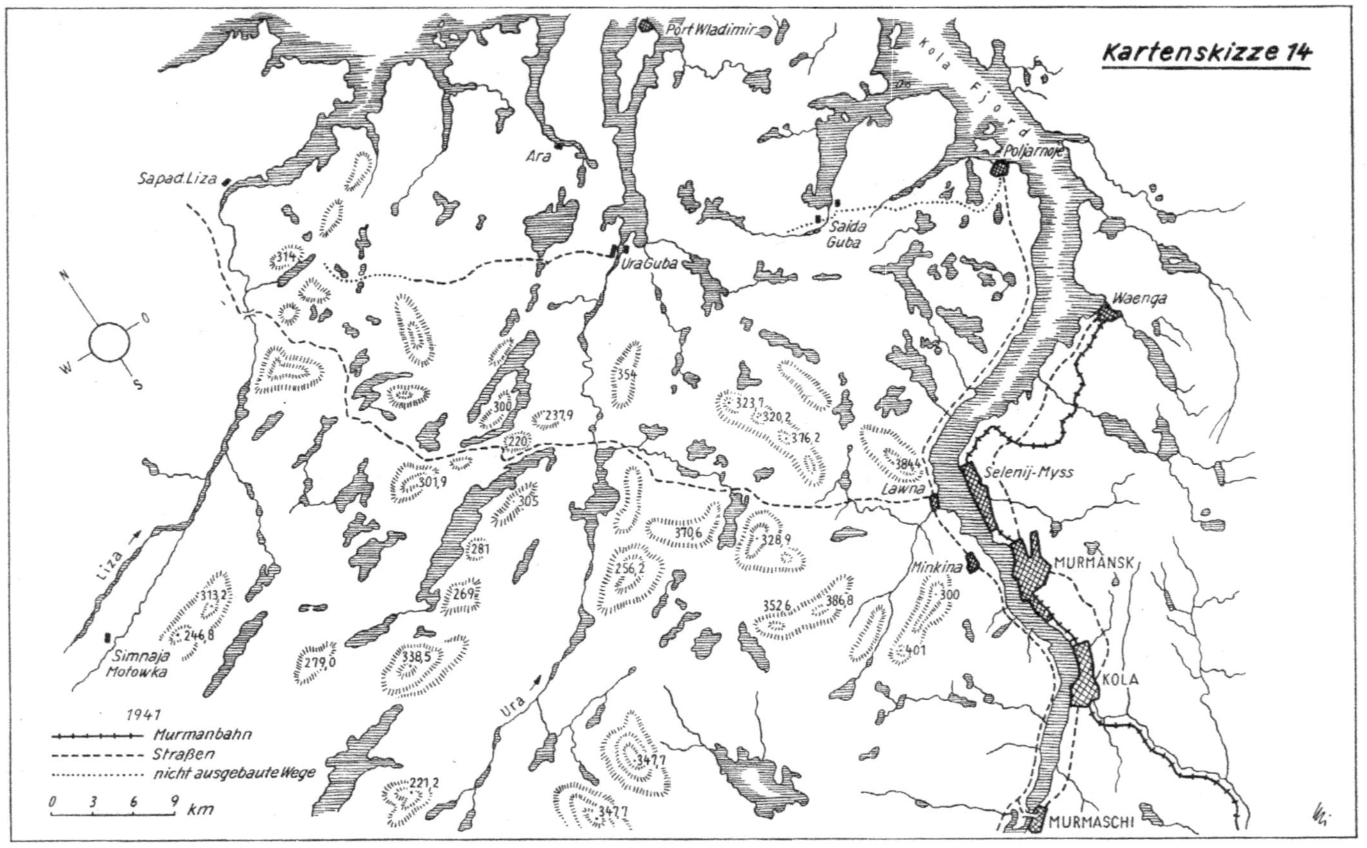

Map 14: The terrain leading towards Murmansk

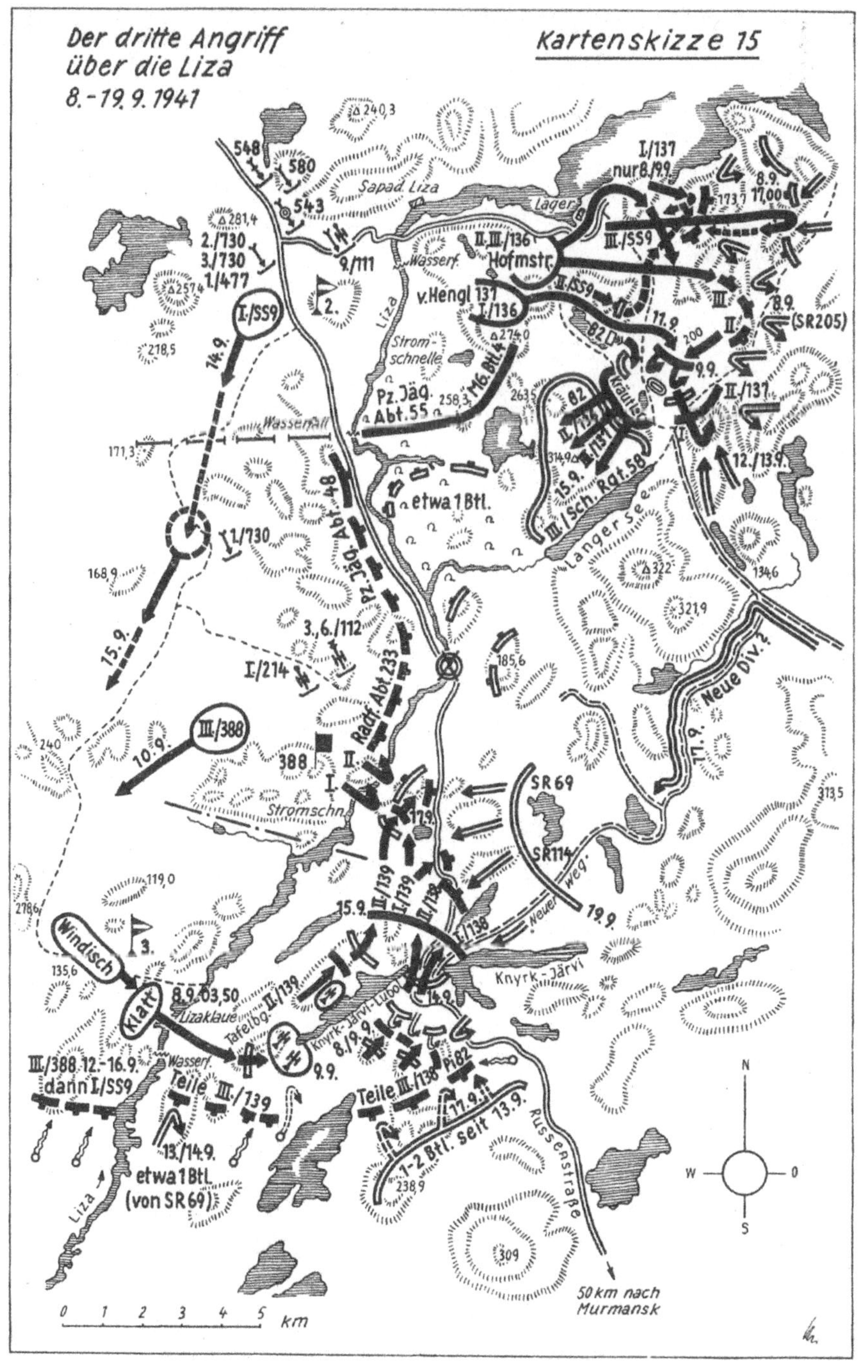

Map 15: The third attack across the Litsa, 8–19 September 1941

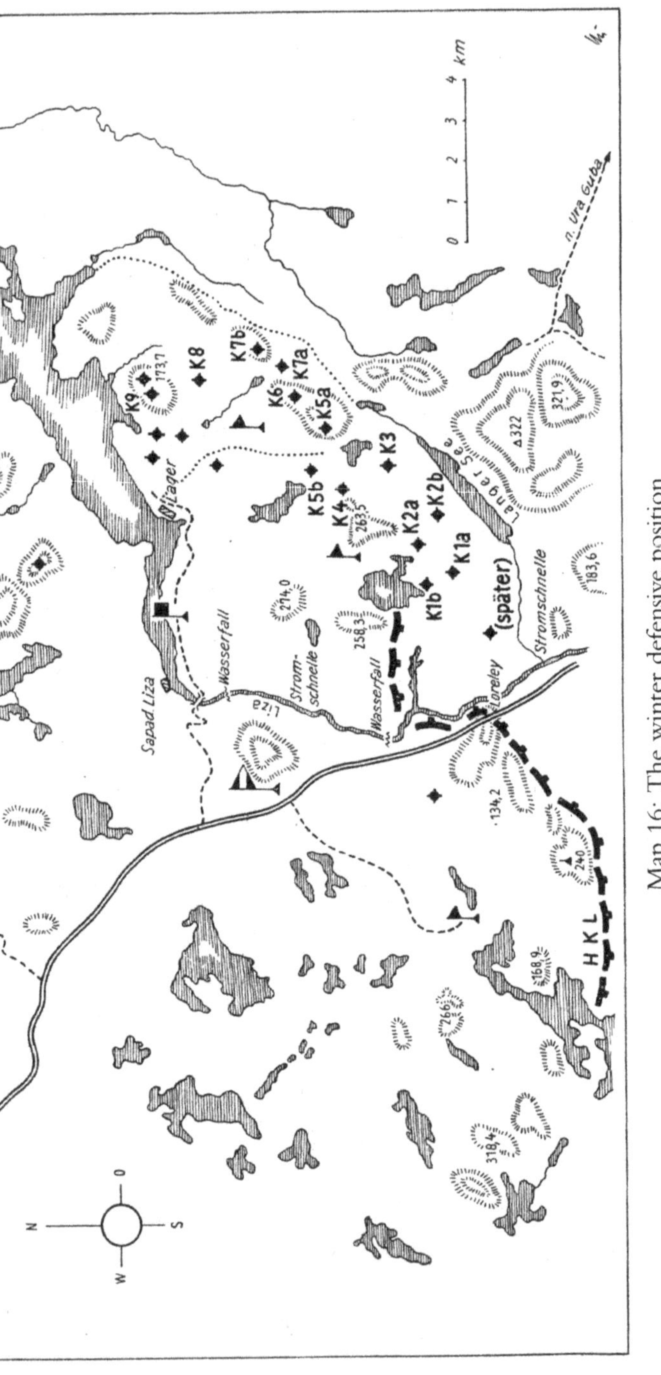

Map 16: The winter defensive position

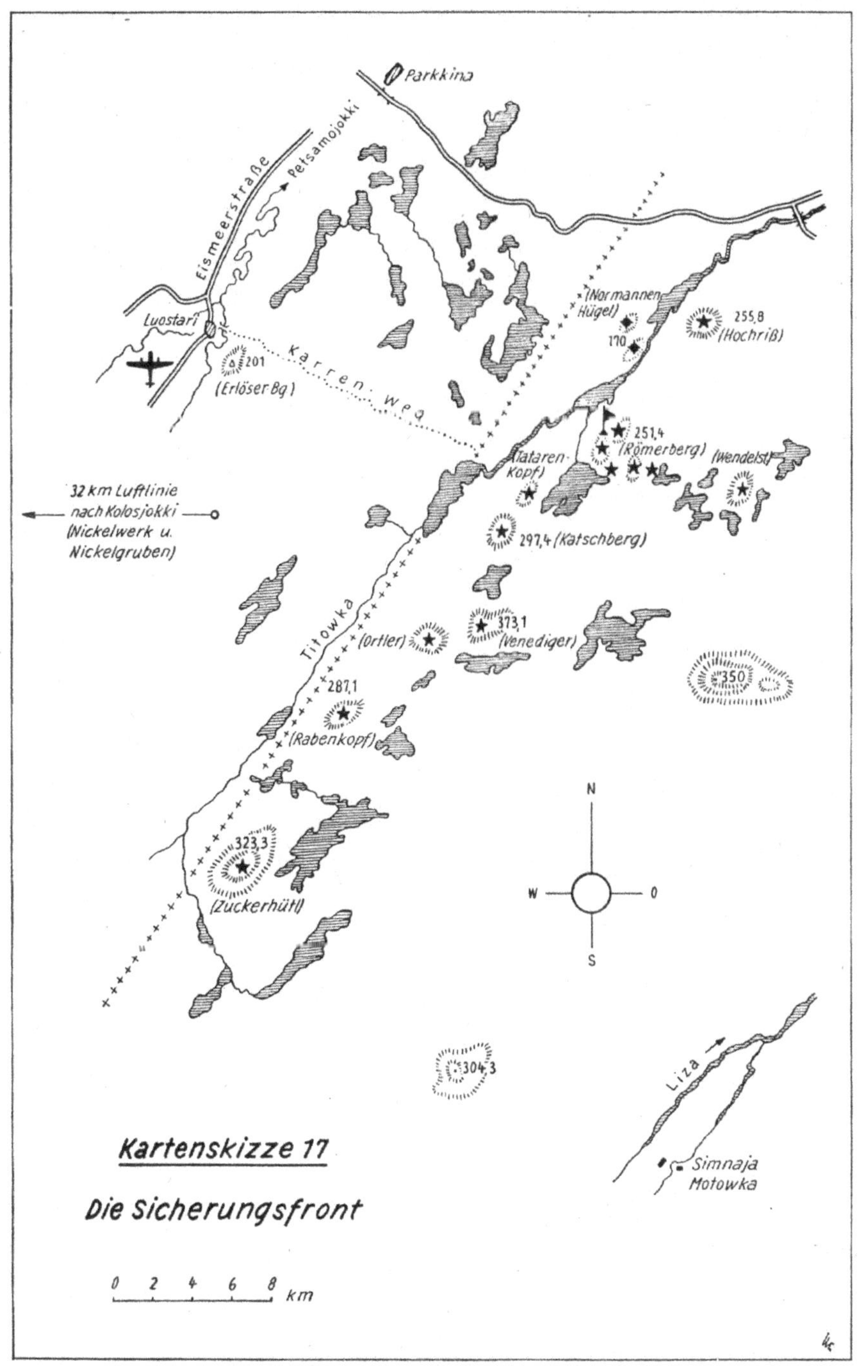

Map 17: The line of security

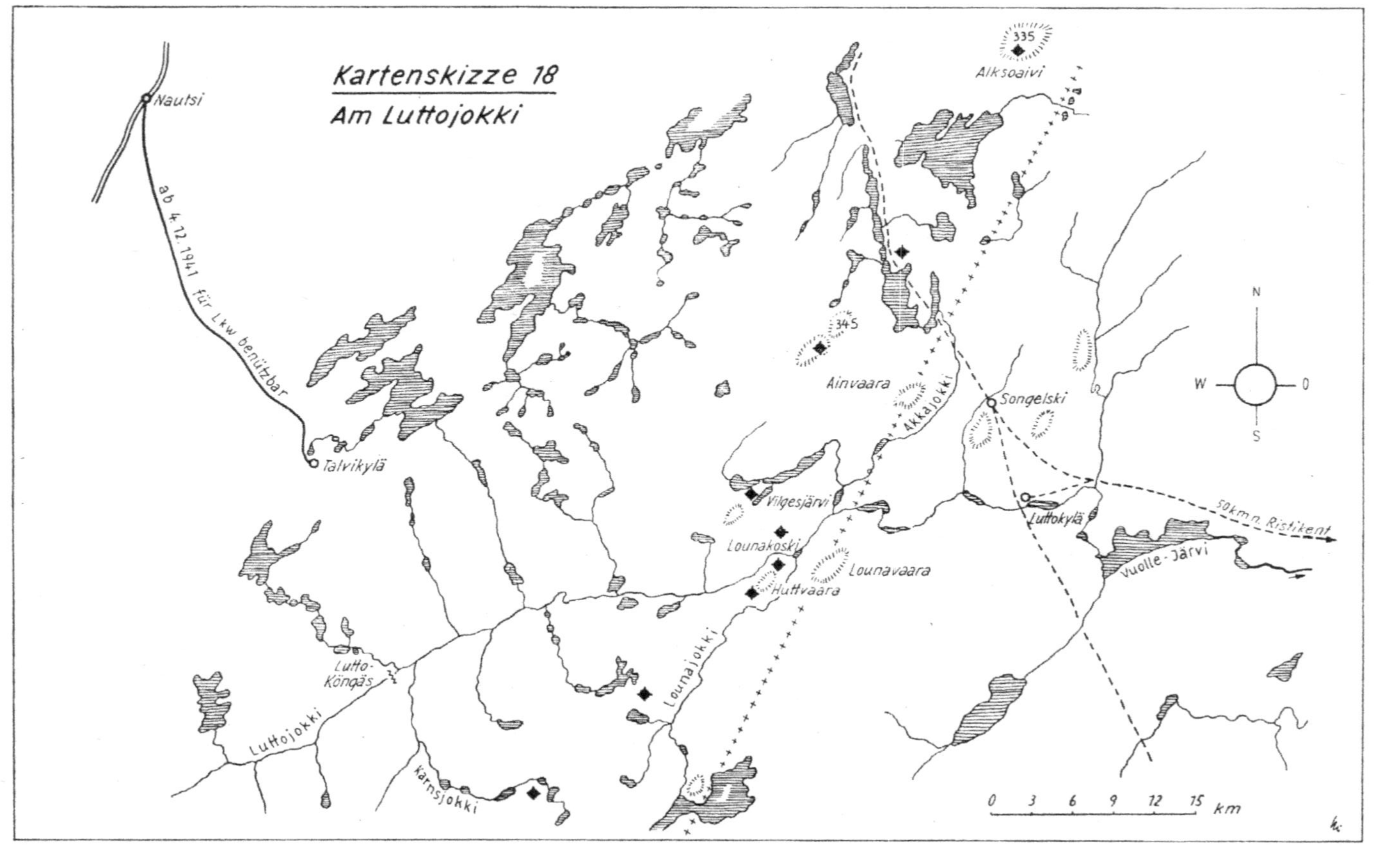

Map 18: On the Luttojoki River

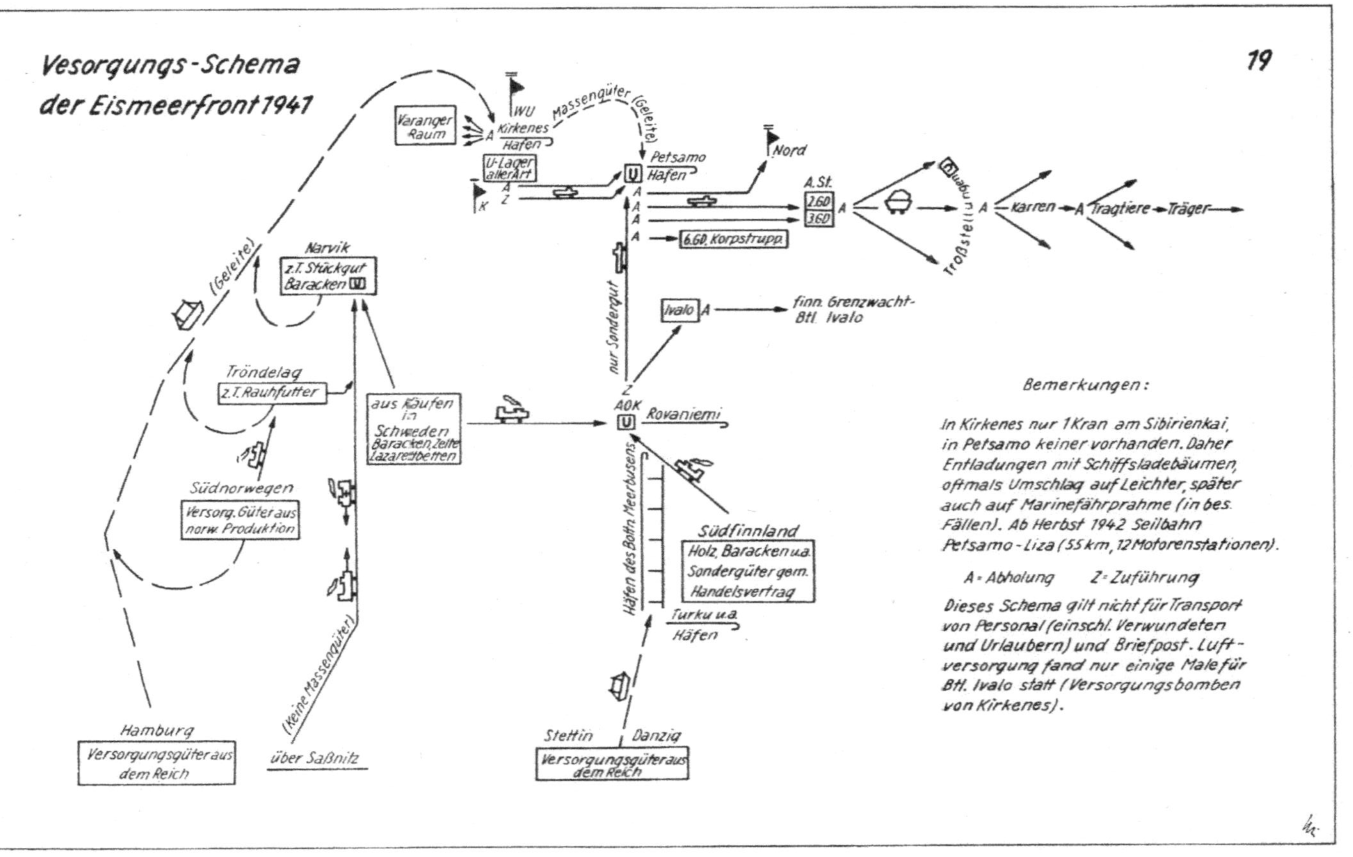

Map 19: The supply of German forces on the Arctic Front, 1941

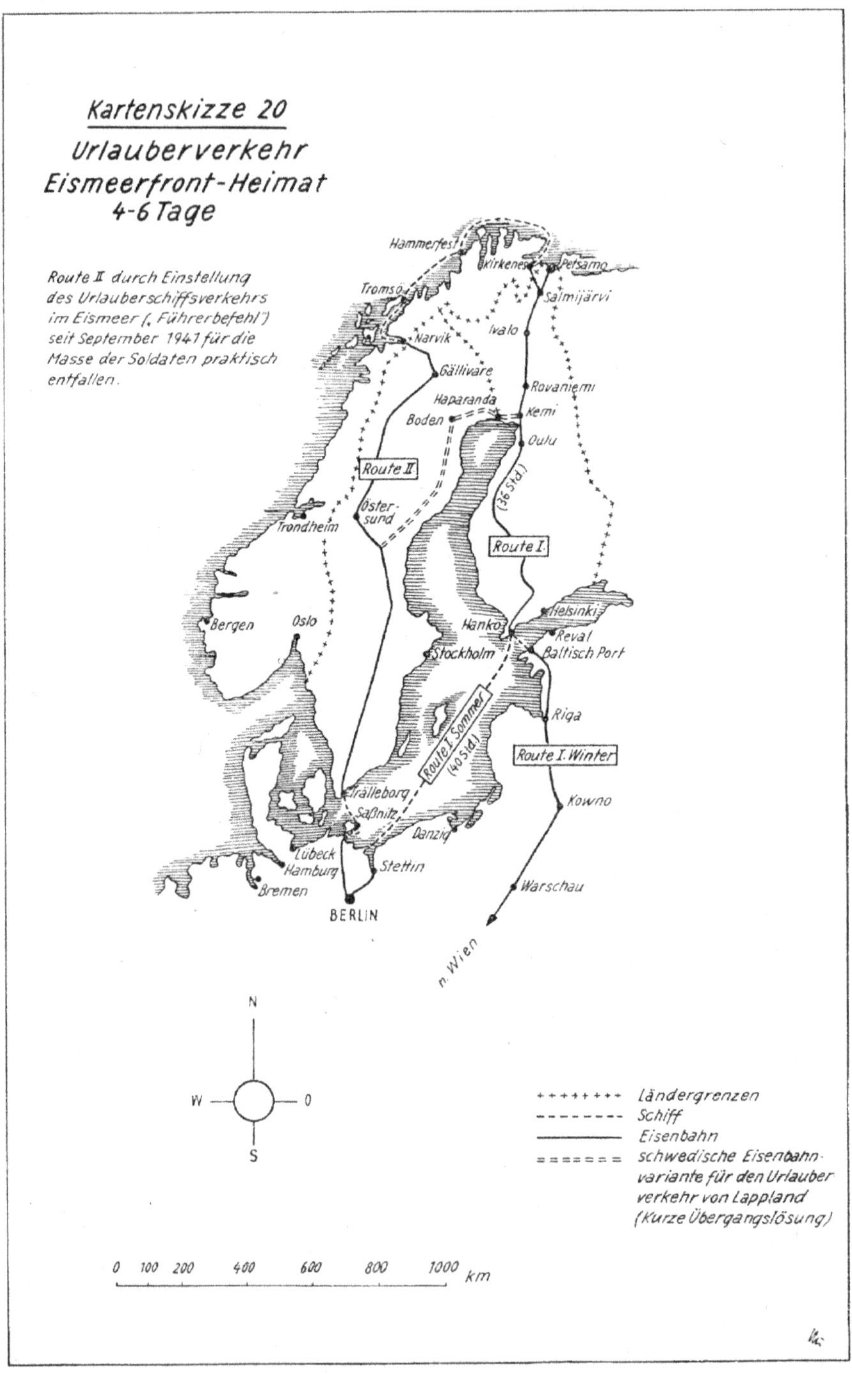

Map 20: Furlough traffic between the Arctic Front and the Fatherland (4–6 days)

CHAPTER I

Mountain Corps Norway

Map 1

The guns had fallen silent in Norway on 10 June 1940. The German leadership did what had to be done in the wake of such a campaign: units were reorganised, our achievements were made secure, our experiences were evaluated, and preparations were made for future tasks.

Group XXI had only been a reinforced army corps made up of the divisions that had taken part in the Norwegian campaign. In order to secure the large area and to stabilise the situation, it had become necessary to divide the units between two new army corps. One of these would be Mountain Corps Norway, created by grouping together the 2nd and 3rd Mountain Divisions. With the 181st Infantry Division of Major-General Woytasch also temporarily under its command, Mountain Corps Norway would be responsible for the defence of the land between the 62nd and 71st parallel north. Covering the provinces South Trøndelag, North Trøndelag, Nordland, Troms, and West Finnmark, this was a stretch of approximately 1,400 kilometres if measured along the axial Norwegian National Road 50. The need to establish a new corps coincided with the desire to give Lieutenant-General Eduard Dietl, who had proven himself in Narvik, a more important role. He was therefore entrusted with the command of this corps, which was formally established on 15 June 1940 with its headquarters in Trondheim.

There was good fortune in the composition of the headquarters of the mountain corps in terms of personnel. The commander of the mountain corps would have alongside him his old friend and company officer, Lieutenant-Colonel on the General Staff von Le Suire. This was an ideal pairing, and there would be several other staff officers from the mountain troops who had shown themselves capable in peace or in war. The number of comrades from other associations was not low; they all possessed a level of commitment and unity of vision that reflected the cream of the officer corps. Dietl's strong and engaging personality left its mark on the spirit of his men from the moment he met them.[1]

As a first step for the formation of the corps troops, the 463rd Corps Signal Battalion was transferred from the former Group XXI, now Army Norway, to Mountain Corps Norway, while the staff of the 477th Corps Supply Service with a number of columns and a supply train were put under the command of the corps. Two half batteries, equipped with captured Norwegian matériel, were combined and designated the 1st and 2nd Batteries of the 477th Artillery Regiment, although they were soon simply designated the 1st Battery of the 477th Heavy Artillery Battalion. The 477th Map Reproduction Office, the 477th Military Police Unit, and the 231st Army Post Office were further additions to the corps in the year of its formation.

Both mountain divisions had been active units of the XVIII Military District (Salzburg) that had been formed from contingents of the Austrian Army following the annexation of Austria in 1938. The zone of the 2nd Mountain Division (based in Innsbruck) was Tyrol (including East Tyrol) and Salzburg, and that of the 3rd Mountain Division (based in Graz) was Carinthia and Styria. Living on in their regiments were the best traditions of the old Austrian elite troops like the imperial rifle troops and imperial mountain troops. They also remembered with pride the folk hero Andreas Hofer, leader of the Tyrolean Rebellion against Napoleon, as well as the spirit of freedom of the Carinthians in 1920.

The mountain divisions were lacking in some units. Before its transfer to Norway in the final days of April 1940, the 2nd Mountain Division had been compelled to leave behind in the Reich its heavy artillery battalion, anti-tank battalion, cavalry troop, replacement training battalion, and five good light motor transport columns. The High Command of the German Army (OKH) had regarded these units as unnecessary for the Norwegian campaign. In a similar fashion, the strength of the 3rd Mountain Division had been reduced. It had then been dispersed amongst the destroyers and merchantmen on the way to Norway and distributed widely between Narvik and Trondheim, although not before much of its matériel ended up on the seafloor. Both divisions still did not have a third battery for each mountain artillery battalion, a situation that prevailed from peacetime. This problem was solved by establishing four batteries with old mountain howitzers. Moreover, an attempt was made to create new heavy battalions with Norwegian 10.5cm guns in the form of the 9th Battery of the 111th Mountain Artillery Regiment and the 7th Battery of the 112th Mountain Artillery Regiment. After some time, both divisions would once more be equipped with anti-tank battalions. They would even have bicycle battalions, a regionally appropriate substitute for what had originally been mountain reconnaissance battalions. The supply troops were also reinforced.

At the outbreak of the war, the tables of organisation of the German mountain troops were rather temporary in character. A long trial period for this organisation of the troops seemed to be necessary. Designed for high-mountain operations, the mountain infantry and mountain artillery units required considerable manpower as well as a large number of pack animals. A single mountain battery equipped with four guns of 7.5cm calibre called for 324 men and approximately 160 horses and pack animals. The first campaigns of the war appeared to demonstrate that such extensive supply trains were a hindrance, that the provisions and equipment for any normal operation must be limited, and that special units should only be assigned when in mountainous or impassable terrain. In the far-flung Scandinavian terrain, motorisation was naturally of greater significance than horses and pack animals during the campaign and in the security phase afterwards. Yet there were differences of opinion as to whether the mountain troops should always maintain a state of readiness for high-altitude operations. The reduction of forces in Norway, accepted by the OKH with reservations, had one very good reason: the many animals could not be sufficiently fed and looked after in the far north. There was not enough animal feed in a land where the growth of grass was relatively rare. Transporting fodder to the Scandinavian front would always remain a problem. Our sea lanes were endangered by the naval superiority of the enemy, and the goods would be large and cumbersome. The decrease in the number of pack animals had been compensated for with an increase in the number of horse-drawn carts. While a pack animal would normally carry 100kg, a horse-drawn cart could manage 200kg. By 1941, both mountain divisions possessed more motor vehicles and carts, and fewer horses and pack animals, than they had in 1939.

The significant quantity of personnel that the mass of horses required had already led to the decision before the war to equip the mountain divisions with just two rather than three mountain infantry regiments and with just three rather than four artillery battalions. This double-pronged deprivation would be regarded with disapproval by the field troops for a long time, as it robbed the divisions of sufficient reserves from the outset. The course of the operations to be described in this book would prove that there was just cause for such disapproval. The bicycle battalion could be no substitute for a third mountain infantry regiment. In making such an observation, it must be noted that a triangular mountain division of the sort that existed in 1939, for example the 1st Mountain Division with approximately 23,000 men and considerably more than 6,000 horses, would be incapable of operating effectively on a narrow front or anywhere other than in mountainous terrain. One possible solution was the creation of a brigade-style battle group that could organise combat elements, traffic, and supply, thereby relieving the division of the need to deal with matériel overabundance and easing the movement of the units of the division.[2]

After the end of the action in Norway in 1940, the 2nd Mountain Division had been committed between Namsos and the area north of Bodø (Sørfolda Fjord), and the 3rd Mountain Division from there to Alta (in the fjord of the same name 150 kilometres south of Hammerfest). The security of East Finnmark, between Alta and the frontier east of Kirkenes, had already taken on an important role in the capitulation negotiations of 10 June 1940. The Norwegian negotiators had requested that the Norwegian troops still in Finnmark be allowed to remain as frontier protection against the Soviet Union, which was only separated from Norway by the narrow Finnish corridor of Petsamo, and that they should remain under Norwegian command.[3] However, after the Norwegian government had escaped to Great Britain with the intention of continuing the fight against the Reich, the German commander felt unable to grant this request.[4] Very soon after the armistice, the 3rd Mountain Division sent the II Battalion of the 138th Mountain Infantry Regiment to occupy the town of Alta with its small Norwegian base. For the protection of East Finnmark, the army transferred an SS battalion, initially under the command of SS-Lieutenant-Colonel Reitz and later SS-Lieutenant-Colonel Deutsch, from South Norway to Kirkenes by sea in June 1940. The Reich Commissioner for the Occupied Norwegian Territories, Josef Terboven, agreed with this transfer. On 15 August, strong elements of the 3rd Mountain Division and then of the 2nd Mountain Division were suddenly sent to the Varanger area. This triggered a regrouping of the forces of Mountain Corps Norway as follows:

- 2nd Mountain Division (Finnmark)
  - Reinforced 136th Mountain Infantry Regiment (Kirkenes–Tana area)
  - Reinforced 137th Mountain Infantry Regiment (Hammerfest–Alta–Kautokeino–Karasjok area)
- 3rd Mountain Division (Troms and the northern half of Nordland)
  - Reinforced 138th Mountain Infantry Regiment (area of Nordreisa, Tromsø, and Balsfjord [southeast of Tromsø])
  - Reinforced 139th Mountain Infantry Regiment (Setermoen–Narvik area)
- Corps troops in the vicinity of Alta

This distribution of forces had been ordered by the army according only to the theoretical strength of the regiments, even though an investigation of actual numbers had been undertaken. The one place in which an adjustment had to be made was the Kautokeino area, with a mountain infantry company instead of a mountain infantry battalion being stationed there. In the meantime, the security requirements inland had been overestimated; frontier sectors that would enable movement out of Kautokeino and Karasjok would have sufficed.

It was a peculiar front as in the rest of Norway: a front without depth and, of concern to the army, almost without outposts; a front of garrisons with limited possibilities for mutual support; a front whose supply had to be brought along what would be the main line of resistance (Norwegian National Road 50).

We must now examine the nature of this land on the periphery of the Arctic Ocean and what it was that led to the expansion of German operations right up to Kirkenes on the Norwegian–Finnish border.

CHAPTER 2

Fennoscandia and Kola

Maps 1–3

Ohthere or Ottar was a Viking from the coast south of Vestfjorden whose account was recorded by King Alfred of England in about AD 880. He was the first to bring tidings of the land that 'receded to the east – or the land into which the sea extended from here'. He had apparently travelled as far as the mouth of the Northern Dvina River in Arkhangelsk. He described the Roof of Europe as a complete wasteland, but the sparse nature of the account means that few details survived into the modern era.[5]

As a matter of fact, if there was no Gulf Stream, Heligoland would already be in pack ice and the northern Scandinavian shores would be as inaccessible as those in northern Greenland. But these areas remained free of ice right up to the Kara Strait and the bay made up by the White Sea. If the sea did not offer an abundance of fish, and the land to its east furs and timber, settlements along these coasts would have been few and far between, for life there is otherwise one of privation. Between Vestfjorden and Nordkapp, an extensive undulating highland of 400–600 metres, and sometimes of 1,000 metres, in height falls steeply to the shores of the Atlantic and offers magnificent scenery with its many fjords and primeval islands. Only here in the Lofoten Islands or amidst the dramatic mountains of Hammerfest can the Old Norse sagas of the frost giant Aegir, of the Sea Halls, or of Niflheim be fully understood. The worship of Baldur, the god of the summer sun, can also be understood, for his return as the midnight sun is awaited with impatience during the long weeks of darkness. Do the ghostly, flitting northern lights shimmer more beautifully anywhere other than in Lapland? The hem of God's cloak flowing across the sky?

Should one manage to surmount the barriers of the coastal mountains and head inland, one would discover more level terrain. Even if the emphasis is still on the massive at the Norwegian–Swedish–Finnish tripoint south-east of Tromsø with its cold and high alpine environment, a high-altitude steppe opens up after that which, according to the description of Sven Hedin, can be compared to the Central Asian plains. While the fjords by the sea sometimes promised protection with their growth of grass, shrubs, birch trees, and pine trees, the vast terrain here presented us with scattered yet wide birch bushes that were twice the size of a man. Right up to the high-altitude areas, the ground was covered in dwarf birches (up to 20cm) and hard moss that was the colour of the wreaths that we would wear in the Fatherland on All Saints' Day. Because it is the food for the sole animal to be found in substantial numbers in this land, the reindeer, it is generally called reindeer moss. Its rich colour in the short northern autumn is remarkably beautiful. The modest growth in the coastal areas also diminishes to the east of the North Cape. The mountains that flank Porsanger Fjord (Banak-Lakselv) and the coast up to the large Varanger Peninsula are barren, steep, and desolate. It almost looks like a lunar landscape from the air. Yet South Varanger, with its coastline around Kirkenes, shows more signs of life. In particular, the valleys of the major rivers in this region are pleasant and sometimes even fertile. These rivers are the Tana, the Pasvikelva (Paatsjoki), which used to mark parts of the Norwegian–Finnish eastern border, and the Petsamonjoki, which flows by Petsamo. The only eyesore is the school of agriculture by the Tana.

Soviet ground lies to the east of Petsamo. This is Kola Peninsula. It was as good as unknown to Europeans until the name Murmansk and the Murman Railway became familiar terms in World War I. The peninsula is bleak on the coast, bewildering in the 'stony sea' of the near coastal zone, but then becomes obscured by gently sloping swamp valleys densely overgrown with shrubs. The shape of the land becomes ever more difficult to ascertain after that, and only from the air can the tree line be perceived in the far distance. While tundra covers the north of the peninsula, taiga covers the south – twin sisters whose dominance stretches from here to other lands of the same latitude in Eurasia and North America. Together, both biomes contain tens of thousands of lakes, especially here in Fennoscandia and Kola. In some places, it is hard to know whether the surface of the peninsula is covered more with lakes and marsh or more with glacial debris. The further inland one goes, the lakes become less clearly defined and their banks become increasingly shrouded by clouds of mosquitoes. No less a scourge for mankind here than in the tropics, the one positive difference is that this genus does not carry malaria. The climate of the 'Cap of the North' is harsh, yet clean: only 0.025 per cent of the personnel of Army Norway were on sick leave in the autumn of 1940, and most of these were due to work injuries.

Norwegians live in the coastal zones, and, in Finnmark, there are gradually more Finns and Russians and, to some degree, Lapps.[6] These Mongoloid people who speak a unique, distant Finno-Ugric dialect might make up approximately 26,000 people in all three northern lands. In accordance with international treaties, they are not bound by borders and so travel with their reindeer herds to the mossy fells of the coastal mountains in summer and return inland in autumn. In the course of time, some of these people (half-nomadic forest Lapps) have developed parishes as settlement centres. Those who move every six months and who live only in their tents are the fully nomadic mountain Lapps, while in the Varanger and, in earlier times, Kola regions the low number of farm and sea Lapps eke out a living from fishing or animal trapping. The lives of the Lapps and their reindeer do not need to be described with any mythological embellishment.[7] It is here that the last primitive people of Europe live, and they appear no more European than their homeland. Our troops did not come into much contact with these people. In order to maintain hygiene, it was forbidden to enter Lapp tents or pit-dwellings. It must not be forgotten that tuberculosis could spread even in Norwegian settlements along the Arctic Ocean.

The reindeer is a semi-wild domestic animal that is capable of roaming freely and finding food. It is suited to pulling a light, troughlike sled (a pulk or an akja) across its native landscape and can dash with its broad hooves at an ever-steady trot over hard and soft snow at speeds greater than that of a horse. Yet these animals would absolutely refuse the unreasonable demand to draw akjas loaded with the components of a mountain gun. They were used by assault squads and outposts if they were no longer required by their Sami owners. The fauna is otherwise unremarkable in this land: mice and lemmings, magpies, capercaillies and black grouses, red foxes and different types of weasel, and occasionally elks. There is also the odd bear further south. Wolves can present a danger to reindeer when the winter is severe. The coasts are frequented by seabirds like auks and seagulls, and probably many other types. The sea offers good fish for meals: halibut, turbot, dogfish, flounder, herring, and cod (especially salted dried cod). Giant salmon can be caught in the fjords and rivers; delicious trout in the streams and lakes. With increasing distance from the northern coast, there are forests with millions of berries (cranberries and cloudberries) and mushrooms (porcini and birch boletes) in complete purity and unfathomable quantities; hardly anyone pays any attention to them.

Soldiers are not exclusively concerned with geography and ethnography, though. With the task of occupying and securing North Norway, it was important that the headquarters of Mountain Corps Norway convey the realities of the situation to the men. The need to partake in fishing and to continue importing ore from Kiruna via Narvik was commonly understood. But there were also good deposits of ore in Bjørnevatn (near Kirkenes) and Kolosjoki (near Petsamo). Whoever had North Norway in their hands had to be able to exert their influence from the air on the sea route from the Atlantic through the Barents Sea into the White Sea. Spitzbergen, which had no military presence in 1940 and was still peacefully supplying coal in early 1941 to Troms and Finnmark, and thereby also to the German forces in Norway at that time, needed to be within operational range. The construction of suitable airfields was therefore of the utmost urgency, whose demands were, quite logically, considerable in terms of labour and resources. It was difficult to find locations for airfields in the mountainous terrain. Only three bases could be identified, and aerial operations would subsequently be conducted from them for the rest of the war: Bardufoss, a small Norwegian airfield which lay between Narvik and Tromsø and which was expanded; Banak, at the inner end of Porsanger Fjord; and Kirkenes-Høybuktmoen. The necessity of discovering the few locations where level ground existed and the problems faced by the airfields in those locations due to the environment can be shown simply by consulting Map 3, taking note of where Banak is situated and of the nature of the surrounding terrain. The occupation of this coast finally allowed German warships access to the North Atlantic, although the naval bases there did not yet, in 1940–41, assume the importance that they would later on when the Allies possessed aerial supremacy over the North Sea.

The map must be consulted to see the settlements where our troops could be stationed. They are almost all to be found along the coast. Tromsø, with more than 10,000 inhabitants, the 'Paris of the North' (a comparison that could only have been made by a polar explorer), was the only major city. Towns like Hammerfest, Vardø, Vadsø, and Kirkenes each have populations of 2,000–3,000. The army was bound to villages on the mainland that were reachable on or connected by roads. Tromsø, Hammerfest, and Vardø were therefore garrisoned by coastal batteries or naval stations. In the many corners of the fjords, there were often at best small school buildings and chapels that the troops could requisition. Finnmark, spanning 500 kilometres from Alta in the west and Kirkenes in the east, had only about 25,000 inhabitants. This number includes all of the island settlements and all of the Lapps in the most remote locations. To station here a modern army of large units, each of approximately the same strength, in a short period of time, before the onset of winter, and in a few small locations was a new experience for everybody involved. In those positions where the German forces were garrisoned, there were typically only a small number of local residents. The barracks and other prefabricated quartering components (plywood and millboard) would last for years. In the difficulties of the initial period of the transfer of forces to North Norway, some troops even dismantled the wooden houses that they had bought in their garrisons in Central Norway and rebuilt them in their new garrisons 2,000 kilometres further north. It is a testament to the energy of the German supply leadership and their organisational capability that they succeeded, between 15 August and Christmas 1940, in accommodating both mountain divisions and all other troops in Troms and Finnmark so that they were more or less safe in the winter.

Many of the points on the map with names are in general individual homesteads. It cannot be expected that the piers in the fjord harbours would have space for anything larger than cutters and small fjord steamboats. Even if the water surface in the bays remains free of ice, this is not always the case underwater. Skerries or lagoons (like the inland Botn Fjord) make the tidal amplitude quite small and allows ice to form on the shores and sometimes also in the bays. Even Kirkenes can be challenging to get to without an icebreaker. Many places are connected, and much trade is conducted, by sea routes. Most roads serve only local communications. Because of the frost, they require constant grading and steamrolling and then layering with sand so that they are kept in good condition. Norwegian National Road 50, which goes right through the country, still lacked some road sections and ferry links in 1940: between Fauske and Narvik due to the fact that six fjords, the 'aquarium', lay in its path (see Map 2); the southern bank of Langfjorden; approximately 70 kilometres between Alta and Repparfjorden; and almost the entire stretch between Lakselv and Tana. Over none of the major rivers was there a solid or ice-resistant bridge at that time. West of Nordreisa was the stormy, 14-kilometre-wide Lyngen Fjord; to the east of it a small fjord near Sørstraumen, downstream from the scenic yet dangerous Kvænangen pass. The road had to go over both fjords. Of the 1,001 kilometres of road between Narvik and Kirkenes, hardly 200 kilometres were secured with snow fences. In peacetime, winter road maintenance or snow clearance was carried out by the Norwegian civil population only when the need arose. This was minimal in winter. Drift-blocked sections of road were often closed off. The horse-drawn light sleigh would be able to reach the parish, the inhabitants would stock up on supplies, and motor vehicle traffic would not start up again until spring. The sun would disappear for a while, meaning that its warmth could not be expected to contribute to the clearing away of snow. The will of the Führer alone would not have been enough to achieve what was necessary. The severity of the conditions compelled our soldiers to develop an industriousness that was second to none, and it was with a shake of the head that the Norwegian fishermen and farmers regarded the so-called 'tyske tempo'. They could not comprehend our sense of urgency. What did so many Germans want here in this remote part of the world? What purpose did their haste have in this land of peace and quiet and the northern lights?

In the summer days of 1940, the grounds for the transfer of Mountain Corps Norway so that it could occupy the whole of North Norway were outlined by Army Norway as follows:

1. North Scandinavia, which lies within the sphere of influence of the Reich, is an essential source of raw materials (Kiruna, Kirkenes, Petsamo) that will aid the German war effort.
2. Finnmark, thus far only lightly occupied by German troops (one battalion in the west and another in the east), must be considered a stray area that might attract the ambitions of foreign powers or inspire in the Norwegian government-in-exile the idea of retaking the area.
3. The intervention of America in the war is not beyond the realms of possibility in 1941. Preparations in Iceland point towards such an eventuality.
4. German forces in their current positions in Central Norway would be powerless in the event of foreign intervention in the Arctic Ocean, especially by a British–American fleet. The German defence against such intervention can only be effective if North Norway is held firmly.
5. The difficulties posed by the distances, the supply, and the conditions mean that the shift of forces to North Norway cannot be started and completed quickly enough for the most essential preparations to be made before the onset of the northern winter in October. It can be expected that the transfer of an entire division with everything it needs would take three months. If this begins in August 1940 – by land! – the corps can be ready to defend North Norway at full strength in February 1941.

CHAPTER 3

The Threat from the West

Map 2

Great Britain was much too preoccupied with the defence of the motherland in 1940 to be able to assemble forces for a new operation against Norway. To what extent it lay within the realm of Allied interests and strategic possibilities to seriously mount an organised landing in Norway with the goal of establishing a foothold in or perhaps even retaking the country was a question that would exercise the minds of the German supreme command throughout World War II. It can reasonably be assumed, in accordance with the facts, that fears in this regard periodically emanated from the High Command of the Armed Forces (OKW) and often directly from Adolf Hitler himself. They may have arisen in part from his imagination or probably more frequently from Allied-leaked disinformation. In contrast to the OKW, the headquarters of Army Norway was hardly ever, and that of Mountain Corps Norway never, seriously worried about an enemy landing. Rather, the German leadership in Norway was far more concerned about local, isolated operations. These questions were tested, taking into account various incidents and experiences thus far, in an operational map exercise led by the commander of the mountain corps on 17 April 1941 and in which unit commanders from the army, navy, and air force took part. The investigation resulted in the unanimous view that the Western Powers, at that time still without the United States, would be unable to afford such an extensive engagement, supported only by fleets, in a secondary theatre of war from their far-distant bases, especially given the increasing success of the U-boat campaign. They would instead employ less costly methods, particularly raids carried out by light forces, to tie down German forces, to disrupt German supply, and to influence the mood of the Norwegian population. One of the most noteworthy chapters of such pinprick operations will be outlined here from the point of view of the mountain corps, whose commander was also the territorial commander of North Norway.[8]

On 3 March 1941, a British force of light naval vessels was spotted, albeit not quite perfectly, from the heights of Trondheim at 1150 hours. They were heading northwards at high speed. Informed of this at 2040 hours, the mountain corps sounded the alarm. The British force, consisting of a heavy cruiser and five destroyers, appeared before Svolvær in the Lofoten archipelago on 4 March at 0700 hours. One destroyer provided protection to the north and another to the south. The action began with the German outpost patrol boat *Krebs* being put out of action; it drifted off course and sank. Then 14 direct hits tore through the valuable fish processing vessel *Hamburg* (6,500 tonnes), at that time the only ship of its type in German ownership. It was a kind of floating factory ship, and its destruction brought to an end the ability to immediately process fish that had been caught in Lofoten. After that, 16,000 tonnes of other German shipping were sunk (*Eilenau*, *Felix Neumann*, *Gumbinnen*, *Bernhard Schulte*, and *Rissen*), as was the Norwegian Hurtigruten steamship *Mira*.[9] The fourth phase began at 0730 hours when approximately 300 soldiers, mostly Norwegian legionnaires, landed, took the town and its ships, requisitioned motor vehicles, and rounded up all German soldiers and Norwegian members of Nasjonal Samling that were in the area.[10] The enemy captured radio communication records and signal code charts from the nearby observation post, taken completely by surprise, in the village of Kabelvåg. Several Norwegian civilians (about 60 men and eight women) who sympathised with the enemy were waiting in prearranged hotel rooms so that they could be easily found by the legionnaires and willingly taken away. The fifth phase was the destruction of facilities that would neutralise the fishing industry: the oil factory and oil tanks in Svolvær; the oil factories, fish oil factories, fish tinning factories, and oil tanks in Stamsund; a fish processing factory in Brettesnes; and the oil factory and oil tanks in Henningsvær. Meanwhile, the destroyer providing protection to the south had seized the Hurtigruten ship *Finnmarken* and arrested all Germans on board. The Norwegian ship was put into harbour in Svolvær after that and left there. Its crew joined the British. Accompanied by the ovation of the population, the commando units disembarked at 1300 hours, though not before they had distributed flyers inviting people to join the Norwegian Legion. At 1418 hours, the British naval vessels set off due south at top speed.

The German–Norwegian radio broadcast at 1300 hours on 7 March 1941, as well as that of BBC London on the morning of the same day, reported what had happened in more or less the same way, embellished and exaggerated according to the tendencies of the time.[11] England claimed to have taken prisoner 215 Germans and 10 Norwegian Nasjonal Samling members. According to the assessment of Mountain Corps Norway, German losses amounted to 10 killed, eight wounded (those left in Svolvær), and 222 taken prisoner or missing.

The reader will notice that a description of the German defence is missing. This is because Lofoten was not occupied by the German Army. There were only observation posts of the Luftwaffe, small surveillance forces of the navy, and a few administrative offices of the Reich commissariat. The Wehrmacht was at that time unable to effectively rule islands like those of Lofoten. That after the sighting of the British naval unit on 3 March no warning whatsoever was sent to the fishing companies around Vestfjorden is an indication of the fact that there existed no military post that liaised with them. The observation post in Kabelvåg may have been careless – probably careless like many then in Norway – although such a raid really ought to have been expected for a long time. Since August 1940, transport after transport had been heading north to Narvik and then, laden with ore, had been returning to Germany. So safe had this shipping remained that not only Wehrmacht commanders of all ranks and smaller groups of soldiers but even Reichsführer-SS Heinrich Himmler, who otherwise took great care about his personal safety, travelled on a regular schedule on the steamboats of the Hurtigruten between Trondheim and Kirkenes, just like tourists in peacetime. Aircraft were sent from the south in the course of the day on 4 March, but it was too late. The arrival of a mountain infantry platoon from Narvik in Svolvær on outpost patrol boats at midnight on 4/5 March was no more than a gesture of reassurance and in response to the following telegram that Field-Marshal Wilhelm Keitel, on Hitler's orders, had sent to Reich Commissioner Terboven on the night of 4 March:

> Inhabitants of the villages involved must be most severely punished if there is the slightest suspicion of even tacit favour of the enemy operation. This will be a powerful deterrent for the future. If necessary, the villages should be annihilated entirely. Ensure this is announced throughout the country. Why cannot fishing companies be run in one place so that they can be better provided with military protection?

Experts would immediately answer the question in the last sentence in the negative. Even General Dietl answered laconically: 'because fish do not orient themselves in accordance with tactical considerations'.[12] But had it not been an indication of what would at some point unfold when, in November 1940, two British warships had stopped Norwegian cutters and had made enquiries about the *Hamburg*, which was at that time moored in Hammerfest? Had the report of this incident been filed away without any attention, or had it been passed on to the fishing industry? Had a deaf ear been turned to the warning? All the details of the British operation had doubtless been carefully worked out not only by the British but also by Norwegian patriots both in and outside Norway. Reich Commissioner Terboven's flight to Svolvær on 5 March, the destruction of the properties of those who had fled, the arrests, the punishments, and the contributions did not cure the damage to German prestige. As collective punitive measures usually did, these actions only made things worse. From the notes I took at the time is to be found the following excerpt: 'had we taken over the condemned houses at demolition value, they would have at least been of use to us'.

General Dietl should have been the one to report on the situation to the highest authority, but Colonel-General Nikolaus von Falkenhorst, the commander of the German forces in Norway, was summoned first and Dietl only afterwards. Falkenhorst set off for Germany on 16 March with all the necessary paperwork. If the OKW had been unaware of how truly weak the German position in North Norway was, it would now, by necessity, no longer be. 165 coastal batteries were subsequently sent to Norway. The mountain corps received a couple of regimental headquarters and 10 battalion headquarters as well as 55 batteries with 10cm–15cm guns (captured matériel from the western campaign) and eight batteries with 21cm guns (the German Mörser). Hitler himself had determined their distribution. They were to cover not only Norwegian National Road 50, which was regarded as a potentially important defensive line, but also, as far as possible, coastal shipping. The 256th Police Battalion strengthened the administrative offices of the Reich commissioner in the area of Narvik and Lofoten. Anything that we were to receive after that was no longer a direct consequence of Svolvær.

This British operation had not caused any noteworthy military damage. The economic impact might have been perceptible for Norway, but it was insignificant for Germany. Its main effect was to strengthen the political resolve of the Norwegian population, something that our troops could very well sense.

CHAPTER 4

Assembly of Forces in the East

Maps 1 and 4

Shortly before Christmas 1940, General Dietl had been informed of the plan to attack the Soviet Union in the summer of 1941. He then conveyed this news to the four general staff officers of his corps headquarters, the corps intendant, and the corps adjutant. Nobody else was permitted to have knowledge of this secret until further notice. For months on end, this circle could say nothing about the plan to anyone and had to make preparations for the future on its own. It was not an easy task, neither in terms of matériel nor psychologically.

It was immediately clear that Mountain Corps Norway was to be assigned a most important role. If it was to be on the left wing of an Eastern Front whilst also remaining on the right wing of the Western Front, then the only objective it could be given would be Murmansk. On that basis, detailed operational planning got underway. Each staff officer focused on his own area of specialisation, and all worked together effectively. The importance of Murmansk was readily apparent, but that of the interconnectedness of the northern region was perhaps less so. While the troops improved their quarters and started training again in defiance of the winter nights, the thoughts of a small number of staff officers revolved around a series of difficult problems.

A book by Vitalis Patenburg was being passed around at that time: *Rußlands Griff um Nordeuropa*.[13] It made very clear the geopolitical and military-geographical situation of Fennoscandia from the point of view of the Soviet Union. Of particular note for the leadership of the mountain corps was the chapter 'Rote Offensivstellung am Eismeer'.[14] The next study we undertook dealt with the lessons of the Finno-Soviet Winter War of 1939–40. We had very few records on this matter, and there was nothing on the fighting in the area around Petsamo. Only gradually could we begin to draw some conclusions. It was noteworthy that, from the very beginning, the Finns did not leave anything intact on any land they relinquished, not even a single log cabin, that could have been of use to the enemy in the subarctic winter. The Finns had set fire to their houses during the retreat of 1939. In a land in which almost everything is built of wood and can also be rebuilt with wood, a strategy such as scorched earth is not really a case of punitive destruction. The idea, in the middle of winter, is to temporarily deprive the enemy of any shelter against the extreme cold, and his vulnerability is all the greater if he is poorly prepared for winter warfare. Soviet forces in North Finland in 1939 had indeed been poorly prepared, and the Finnish scorched-earth strategy had been a legitimate course of action. Amidst cold waves that were measured at lower than minus 50 degrees Celsius, up to 22,000 cases of frostbite had been reported in the two divisions that had advanced on Petsamo and Nautsi. This advance had finally been cut off by a single Finnish battalion of hardened rangers whose assault squads struck the flanks, which were 150 kilometres in depth, and did the enemy the utmost harm. The German leadership thus formed the following picture of the enemy forces: composed of Siberians and people from northern or cold zones, they were fierce fighters and good defenders, but they possessed very little mobility. That the Soviet forces had managed to advance in this area in the end did not point to anything in particular. On the question of German forces being able to push forward in the direction of Murmansk, four problems required contemplation.

The first was the terrain. This has already been described in general terms, and the details of certain locations will be outlined in the analysis of subsequent operations. But, for the time being, the mountain corps had too little knowledge of the important details. No one had any information on what the terrain of Kola Peninsula looked like. Even in June 1941, the month of the commencement of the attack, the Finns in Petsamo could shed no light on what lay ahead. Nobody had been there or knew of sources for a theoretical study. We received some maps at a rather late stage, but they depicted the land on a large scale and were obviously copies of imprecise, non-military publications. Monochrome areas full of arbitrarily drawn lakes and hill-shading may have been able to convey a basic idea of the land, but they did not provide any real insight. The terrain was covered with snow right up until the beginning of the operation. This prevented our reconnaissance flights from being able to map the terrain, even when they flew beyond the frontier. Judging from the character of the terrain of the narrow Finnish corridor of Petsamo, we could reasonably conclude that that on the other side of the border would be of the same kind to begin with and would probably remain roughly the same for the next 25 kilometres. The terrain conditions beyond the Litsa River, however, remained a mystery, as did the entire stretch of land and lake-dotted area up to Murmansk. Even in the months before the beginning of the offensive, the layout of the lakes in particular was still unknown.

By sending these maps on to us, the headquarters of Army Norway demonstrated that it was a little too trusting and not enough discerning. We could not be confident about the accuracy of the routes marked on them, and we were still in doubt at the beginning of the campaign. This was the second problem we had to deal with. We immediately noticed one error, for there was certainly no road along the old Finno-Soviet border. Despite our many reservations, we at the mountain corps had to trust the rest of the information that was passed on to us from above regarding the road network. From these documents, we assumed that the following streets or road connections existed: roads going around the southern half of Rybachy Peninsula and from there through Titovka, Zapadnaya Litsa, and Ura-Guba to Polyarnoye; a road from Murmansk (west bank of Kola Bay) via Motovsky (also Zimnyaya Motovka) to the Finno-Soviet border in the direction of Luostari; a direct connection between Motovsky and Zapadnaya Litsa as well as between Motovsky and Titovka; the Titovka Valley Road and a connection from there going past the south of Zapadnaya Litsa in the direction of Murmansk; and another road along the Tuloma and the Luttojoki (different names for the same river) from the border area via Ristikent towards Kola. It was of great importance to have knowledge of the road network. Any major movement of forces in the tundra region would be dependent upon these roads. Even horse-drawn carts would make little progress without them. Only half a dozen placenames were shown on our maps, but that could be considered normal for this largely deserted area. But could a village on the map be regarded as a village in reality? Did places like Titovka, Zapadnaya Litsa, or Motovsky actually exist? Did they have fishing populations and Lapps like such places in North Norway or North Finland?

Since there was no road on the Finnish side that led to the frontier, it was a natural course of action to examine what would be involved in constructing a road that would connect with the possibly existing network on the other side of the border and that would be on the scale needed for two mountain divisions. The supply was our third and most critical problem and was bound to be very difficult in the first few days of the campaign. Shortly after those first days, according to our assessment, our supply lines could run along the aforementioned roads or, provided Rybachy Peninsula was in German hands, via the habour in Liinahamari and the west coast of Rybachy Peninsula to Titovka. In any case, the main supply base would be in Kirkenes to begin with, and it was hoped that it would be moved forward to Petsamo soon after that.

Of the various tactical problems, the one the mountain corps thought about the most was that presented by Rybachy Peninsula. Opinions varied as to whether it ought to be feared as an operational flanking position against our planned advance on Murmansk. The enemy presence there was probably minimal. At any rate, there were few who believed that the peninsula was heavily occupied. We were generally inclined to think that the enemy would prefer to adopt a fierce defensive stance before Murmansk, but it was too optimistic to expect that his forces would completely crumble in the event of a rapid advance. To carry out a successful attack, it would be of great importance to constantly scout the land ahead and to be aware of the location of the enemy troops.

As an experienced mountain infantry officer, General Dietl was more critically minded than the leadership of Army Norway or that of the OKW. Although all general staff officers from the rank of major and above had been working on an operational study so as to be able to anticipate the possible plans of the opposing side (i.e. the Soviet high command in Murmansk), it did not require such an operational study for it to be clear to General Dietl that an advance in this area would be difficult.[15] Four mountain infantry regiments organised into two barely reinforced mountain divisions seemed to him, as he explained during a meeting with the Führer in Berlin at the end of April 1941, to be 'like a journeyman's kit' for conquering a 120-kilometre-wide tundra zone which was peppered with natural fortifications, which had an unknown road network, and which was bound to be defended fiercely given the importance of Murmansk. Although mountain divisions could manoeuvre far into the mountains, they could only do so for a short time and at the cost of striking power. The number of pack animals and the supply of animal feed were not much greater than they had been in the second half of 1940. It had been necessary to make dirt tracks, but the forces that did so ended up going missing from the front. General Dietl told us that Hitler had been most impressed by his report and by the seriousness of his arguments, and, although Hitler had not reached a decision at that time, he had held on to the documents that Dietl had brought with him. But the decision was made soon afterwards in favour of an attack with what was available. The commander of the corps could only explain this as the result of other advisors trivialising the difficulties of the Arctic Front and thereby dispelling Hitler's doubts. Whoever it may have been, he was probably a layman in mountain warfare or infected by the prevailing tendency to underestimate the enemy and the land.

Between April and June 1941, whilst our minds were focused on the east, the troops of the corps, including the rear units, were assembled in North Norway.

Mountain Corps Norway requested from Army Norway that, among other things, there be close cooperation with the Finnish armed forces, that the area east of Petsamo be carefully scouted, that useful maps be provided, that the kind of support to be provided by the other arms of the Wehrmacht be established, and that questions regarding security and organisation in North Norway, in particular the setting up of army coastal artillery, be addressed. In addition, the mountain corps recommended the construction of roads and bridges in North Finland, the provision of supplies along the Arctic Ocean Highway, the diversion of some supply transports headed to Petsamo (men of straw for the benefit of the Finnish armed forces), and, not least, the delivery of all of the equipment that would be needed by the front-line units. Army Norway helped in any way it could, and the transport administrative offices accomplished the incredible. The enemy in the west hardly disturbed us at all. Of the many unknown yet hardworking cogs in the machine, particularly worthy of mention is the office of transport and supply of the mountain corps in Narvik under the tireless and resourceful Captain Habel.

There were four sea transport operations that brought forward the troops to be assembled for action. In Operation *Fish Haul*, beginning in the middle of April, SS Battle Group North, which was allocated the area in southern Finnish Lapland, was to be transported to Porsanger Fjord with its two infantry regiments, one artillery battalion, and one signal battalion. From there, it was to assemble in the area of Kirkenes by the start of June and then depart for Finland. It had to wait for some time in the Porsanger area whilst the roads were being improved and there was still drift ice on the Tana River. It finally set off for Rovaniemi on 7 June and was placed at the disposal of Army Norway. The movement of this battle group through the area of the mountain corps was due to the fact that passage through Sweden had been denied. The battle group had thus made a detour of approximately 1,500 kilometres. A third regiment that had been transported in *Fish Haul* remained in the Varanger area. There were the 4th and 14th Machine-Gun Battalions, 12 units of the Reich Labour Service (RAD) with their headquarters personnel, and army coastal artillery. The 4th Machine-Gun Battalion arrived along the national road east of Nordreisa and was to undertake snow clearance, while the 14th Machine-Gun Battalion relieved the mountain infantry in Porsanger Fjord and, in addition to maintaining the road there, often had to be responsible for transport operations. The RAD units were soon distributed throughout Finnmark, as they would be needed for the maintenance of the national road at several points, but what precisely these units would do in the upcoming operations was not yet certain.

Operation *Pilgrimage* was the transfer of the 199th Infantry Division from South Norway to Troms. Operation *Hercules* was then the transfer of those elements of the 3rd Mountain Division that had thereby been relieved from Troms to the area around and to the west of Neiden in East Finnmark. All the transport ships that came from the south in *Pilgrimage* subsequently proceeded further, each with a new unit on board, in *Hercules*. Since Neiden did not have a suitable port for large ships, Vadsø was instead the destination for transport ships of up to 3,000 tonnes. A small number of ships were even larger than that and could only unload in Kirkenes. By the beginning of June, the 3rd Mountain Division began to assemble near Neiden. *Pilgrimage* had lasted from 25 April until 3 June 1941, while *Hercules* had commenced at the end of April and, fortunately, ended with the arrival of the last transport in Kirkenes on 21 June 1941, 12 hours before X-Hour.

Most of the units of the 2nd Mountain Division were already scattered around Finnmark. Operation *Siegfried* involved the concentration of those units and of the troops of the mountain corps in the area near and to the south of Kirkenes. Moving the troops in one go was out of the question here. The I and III Battalions of the 137th Mountain Infantry Regiment had to make do with just two ships, the untiring and midsize MS *Stamsund* and MS *Vardø*, with which they were transported from Alta to Lakselv one company at a time. Meanwhile, the regimental commander successfully covered 350 kilometres with his reinforced II Battalion in conditions that resembled the depths of winter. Every man, steed, and cart made the journey over the ice of the Tana and along the shores of Varanger Fjord in temperatures at and below minus 30 degrees Celsius from Karasjok to Kirkenes.

Aside from these movements, several motorised units had been sent by the overland route from Narvik to Kirkenes so as not to overburden the sea transport operations. Those that did not make too much haste were able to reach their destinations relatively easily thanks to the sun and the thaw; those that tried to surge forward as quickly as possible along National Road 50, like the 48th Anti-Tank Battalion of the 3rd Mountain Division, wore out their motor vehicles considerably. Even the 4th Machine-Gun Battalion proceeded along the road to Varanger Fjord after completing its work in Nordreisa. It was dispatched to Rovaniemi at the end of June, where it would be at the disposal of Army Norway.

In the course of these eastward movements, the headquarters of the mountain corps, in multiple trips, relocated itself in the middle of June to Nyborg, where the small, formerly Norwegian camp at Nyborgmoen was located. However, the unsuitability of this place for traffic and communications compelled the corps headquarters to move just a few days later to Bjørnevatn, a mining town 10 kilometres south of Kirkenes. The headquarters of the 2nd Mountain Division and that of the 3rd Mountain Division had each found small tourist hotels, the former in Kirkenes and the latter in Neiden. These two hotels were the only suitable buildings in the entire region of South Varanger. By 0230 hours on 22 June 1941, the divisional and corps troops stood in long march columns on the banks of the Pasvikelva (Paatsjoki) before the border post of the small, previously Russian, Boris Gleb Monastery. But, in contrast to the rest of the large Eastern Front, the fighting did not begin here just yet. Rather, the troops moved into the Petsamo area in Finland as a prelude to the commencement of the attack.

The relationship between German plans and the Finnish political situation will be discussed in Chapter 6. The headquarters of Army Norway, in accordance with the intentions of the OKW, was to maintain security in Norway with as few forces as possible and was to organise the rest of its forces into multiple attack groups that would advance from Finnish Lapland towards the Murman Railway. The railway would then be rendered inoperative for the Soviet Union through the seizure of Kandalaksha and Murmansk. Also participating in the offensive was the Finnish III Corps. With the Finnish 3rd and 6th Divisions under its command, it was to advance from the Kuusamo area against the Kiestinki–Louhi line. A further 150 kilometres to the north was the XXXVI Army Corps, which was to proceed with the 169th Infantry Division and SS Battle Group North from the Kemijärvi region towards the Salla–Kandalaksha line. Another 400 kilometres further north as the crow flies was Mountain Corps Norway, which was to advance on Murmansk from East Finnmark via Petsamo. No reserves could be created, for Army Norway had barely anything else. Army Norway command post in Finland would be in the capital of Finnish Lapland, Rovaniemi, and it was from there that operations would be coordinated.

CHAPTER 5

Operational Plans

Maps 4 and 5

The first task of Mountain Corps Norway was laid out in Army Norway order of 7 May 1941:[16]

> From 22 June at 2:30 am, Mountain Corps Norway is to occupy Finnish Lapland along and to the east of the Arctic Ocean Highway in the Nautsi–Petsamo sector, especially Petsamo, Liinahamari Harbour, and the ore mines of Kolosjoki. After that, the forces are to be organised so that:
> (a) the occupied area, in particular the ore mines of Kolosjoki and the harbour area of Petsamo, can be defended against any attack from land, sea, and air; and
> (b) when the order is given (codeword 'Platinum Fox'), and with the harbour area of Petsamo and the ore mines of Kolosjoki fully secure, the attack over the Soviet–Finnish border in the direction of Murmansk can be commenced.

This order did not outline what to do in the case of Soviet preventive measures. Special orders would have to be issued by the ever more distant Army Norway as necessary.

The occupation of the Petsamo area (codename 'Reindeer') that was to precede the advance on Murmansk was without tactical difficulty, although there was some friction whilst preparations were made due to the limited room for traffic, the political entanglements, and the need for absolute secrecy. It was important that this phase be carried out smoothly, for it could have an effect on the development of the situation and on the future operational use of the mountain corps.

The intelligence on the enemy that the mountain corps possessed was vague. We believed that the Soviet 14th Rifle Division was in the vicinity west of Murmansk. According to the observations of the Finnish outpost in Ofonjanvaara, 8 kilometres east of Petsamo, the construction of a line of concrete emplacements and pillboxes approximately halfway between the new Finno-Soviet frontier and the Titovka River was underway. Its extension southwards in the direction of Kuosmejärvi and northwards in the direction of Maattivuono Bay, which lay west of the neck of Rybachy Peninsula, had not been detected. We could presume that the enemy was ready to defend himself and that the defensive line would be armed to the teeth. No evidence could be found of any enemy forces or installations in the tundra region between Luostari and Motovsky. We suspected that there would be a strongpoint near Motovsky, as with most places marked on the map. Our assessments indicated that there was a strong enough artillery and infantry presence on Rybachy Peninsula for fierce resistance to be put up should we attempt to land there, even though the enemy forces there would most likely be composed of naval and special units rather than regular army formations. That there existed a formidable array of fortified defensive systems in Murmansk and at the naval base in Polyarnoye, on the western side of Kola Bay, was beyond doubt, but we lacked any detailed diagrams of or information on their layout. The mountain corps expected not only that it would encounter a number of outpost fortifications positioned far to the west; it could also, above all, count on the presence of a permanent field of fortifications that extended all the way from the east coast of Rybachy Peninsula to the deep flanks of Kola Bay. This field of fortifications was independent of the city of Murmansk and would allow any operation by German forces from the sea little chance of success. Even if conditions were favourable and a rapid advance on Kola Bay could be carried out, it would be impossible for Murmansk to be seized immediately. The garrison in Murmansk would be made up of components from all branches of the Soviet armed forces. We certainly suspected that the 52nd Rifle Division would be there or, if not, somewhere in the vicinity. The element of surprise was bound to be inadequate by the time the German advance reached Murmansk, and we had to be prepared for the garrison there to confront us and to make the conquest of the tundra of the utmost difficulty. The precise strength of the Soviet Air Force and of the Soviet Arctic Fleet in the area of Murmansk was not known, but we did know that they were there and that their offensive capability, especially their ability to intervene against our sea lanes and the flanks of the mountain corps, would depend upon the agility of their leadership. Finally, there was the Murman Railway, which would enable the enemy to quickly bring in reinforcements when needed and would ensure that his front was sufficiently supplied at all times.[17]

For the conduct of operations, the mountain corps had not only the 2nd and 3rd Mountain Divisions at its disposal but also: the Finnish Ivalo Border Guard Battalion, which was tasked by Army Norway to secure the Lutto sector; a reinforced Finnish border guard company in Petsamo, which was to carry out local tasks; and German corps troops, without signal battalions and supply services, which comprised a company of captured French tanks (1st Company of the 40th Panzer Battalion for special purpose utilisation), three batteries of 10.5cm Skoda M.35 guns (730th Heavy Artillery Battalion), and a battery of Norwegian 10.5cm guns with obsolete ammunition (1st Battery of the 477th Heavy Artillery Battalion). Construction troops under the command of the mountain corps were organised into the 405th Construction Pioneer Battalion and the 27th Section of the RAD. The latter had at first eight but eventually 12 RAD units. Also promised was the assistance of a Finnish civil road construction unit of approximately 700 (later 1,000) workers in the middle of July under Savolainen Engineering (the advance party arrived on 27 June 1941). Anti-aircraft protection for the mountain corps was provided by the I Battalion of the 5th Flak Regiment. It was possible that some of the army coastal batteries attached to the mountain corps for the security of Petsamo would be relocated further east later on, but their immobility meant that they would always remain in the role of coastal defence. With 12 mountain infantry battalions, two mountain pioneer battalions, one panzer company, and 16 mobile batteries of varying calibres (of which 12 were mountain batteries), the forces available for the attack in the direction of Murmansk were quite weak. Both bicycle battalions and both anti-tank battalions could only really be expected to undertake defensive and security duties.

Two operational options were considered. The first was to carry out an advance on a wide front (i.e. against Motovsky, Zapadnaya Litsa, and Rybachy Peninsula) so as to probe for the weakest point and then apply the greatest effort against it. The direction of advance to be chosen after that would be the one which would open up the road network for the flow of supplies at the earliest possible moment. Rybachy Peninsula, on which enemy resistance was anticipated to be weak, would ideally be occupied and secured so that the harbour in Petsamo could be used without disruption and so that a sea route could perhaps be established between Liinahamari Harbour and Maattivuono Bay.

The second operational option was to commit both mountain divisions, minus the troops needed for the seizure of Rybachy Peninsula, one after the other for a powerful thrust against a single point. But which road would have been the best to use? Which road was poorly defended or held by the enemy? Contact would have had to be maintained with German troops in Rybachy Peninsula. The flank between this peninsula and our spearhead could not be left unprotected. Yet the commitment of all forces along a single road would have been risky, as we could not be certain whether any particular road was suitable or whether it even actually existed.

According to our appraisal of the terrain, the two routes that were available, one leading to Motovsky and the other to Zapadnaya Litsa, offered similar chances. Either way, the defensive bunker line could not be allowed to stay where it was. It had to be attacked and eliminated. The advantage of the northern road towards Polyarnoye was that it promised the possibility of closing off the mouth of Kola Bay without having to storm Murmansk. However, the road towards Motovsky would similarly avoid Murmansk whilst raising hopes of a thrust towards Kola and thereby over the bridge we had detected over the Tuloma River. The Murman Railway would then be within range.

Our aerial reconnaissance between 21 and 26 June had been unable to adequately map the layout of the roads. We had identified the road from Zapadnaya Litsa to Murmansk with the turnoff to Ura-Guba and the bridge over the Litsa River approximately 12 kilometres south-west of

Zapadnaya Litsa. We had also spotted camps of at least battalion strength on the south bank of Litsa Fjord east of Zapadnaya Litsa, on the east bank of the mouth of the Titovka River, and on a terrace east of the western bend of the Titovka Valley Road. The bridge that we had recently discovered over the Litsa River and the good road that led from there to Murmansk caught our eye, especially as a reconnaissance report from 26 June described the presence of a bridge over the Titovka River and of a road, even if in poor condition, that led from there to Zapadnaya Litsa. We did not have a perfect picture of the start and end of this stretch of road, in particular to the west of the Litsa, as the snow cover was still considerable.

After considering the situation, and without any clear picture as to how the advance over the Litsa might unfold, General Dietl issued the following order, reconstructed from a note in the war diary of the mountain corps, on 26 June 1941 regarding the assembly of the troops and the launch of the attack:

> After moving into position, the mountain corps shall attack on 29 June at 0300 hours on either side of Lake Kuosmejärvi over the Finno-Soviet frontier in the direction of Murmansk and Polyarnoye.
>
> The 3rd Mountain Division is to proceed over the Titovka, seize the heights north-east of Lake Chapr (the first objective), and thrust eastwards from there towards the road connecting Motovsky and Zapadnaya Litsa.
>
> The 2nd Mountain Division is to overcome the bunker positions near the border and cross the Titovka so as to be able to reach the Motovsky–Titovka road. A secondary group will accompany the advance eastwards beyond Maattivuono Bay and cut off the neck of Rybachy Peninsula.

The task for the foreseeably independent Finnish Ivalo Border Guard Battalion as issued on 27 June was to lunge over the Luttojoki and over the Finno-Soviet frontier as far east as the orderly flow of supplies to the battalion would allow. It would then reconnoitre and secure the Lutto–Songelsky area. The original directive of 21 June had envisaged a holding attack against enemy forces we believed to be in the vicinity of Ristikent. But this would not be able to be easily sustained, as the battalion would most likely begin to experience difficulties with supply after making the 90-kilometre trek to the frontier, which it would have to do not on roads but rather over the strong currents of the Luttojoki. Its advance would initially be expeditionary in nature. Roads would need to be built in this area in order to establish lines of communication that would run uninterrupted across the border.

With such a strong commitment in the east, it would be impossible for the mountain corps to be simultaneously responsible for the defence of the more than 1,200 kilometres of coast of North Norway. Army Norway therefore relieved General Dietl of the need to take care of this defence and handed it over to the newly created High Command of North Norway under Lieutenant-General Emmerich Nagy. It later turned out to be an inconvenience. With the 702nd Security Division as the garrison force, the defensive area covered Finnmark in its entirety, reaching as far as the eastern border of Norway and including the region of South Varanger. Yet this area was where the supplies for the mountain corps had to pass through, and it was also where the rear combat zone of the mountain corps would lie. Of course, it was only the leadership of the mountain corps that noticed that its replacements and supplies always had to flow through three areas of jurisdiction: the Reich Commissariat of Norway, the close ally Finland, and the combat zone of the Soviet Union.

Unfortunately, the weakness of the mountain corps on land was matched by that of the forces made available by the other arms of the Wehrmacht. On 19 June, the chief of the command group of the Fifth Air Fleet reported to the commanding general in Bjørnevatn that the following units of the Luftwaffe were available for the support of the advance of the mountain corps and for the operational conduct of the air war:

> Ready for action: 1 fighter squadron, 1 Stuka group, 1 bomber squadron (Junkers 88), 1 long-distance reconnaissance flight.
> Subordinated to the mountain corps: 1 short-range reconnaissance flight.
> Approaching (due to arrive 24 June): 1 fighter squadron.
> Probably to be sent: 1–2 bomber squadrons (one of which might arrive on 24 June), 1 transport group.

The tasks for the Luftwaffe were outlined as follows:

(a) Fighting the Soviet Arctic Fleet.
(b) Laying mines around the Soviet Arctic harbours.
(c) Interruption of the Murman Railway.
(d) Striking the enemy air force in the air and on the ground.
(e) Reconnaissance for the mountain corps to assist it with its combat tasks and reconnaissance over the sea.
(f) Setting up an aircraft warning service on the Norwegian–Finnish border before 22 June and on the Finnish–Soviet border before 29 June.

And the following was promised to Mountain Corps Norway by the Luftwaffe:

(a) Fighter cover and anti-aircraft artillery protection during the assembly of the troops and the occupation of Petsamo between 19 and 22 June.
(b) Special reconnaissance flights to identify the main roads between Petsamo and Murmansk.
(c) Support of the attack of the mountain corps on 29 June by striking the fortified position east of Petsamo and the enemy batteries on Rybachy Peninsula near Maattivuono Bay, the latter if possible before 29 June.

Constant low-lying cloud cover in the preceding 10 days made operations from the aerodrome in Kirkenes very difficult and prevented any appreciable success by the Luftwaffe. An initial reconnaissance flight had spotted most of the Soviet Arctic Fleet still in Polyarnoye, but this fleet was able to evade detection after that. While German aircraft could not easily take to the skies, seemingly better weather conditions in the vicinity of Murmansk enabled Soviet aircraft to make a number of sorties.

Regarding the ground organisation of the Luftwaffe, the most important base for operations in the east was the Kirkenes–Høybuktmoen Aerodrome, approximately 6 kilometres west of the town of Kirkenes. In Luostari, 20 kilometres south of Petsamo, was an airbase that the Luftwaffe started to make use of from 22 June. It was near enough to the front for close reconnaissance planes and fighter aircraft to be employed. Banak Aerodrome, adjacent to Porsanger Fjord, was used for bombers (Junkers 88) whose main operational area was the Arctic Ocean, although these aircraft would also be employed for sorties in the new theatre of war in the east. With so few German aircraft in the region, the danger for Kirkenes was considerable. The town had a port, was a base of supplies, and was also an industrial centre, so it was bound to attract the enemy air force. The first air raid on the town took place on 24 June 1941. It was a challenge to ensure that there was sufficient anti-aircraft protection for the aerodrome, the town, the harbour, the ore factory, and the Langfjord and Pasvikelva bridges (Elvenes and Boris Gleb), as well as for the nickel factory and ore mines of Kolosjoki. This is because there was not enough anti-aircraft artillery to begin with, and only after several months were they reinforced to our satisfaction.

The German Navy was not in a position to support the mountain corps before 22 June. While numerous personnel (600 sailors) had already been made ready in Kirkenes for duty with a planned but not realised Coastal Command T (Murmansk/Teriberka), Coastal Command Kirkenes itself was still lacking in coastal security forces and so could not guarantee safe conduct for the first supply ships to Petsamo with any certainty. The possibility of partially mining Petsamo Fjord was considered, and preparations were made for the departure of any ships that had been there before 22 June, but it soon turned out that such preparations were unnecessary. Provisions had not been made by Naval District Polar Norway for the placement of naval coastal batteries at the entry of Petsamo Fjord, presumably because the anticipated occupation of Murmansk would quickly render the fjord and harbour of Petsamo useless.

To be mentioned at this point is the attempt from 25 June to fabricate evidence of a 17th Mountain Division in the vicinity of Ivalo. Fake signs and other clues were created for this purpose. It is not known whether reports of such a division reached the enemy or, if they did, whether he paid them any attention.

CHAPTER 6

Petsamo

Maps 4 and 6

Following the conclusion of the Soviet–Finnish Winter War, the relationship between Finland and Germany had gradually become closer. And then after the German victory in the west in 1940, many people in Finland had been of the opinion that only Germany would be able to provide assistance against the Soviet Union. Since the supply of the Soviet strongpoint in Hanko demanded constant rail transport through South Finland from Leningrad, it did not seem unreasonable to the government in Helsinki to grant the German Reich transit to Kirkenes via Finnish Lapland. The agreement in this regard was concluded on 22 August 1940. German troops in East Finnmark were able to make the most of this arrangement when they went on leave, and the supply traffic to the region also benefited. The army received temporary barracks for 7,500 men and 1,000 horses in this manner. Soviet Foreign Minister Vyacheslav Molotov, during his visit to Berlin in the middle of November 1940, had demanded the cessation of this traffic and the withdrawal of any German agencies in Finland at that time. Hitler had not responded to this. The deterioration of German–Soviet relations had not escaped the attention of Finland. On the initiative of the German government, several meetings between senior military figures had taken place in the first half of 1941. An agreement on how to wage joint warfare against the Soviet Union had not yet been reached by the end of May 1941. At a conference with the Finnish chief of the general staff, General Erik

Heinrichs, in Salzburg on 25 May 1941, the chief of the operations staff of the OKW, General of Artillery Alfred Jodl, made it clear for the first time that, in the event of a German–Soviet conflict, German troops would need to proceed through Finnish territory in an advance from North Norway against Murmansk. General Heinrichs declared that Finland would only take up arms if it were attacked by the Soviet Union. No agreement was reached in Salzburg. Further discussions after that always revolved around this Finnish condition of renewed Soviet aggression, but it nevertheless became clear to the Finns that they could hardly adopt a position of neutrality in the event of a German–Soviet war. Colonel-General von Falkenhorst arrived in Rovaniemi on 15 June 1941 and took command of the German and Finnish troops that had been assembled for action in North Finland, but this was done in preparation for the hypothetical case that Finland found itself drawn into the imminent war by a Soviet attack. Neither at that time nor at a later stage did the Finns enter into a formal alliance with the German Reich. The relationship of the Finnish soldier with the German soldier was always one of a brother-in-arms fighting against a common enemy, albeit for quite different reasons. Germans and Finns had a warm and comradely relationship in those years. Even the bitter events at the end of the war, fuelled by military and political necessities, could not cast a cloud over the relationship for long.[18]

Right up until the outbreak of war with the Soviet Union was nigh, Mountain Corps Norway had been unaware, or perhaps only peripherally aware, of the development of the Finno-German relationship. There were delays in the fulfilment of so many urgent demands, but, on top of that, there was an overwhelming atmosphere of reserve and uncertainty filled with rumours and contradictions. It was hard to know if the Finns were being obstructive or the German leadership was engaging in cover-up manoeuvres, or if everything was just the result of the enormous political tension before the onset of new world-shaking events.

With this prevailing political situation in Finland, the German forces in Lapland did not commence their advance into the Soviet Union on 22 June 1941 as did the German troops along the rest of the Eastern Front. All that the mountain corps did on this day was to occupy the Petsamo area. Although an immediate Soviet reaction could not be completely ruled out, this occupation was in essence a tactical practicality.

The one way to enter the Petsamo area was along the so-called Nikel Road from Kirkenes to the north of Salmijärvi and from there along the Arctic Ocean Highway. The highway started in the south from the capital of Lapland, Rovaniemi (approximately 6,000 inhabitants), and ran northwards via Ivalo, along the south-east side of Lake Inari and its outlet, the Paatsjoki (Pasvikelva), and through Salmijärvi. From there, the highway followed a curve roughly parallel to the Norwegian–Finnish eastern border past Luostari (or Ylä-Luostari, to be precise) and then bent sharply to the north and led to Petsamo. There was a second, but only partial, route of advance along the Norwegian side of the border, the Kirkenes–Svanvik–Nautsi road. To be able to occupy the Petsamo area from this direction, the question that had to be resolved was how German forces would cross the enormous width of the Paatsjoki from Svanvik to Salmijärvi. It was clear that this second route of advance would not quite work and would be unable to reduce the flow of traffic along the Arctic Ocean Highway. All that we could send along this route was the 68th Bicycle Battalion of the 3rd Mountain Division for the security of the nickel ore mines of Kolosjoki. The rather unimportant Svanvik–Nautsi road had only been of use for the southward departure of SS Battle Group North.

The assembly zone for marching into the Petsamo area was therefore placed along the part of National Road 50 south-east of Kirkenes, between Neiden and the border post in Boris Gleb. Both mountain divisions would advance along this road, although they still had different destinations. While the 2nd Mountain Division would set off first and would head towards the area around and to the south-east of Petsamo, the 3rd Mountain Division would get going afterwards and would occupy the area around and to the south-east of Luostari.

So that we could reach the east bank of the Petsamonjoki as soon as possible, establish a secure position along the Finno-Soviet frontier, and, above all, undertake urgent road construction work, Army Norway gave its approval on the afternoon of 20 June for construction forces to be sent ahead as per our request. The companies of the 405th Construction

Parkkina – Ala Luostari

Pioneer Battalion and several units of the RAD were thus dispatched in a number of vehicles on 20 and 21 June to start work on building roads and bridges. Not only in Luostari but also south-east of Parkkina, 8-tonne emergency bridges were completed over the 80-metre width of the river by the afternoon of 23 June. The participant in the campaign can vividly remember these pioneer commandos going in ahead of the rest of us in their scruffy old clothes, completely unmilitary in appearance and, incredibly, able to escape the notice of the Soviet consulate in Petsamo.

An explanation of the term 'Petsamo' must be given here. Petsamo was the name of a town as well as of an administrative district. Yet the town of Petsamo was not a clearly defined settlement. Regarded as geographically within the area of the district were the villages of Parkkina, with the Ala Luostari Church, at the upper reaches of the fjord; Trifona, 2 kilometres further north, with a small pier; and Liinahamari, almost another 10 kilometres further north, with a large semi-circular harbour. The scattered settlements of the lower Petsamonjoki Valley and of the fjord were not politically linked. The river and the district simply took their names from the town. The company that ran the nickel ore mines and the Kolosjoki works called itself Petsamo-Nikkeli, a good example of the mode of expression that had become common there. The ore mines were regarded as the nickel deposits of Petsamo, even though these deposits lay approximately 80 kilometres away from the town of Petsamo. For the immediate processing of the ore, a large smeltery had been constructed in which a matte of 60 per cent nickel and 30 per cent copper content could be formed through a converter. The weight of this matte was only 10 per cent that of the ore, an important factor in its transportation by road to Kirkenes (approximately 50 kilometres) and then by sea to Germany. To reduce risks, each freighter was permitted to carry no more than 500 tonnes of matte. The transportation of matte southwards along the Arctic Ocean Highway had been carried out by the interested parties of Finland and Sweden before the German occupation of Petsamo. The highway owed its existence to the need to exploit the ore mines and to use the single Finnish harbour that connected to the Arctic Ocean. It had come into being in 1929 out of a number of small stretches of unpaved road that connected various towns and had by 1940 grown into a major road along which traffic flowed continuously. This was a feat that was proof of the drive and vision of the Finns despite their recent defeat in the Winter War. The distinctive landmark of Kolosjoki and the works there was the 165-metre smokestack, without which the sulphuric exhaust gases would have caused the flora of the surrounding area to disappear, leaving only rusty-red desolate terrain.

The advance of the mountain divisions along just one road and the first measures that were taken, more organisational than tactical in nature, had led to all of the supply troops and supply columns being sent forward after the advance guard but before the bulk of the combat troops. Most of those combat troops had to proceed on foot and would take an average of four days to reach their destination. It was therefore the responsibility of the motorised units to carry out the initial security measures. Divided up into 10 march groups, the movement of the mountain corps ran according to schedule once the Finnish barrier was raised at 0230 hours, underneath the overcast sky that obscured the midnight sun, on that fateful day of 22 June.

On 19 June, the possibility of committing the Ivalo Battalion along the Luttojoki had been discussed with the commander of the troops of the Lapland Border Guard, Colonel O. J. Willamo, who was at the same time the commander of the Finnish liaison staff at the headquarters of Army Norway. On the same day, the Finns had cleared the airbase in

Luostari of mines that had previously been laid as a precaution against a Soviet invasion, and had made it available to the Luftwaffe.

We finally received maps of Soviet territory on a scale of 1:100,000 on 22 June. With the monochromic dark brown drawings of these first maps, we always had to take care not to mix up or interpret in reverse the markings of the innumerable lakes with the contour lines of the similarly countless mountains and hills. Unfortunately, these maps were missing two very important pages that covered the Finno-Soviet frontier.

The first Soviet action took place in the late evening hours of 22 June. The coastal battery in the village of Maattivuono, on the western edge of Rybachy Peninsula, opened fire on a cutter near the mouth of Petsamo Fjord. Over the next few days, Soviet aircraft conducted reconnaissance missions and dropped bombs on Kirkenes and Svanvik as well as on the bridges of Luostari and Parkkina, but no damage was caused. The weak Finnish outposts east of Luostari (Pikka Heinäjärvi) and east of Parkkina (Ofonjanvaara) had been taken over by German forces. So as to allow the divisions to completely focus on preparing for the advance to the east, the following forces were assigned for the security of the Petsamo district by 26 June (see Map 6):

> Under the leadership of Major Lindinger, the entrance to Petsamo Fjord is to be secured with strongpoints in Numeroniemi and Numerosätti with anti-tank artillery, machine guns, and radio stations from the 2nd Company of the 55th Anti-Tank Battalion. A machine-gun security detachment is also to be posted 12 kilometres to the north-west at the entrance to Peuravuono Fjord. Around the harbour bay of Liinahamari, at the end of the 531-kilometre length of the Arctic Ocean Highway, are to be placed the 546th Army Coastal Battery (equipped with four Polish 10.5cm guns) and the 548th Army Coastal Battery (four French 15cm guns), both of which will be under the command of the 504th Army Coastal Artillery Battalion. Also to be placed there will be the 3rd Battery of the 5th Flak Regiment (8.8cm guns), the Finnish border guard company of Captain Tiitola, and, subordinated to him, the auxiliary motorised battery of Captain Tähtelä (Russian 7.62cm guns). Trifona is to be protected by the 1st Company of the 40th Panzer

> Battalion, the 1st Company of the 55th Anti-Tank Battalion, the 16th Anti-Tank Company of the 136th Mountain Infantry Regiment, half of the light battery of the I Battalion of the 5th Flak Regiment, and a platoon of mountain infantry from the 136th Mountain Infantry Regiment. The remaining elements of the 55th Anti-Tank Battalion will probably also be sent there. To be grouped around Parkkina and the bridge there over the Petsamonjoki are the 562nd Army Coastal Battery (four French 10.5cm guns), the 869th Army Coastal Battery (four German 21cm Mörser guns), the auxiliary motorised 9th Battery of the 111th Mountain Artillery Regiment (three Norwegian 10.5cm guns), elements (probably an additional platoon) of the 1st Battery of the 5th Flak Regiment (8.8cm guns), and, for the maintenance of the bridge, a platoon of the 82nd Mountain Pioneer Battalion. For the duration of its presence in Parkkina, Group Lindinger will also have the 67th Bicycle Battalion, elements of a company of the 137th Mountain Infantry Regiment, and elements of a battery of the 111th Mountain Artillery Regiment.

It may be anticipated here that the composition and leadership of the units entrusted with the security of the area around Petsamo Fjord changed frequently throughout the second half of 1941. For some time, we had to make do with assembling troops from whatever was left over or from what could not really be used at the front, but then, in the course of 1942, we were successful in establishing in this area and in the neighbouring zones our own security divisional group, composed of a number of fortress infantry battalions, under the command of Major-General Franz Rossi.

From the early hours of 25 June, Army Norway was able to give permission for reconnaissance patrols to be conducted over the Finno-Soviet frontier. The attack of Mountain Corps Norway was to commence on 29 June, and that of XXXVI Army Corps, near Salla, on 1 July. The Finnish III Corps would follow a few days later from the Kuusamo area in South Lapland. The Soviets had already bombed Finnish coastal ships in the skerries of the Gulf of Finland on 22 June and had laid down artillery fire on Finnish targets from the territory that had been leased to them, Hanko Peninsula. Similar border violations had followed after that. Air raids befell Helsinki, Turku, and other cities on 25 June. So it was that the Finnish president declared in a radio address on 26 June that there existed a state of war between Finland and the Union of Soviet Socialist Republics, and that there also existed a brotherhood in arms between the Finnish armed forces and the German Wehrmacht.[19] With the shift of the corps headquarters to Parkkina on 28 June, General Dietl was in a position where he would be directly behind the offensive forces that had been made ready along the front. His quarters were in Parkkina with Karl Türk, who was the German consul in Petsamo. Türk welcomed Dietl into his small home and was able to provide much valuable advice that was of use to the general and the mountain corps. However, the consul ended up being recalled to Germany a few weeks after the outbreak of the war in the east.

CHAPTER 7

Cutting off Rybachy Peninsula

Map 7

The 136th Mountain Infantry Regiment, reinforced with the 5th Battery of the 111th Mountain Artillery Regiment (four Skoda M.15 mountain guns), had been given the task by the 2nd Mountain Division of conducting the attack that would cut off Rybachy Peninsula. On 28 June, the mountain infantry regiment had worked its way forward from a position on the east bank of Petsamo Fjord that lay opposite Parkkina and had proceeded slightly inland along the Lapp trail to the border area east of Maattivuono Bay.[20] By means of cutter transportation from Liinahamari, it had then set up a food supply and medical base on the bay for any evacuation of the wounded that might be necessary. The movements and engagements of this regimental group will be described here because they were not always directly related to the operations of the mountain corps, the bulk of which was to head straight towards the Litsa River. The isolation of Rybachy Peninsula was regarded as a secondary operation against a relatively weak enemy.

Our advance from the rocky and lake-dotted wilderness against the neck of Rybachy Peninsula took the enemy by surprise. It seemed as if he had expected a landing somewhere on the northern end of the peninsula, in the vicinity of Pumanki, for he had committed there and on the west coast several batteries and at least one machine-gun battalion. The first encounters of the regiment were with the enemy border posts.

In order to give the reader a reasonable picture of the terrain, Map 7 (as well as the maps that follow) shows the most important elevations, hill numbers, lakes, and watercourses. However, only a fraction of the mountains and bodies of water can be depicted. It was necessary here to traverse something resembling a lunar landscape, an enormous challenge for the movement of troops and the flow of supplies. A decisive, though not the largest, peak at the neck of the peninsula was Mustatunturi Mountain, which rose roughly 240 metres above sea level. It was an imposing, windswept rock beside the Arctic Ocean, a significant landmark on the right wing of the Western Front and on the left wing of the Eastern Front. From the moment it was taken by the II Battalion of the 136th Mountain Infantry Regiment on 29 June at 1100 hours, the period of static warfare in this area had begun. With German heavy weaponry able to open fire from the slopes of the mountain, the position of the Soviet batteries at the corner of the bay had become untenable. The difficulties presented by the terrain, especially the slopes of the summit, meant that it was not until the next day that the battalion could push further eastwards. Meanwhile, the I Battalion needed one more day to make progress. It had reached Hill 270 on the evening of 29 June, but only on the morning of 1 July did it take Hill 122 in the face of much heavy machine-gun fire. Regardless of the resistance on the slopes, the regiment had cleared the dominant Hill 388.9 of the machine-gun security forces of the Soviet Border Troops towards 2000 hours on 29 June and had marched into a long depression. The III Battalion moved through this depression from the eastern slopes of Hill 388.9 along a chain of lakes towards the south-east so as to head for what we saw as an important objective, Titovka. At noon on 30 June, the battalion reached the Titovka–Kutovaya road, which, as it turned out, had already been opened by the 67th Bicycle Battalion from the south. Meanwhile, at the neck of Rybachy Peninsula, the enemy had begun to put up greater resistance.

The headquarters of the mountain corps had been of the view on the afternoon of 29 June that a single battalion would be enough to cut off the peninsula. But the firepower of the roughly three enemy batteries in the vicinity of Kutovaya proved to be too strong, and, by 1830 hours,

Stuka dive bombers were needed to take them out. At 0500 hours on 30 June, the first destroyers or similarly small warships of the Soviet Arctic Fleet appeared in Motovsky Bay, just outside Kutovaya, and Soviet troops were observed landing there. In the slopes that led from Hill 122 to Kutovaya, there was little cover against the overwhelming fire of the land and naval artillery of the enemy. The only thing on the German side that could return fire was a single mountain gun battery of 7.5cm guns. The 2nd Company of the 67th Bicycle Battalion, which had approached along the road to Titovka and had arrived on the evening of 30 June, was able to extend the defensive line to the coast of Motovsky Bay, but it could not help with any territorial gain in the direction of Kutovaya. Any idea of supplying the front via Maattivuono Bay could not be entertained for the time being.

It was reported on the morning of 1 July that the bicycle company had been temporarily encircled. Fortunately, the situation was brought under control thanks to the II Battalion of the 136th Mountain Infantry Regiment, which had advanced from Hill 246 and had gained ground later that day to the west of the bicycle company. By 1300 hours on this day, it had become certain from our observations and from prisoner statements that what we were facing in that area was an enemy regiment with at least four mobile coastal batteries. A new attack by the II Battalion of the mountain infantry regiment that had been planned for 1700 hours was postponed until 2 July. After defending against a heavy Soviet attack in the early morning (0200 hours on 2 July), the battalion commenced its own attack at 1550 hours. It had wiped out the bothersome pockets of resistance on the lower slopes by the evening, but the attack lost momentum soon after. The line that cut off the peninsula was now held by the 67th Bicycle Battalion on the right and the II Battalion of the mountain infantry regiment on the left. No further advance needed to be carried out. From the positions that they had reached, German forces would be able to open fire on any Soviet troops that appeared in the neck of the peninsula. The enemy had established a deep defensive zone on the gently terraced slopes that rose up on the peninsula. It is unlikely that this defensive zone had only just been set up, for we would have noticed any extra activity given the good sunlight of the preceding three days. Rather, it is reasonable to assume that the defences on the peninsula at that time had been prepared as part of the enemy plan to permanently fortify the coastal zone. As we had suspected, the peninsula had received high priority in the Soviet defensive plan. The German forces that were committed to that area would not have had any chance of success if they had attempted to continue with the attack. The result, though, was that they were tied down there for an undesirably long time. Even the chief of staff of Army Norway confirmed over the telephone that German forces near the peninsula would have to go over to the defensive. As time passed, both sides would consolidate their positions. Kutovaya would remain an abandoned pile of stones between the two lines. Three warships appeared and opened fire outside Kutovaya and Titovka on the night of 2/3 July, and it is possible that troops landed on the peninsula that same night, but, from then on, nothing would change. With the arrival of German artillery in the form of the 1st Battery of the 730th Heavy Artillery Battalion on the evening of 30 June, and then one to two army coastal batteries after that, enemy shipping along the stretch of coast under German control started to diminish. This was not the case in the bay in the middle of the peninsula. Soviet ships would continue to go there for several weeks. The enemy therefore had the resources he needed to maintain constant pressure against the German obstacle line throughout the summer. Since each individual enemy thrust was never in excess of battalion strength, it was always possible for the determined defenders to hold the line. Mustatunturi Mountain became the blood-drenched cornerstone of the Arctic Front for both sides.

The supply situation of the reinforced 136th Mountain Infantry Regiment had become critical on 2 July, but it gradually improved thanks to the fact that supplies were able to start flowing along the Titovka Valley from 3 July.

Associated with the isolation of Rybachy Peninsula was the occupation and security of the mouth of the Titovka River. On 30 June, the 67th Bicycle Battalion, which was pursuing the elements of the Soviet 14th Rifle Division that had been thrown back towards Titovka, reached a ferry embarkation point at the opening of the bay at 0815 hours. The village of Titovka, which lay on a long gravel headland on a bend in the river, was found destroyed and uninhabited. The camp to the east of the bend in the river and the small airfield there had been hastily abandoned and destroyed by the Soviets. Although the remnants of the garrison carried out a number of weak attacks from the east and south-east on 1 July at 0100 hours, they were repelled by those troops of the bicycle battalion that were in the area. Fire from enemy ships no longer disturbed us, but the danger of a landing had not been averted just yet. We had to assume that the enemy would want to threaten the defensive line at the neck of the peninsula just as much as he would want to attack the flank of the mountain corps. The III Battalion of the 136th Mountain Infantry Regiment conducted a reconnaissance of the area south-east of Titovka on the morning of 1 July and made a tactically significant discovery: the road that, according to our maps, was supposed to connect Titovka and Zapadnaya Litsa did not in fact exist. What was there instead was a telegraph line that ran through the roadless tundra. This line could only be followed with an exhausting march on foot. The land was a deserted wilderness all around.

Neither the 136th Mountain Infantry Regiment nor the 2nd Mountain Division could take care of the border area west and south-west of the aforementioned Hill 388.9. As a result, there were some isolated units of the Soviet Border Troops that still remained and that had not yet been attacked. Several days later, presumably because they had run out of provisions, they sought to break through to Soviet lines, launching assaults here and there far behind the German front.

CHAPTER 8

Overcoming the Border Fortifications

Maps 5 and 8

In the seven days between 22 and 29 June, feverish work had been done on the construction of roads leading from both Luostari and Parkkina towards the east. Observers at higher-level headquarters, even those who just simply looked at their maps, would have shaken their heads upon the sight of this tundra, consisting as it did of fields, boulders, marshes, shrubs, and lakes. Still partially covered with snow, the landscape resembled something from the time of the first days of the Creation. The character of this landscape and of the climate can be highlighted by comparing it with that of the Alps. The conditions on the shores of the Barents Sea correspond to what one might encounter at a height of 1,600 metres in the Alps. A difference in altitude of 100 metres on the Arctic Front was equivalent to a difference of 300 metres in the Alps. An altitude of 300 metres above Petsamo Fjord was like an altitude of 2,500 metres in the Alps, roughly at the crown of the Grossglockner High Alpine Road. This was perhaps trivial in summer, but in winter it was significant. The wind and storm possessed greater force on the Arctic Front than in the Alps. The construction of roads required consideration as to how they would be kept open in winter. If it is at all possible, subarctic roads have to remain passable in winter, ideally leading over hills and summits so that the snow falls aside more easily. Also, alternatives to driving over lake surfaces that have frozen over are desirable. The Lapps have their own lines of movement. Building a good road quickly required enormous effort. The only question that arose was where the focus of our work should be. In its planning, the mountain corps had hoped that the 3rd Mountain Division, upon crossing the Titovka River, would be able to find a road to Motovsky and then, from there, more roads to Murmansk, Zapadnaya Litsa, and Titovka. It had therefore already been decided in Bjørnevatn that the 3rd Mountain Division, with the help of its regiments as well as of two or three RAD units, would dig a dirt track from Luostari towards Lake Chapr.

But the 405th Construction Pioneer Battalion, which always followed the combat troops on foot, and the bulk of the 27th Section of the RAD, which consolidated the routes marked out by the construction pioneers, had been committed from the first day of the occupation of the Petsamo district to the construction of the single road that would be used by the mountain corps. This road would lead from the east bank of the Petsamonjoki near Parkkina over the gradually climbing ridges (Pieni Tartuoavi, Ofonjanvaara, etc.) in the direction of the southern slope of Kuosmoaivi. From there, it was hoped that, after the commencement of the attack, a connection could rapidly be established, perhaps within two or three days, with the high-altitude line of bunkers or with the road along the Titovka Valley,

Road construction in the tundra

both of which had been observed by German aerial reconnaissance, and thereby with the Soviet road network. There is no record of how many broken springs and axles were accumulated on this 10-kilometre stretch east of Parkkina. The truck platoons of the light columns of the four mountain infantry regiments came to an abrupt stop here.[21] Very few of the military postal vehicles from Tyrol or Vorarlberg managed to survive. Only the medium and heavy German-built tractors prevailed. They brought most of the heavy artillery of the 1st Battery of the 5th Flak Regiment and all of the heavy artillery of the 1st and 2nd Batteries of the 730th Heavy Artillery Battalion to the assembly area on 28 June.

It was with the 2nd Mountain Division, minus the 136th Mountain Infantry Regiment and the 5th Battery of the 111th Mountain Artillery Regiment, that the point of main effort of the mountain corps lay. The fortified positions of the enemy had to be taken here, for they would have been a permanent threat if we had simply tried to bypass them. They would have made road construction quite impossible. A frontal assault against them would have been a mistake. The terrain allowed an attack to be carried out against them on the southern flank. The main problem was the strength of the concrete emplacements on Hill 204.6. The preparations for the attack were such that the reinforced 137th Mountain Infantry Regiment, starting from the hollow south-west of Hills 263 and 294, would circle the lakes near Hill 204.6 to the south and, if possible, even push beyond the hill in the direction of the Titovka Valley. Only one specially organised mountain infantry company would be employed to tackle Hill 204.6. To the east of this hill, the II Battalion of the 137th Mountain Infantry Regiment, reinforced with the 2nd Company of the 82nd Mountain Pioneer Battalion (with all of the flamethrowers of the battalion) and the 2nd Battery of the 111th Mountain Artillery Regiment, was to pivot to the north and then roll up the entire line of approximately 27 dugout bunkers, mostly machine-gun shelters, between Hills 189.3 and 255.4. The mountain guns of the 3rd, 4th, and 6th Batteries of the 111th Mountain Artillery Regiment and the abovementioned heavy batteries were to provide fire support. Even the 1st Battery of the 5th Flak Regiment would take part by firing directly at the bunkers.

As early as 28 June, two or three Soviet batteries, one of them a heavy battery, had fired upon the assembly area of the 2nd Mountain Division. A number of air assaults had been carried out by Soviet Rata fighters. The enemy had obviously been fully aware of the preparations to the east of Parkkina. In contrast, it had remained relatively quiet on the front of the 3rd Mountain Division. The Luftwaffe had promised at that time that it would launch a Stuka attack against the enemy bunkers and batteries.

It had been left up to the mountain corps to decide at what time the offensive would begin. The date and time that had been chosen was 29 June at 0300 hours. The troops had moved forward according to schedule. Only at one point on the front of the 3rd Mountain Division was there a single mountain infantry company that had set off early. It had crossed the Titovka River north of Lake Chapr at 0200 hours, had driven away some machine-gun security detachments, and had also broken weak enemy resistance. This early advance had not been planned, but it paved the way for the subsequent crossing of the river by the 138th Mountain Infantry Regiment.

A thick fog concealed the line of fortifications at 0300 hours. The Stuka attack could not yet be carried out. Our forward observers could not see a thing, so our artillery remained silent for the most part. But the fog did enable the movements of the 137th Mountain Infantry Regiment to be conducted surreptitiously. At the command posts of the 2nd Mountain Division and the 111th Mountain Artillery Regiment on Kuosmoaivi (Hill 367), only distant objects could be seen. The commander of Army Norway and the commander of Mountain Corps Norway were present. Soviet artillery zone fire was constant. At 0500 hours, the 13th Company of the 137th Mountain Infantry Regiment stormed Hill 204.6. It suffered considerable losses, for the hill was defended by two or three platoons with heavy machine guns. At the same time, the leading battalion of the 3rd Mountain Division stood with a mountain battery on the east bank of the Titovka before a weakened enemy, probably border troops.

By 0630 hours, the leading elements of the I Battalion of the 137th Mountain Infantry Regiment headed for the Titovka Valley via the slopes about 3 kilometres east of Hill 204.6. Losses were light, although the difficulties presented by the terrain were considerable even for mountain troops. The fog began to lift at 0700 hours. The air support officer at the 2nd Mountain Division contacted the airbase in Kirkenes to request that the Stuka group commence its attack immediately.

In accordance with the plan of attack, the reinforced II Battalion of the 137th Mountain Infantry Regiment, organised into assault companies, pivoted to the north on the eastern side of Hill 204.6. Not only multiple bombing raids but also the direct fire of the 1st Battery of the 5th Flak Regiment put several bunkers out of action, thereby providing good support for the battalion. Hill 189.3 was taken at 1000 hours, so the attack turned towards Hill 255.4. The III Battalion of the mountain infantry regiment stood ready to the north-east of Hill 204.6. Depending on the development of the situation, it was to follow either the I Battalion or the II Battalion. By 1015 hours, the 2nd Mountain Division reported to the mountain corps that the I Battalion of the 137th Mountain Infantry Regiment had pressed forward as far as the west bank of the Titovka in the direction of the bridge that we had detected 2 kilometres north-east of the camp. Exploiting the favourable development of the situation and the weak point of the enemy, who occasionally fought tenaciously but mostly fell back swiftly, the 137th Mountain Infantry Regiment sent its III Battalion from the already abandoned camp over the Titovka so that it could conduct a flank attack on the bridge site. On the evening of the first day of the attack, the line of bunkers was taken whilst the II Battalion of the same regiment advanced in the direction of the Titovka bridge so that it could be stationed there in regimental reserve. Our defence against the enemy positions that we had identified or that we presumed to exist in the north near Hills 221.4 and 286 was weak. On the night of 29/30 June, the advance on the bridge by the I Battalion of the mountain infantry regiment and the 1st Company of the 40th Panzer Battalion from the north and by the III Battalion of the mountain infantry regiment from the west had pushed so far forward that the enemy defence there was compelled to fall back. The bridge, fully intact, was in German hands by 0300 hours, and, by 0600 hours, a bridgehead had been established which extended as far as Hill 228.9. A pursuit formation of the reinforced 137th Mountain Infantry Regiment set off in the direction of Zapadnaya Litsa.

View of the tundra east of the Titovka River

The day produced contradictory news on the advance of this spearhead. The 2nd Mountain Division still faced Soviet infantry and artillery. The I Battalion of the 138th Mountain Infantry Regiment of the 3rd Mountain Division therefore turned from Lake Chapr towards Hill 288 in order to apply additional pressure against the enemy. On 30 June at approximately 1750 hours, the battalion appeared between Hills 288 and 228.9 to the rear of the Soviet artillery positions. It brushed aside the little resistance the enemy put up and captured four guns with horses, a light armoured reconnaissance car, three tractors, and 25 trucks. More guns and vehicles, all blown up, were found in the surrounding area. The advance guard of the 2nd Mountain Division could now continue to press forward more easily.

At that time, on the evening of 30 June, the 2nd Mountain Division and Mountain Corps Norway realised that the road that had been observed from the air and that had been reported to lead from the Titovka bridge to Zapadnaya Litsa was in fact not as extensive as had been assumed. The road ended about 5 kilometres south-east of the Titovka bridge. It was for this reason that the guns and supply trains of the Soviet artillery, which had been pushed back here by the German attack from the Titovka Valley and from what would have been the Soviet line of retreat to Titovka, did not manage to retreat any further. The mountain corps was faced with a roadless area of tundra rather like that that had existed east of Petsamo. At 2105 hours, the 2nd Mountain Division reported to the mountain corps that the bulk of the 137th Mountain Infantry Regiment had set up a defensive position in the area that had been reached. With overtaxed pack animals and no roads, a further advance by substantial elements of the regiment was impossible at that moment. All the tanks of the 1st Company of the 40th Panzer Battalion had broken down.

At 0600 hours on the same day, 30 June, the 67th Bicycle Battalion had started to proceed downstream from the Titovka bridge. There was no enemy presence on the south-east bank of the river. The battalion had reached the bend in the river by 0815 hours and was in possession of the town of Titovka and the camp there by 1000 hours. Lunging further along the road to Kutovaya, the spearhead of the battalion met that of the III Battalion of the 136th Mountain Infantry Regiment at noon.

Until 0800 hours on 29 June, the bulk of the 138th Mountain Infantry Regiment was in the process of crossing the river at a point to the west of Lake Chapr. The hills to the south-east and east of this lake were in German hands. The regimental bicycle platoon, naturally without bicycles, had been sent to conduct a reconnaissance of the terrain in the direction of Motovsky and had disappeared somewhere to the south-east.

There had been no contact with the enemy for several hours. The 139th Mountain Infantry Regiment had handed over all of its carts and pack

Lapp trail

animals for the supply of the 138th Mountain Infantry Regiment. Hour after hour, it was hoped that the road to Motovsky could be reached. In the late morning, our ground and aerial reconnaissance had to report that there existed neither a road to Motovsky nor a road linking Motovsky with Zapadnaya Litsa. Given the fact that the weather had cleared by this time, we could regard these observations as accurate. A Lapp trail was the only thing that seemed to lead to Motovsky. We had once again misinterpreted the maps available to us. The main problem for the German map analysts was that the broken double lines so frequently marked on Scandinavian maps indicated not just roads, as would be the case with central European maps, but also winter trails. Despite the fact that the mountain corps had suspected the worst, it had nevertheless, perhaps for the sake of wanting to be able to exploit any ideal situation, held on to the hope that the roads actually existed. The poor weather conditions in the week before the offensive, together with the unfamiliarity of the Luftwaffe observers with the tundra, made it difficult to correct the false impression we had gained from our maps. It no longer made sense for the 3rd Mountain Division to pursue its original objective.

The mountain corps decided that the direction of the advance of the 138th Mountain Infantry Regiment should be altered immediately. Its I Battalion was to head due east and take Hill 289.6, after which it was to pivot to the north-east in the direction of Hill 288. We estimated that it would arrive there on the evening of 30 June, whereupon it would be at the disposal of the mountain corps. The rest of the 138th Mountain Infantry Regiment would proceed along the Titovka River to the bridge. The 3rd Mountain Division would ensure the secure flow of supplies to the regiment and then, without the regiment, would return to the Arctic Ocean Highway via Luostari so that it could follow in the wake of the 2nd Mountain Division. General Dietl confirmed this decision at 1500 hours: the mountain corps would gather the bulk of the 2nd and 3rd Mountain Divisions in the area of the Titovka bridge and Hill 228.9, and would hold the bridgehead there until the road to its rear had been completed.[22]

The spearhead of the I Battalion of the 138th Mountain Infantry Regiment had broken weak enemy resistance and had already arrived at a point to the north-east of Hill 289.6 at 1240 hours on 29 June. But it was not until 0400 hours on 30 June that the whole battalion had a chance to stop for a much-needed rest, after having made the tiring march through the tundra to a position halfway between Hill 289.6 and the end of the supposed road south of Hill 228.9. The battalion did at least, as described earlier, prevail against the Soviet battery in the late afternoon. By the evening of 30 June, the 138th Mountain Infantry Regiment, without the I Battalion, was on its way to the Titovka bridge. The headquarters of the 3rd Mountain Division departed at once so that it could set itself up in a new position closer to that of the 2nd Mountain Division. The latter was located where the Russian camp had been.

In the area 8 kilometres north-west of Motovsky, our ground reconnaissance had spotted weak forces of the Soviet Border Troops. The observations by the Luftwaffe of the movements of Soviet forces around the Litsa Valley were contradictory. The conclusion to be drawn was that the enemy was most likely bringing forward reserves from Murmansk as quickly as possible. Mountain Corps Norway submitted a report to Army Norway in the evening on the impression that had been gained of the enemy as a result of the first couple of days of the offensive. The following paragraph summarises what was contained in that report.

The border fortifications had been stronger than expected. The temporary construction roads that had been found there indicated that it would not have been long before a coherent line of fortifications would have been completed from Rybachy Peninsula to a point 30 kilometres further south, such that it would have run parallel with the Finno-Soviet frontier. The bunkers had been fiercely defended. Even flamethrowers had not compelled the garrisons to retreat. The number of Soviet troops taken prisoner barely exceeded 100. Most of them were Siberians of various tribes. The bulk of the enemy forces were composed of the 14th Rifle Division with the 95th Rifle Regiment and elements of the 149th and 241st Artillery Regiments. In addition to that, there were parts of the 52nd Rifle Division from the 58th and 205th Rifle Regiments and the 158th Artillery Regiment that had been spotted. A clear picture of the tactical organisation of these forces could not be gained. It was possible that the 14th Rifle Division had been stopped. Elements of the division had immediately fled to the sea or to Rybachy Peninsula via

Titovka, and some had retreated in the direction of Zapadnaya Litsa on foot. The observation of motorised vehicles in the Litsa Valley south of Zapadnaya Litsa indicated that the road that had been reported leading to Murmansk did at least exist. The precise location of its north-western end had not yet been ascertained. Also, the fact that a rearguard unit of the I Battalion of the 138th Mountain Infantry Regiment unexpectedly came across 70 Soviet troops in the southern no man's land on the night of 1/2 July indicated that it was highly likely that stragglers as well as organised enemy reconnaissance detachments could have been anywhere in the deep flanks of the mountain corps at that time. Painstaking reconnaissance and security measures were necessary. This was emphasised in an order from the mountain corps on 2 July at 1800 hours.

The unsuccessful advance of the 3rd Mountain Division leads to the question as to how it could have been used if we had possessed a more accurate picture of the layout of the roads. We had discovered that there were few roads and that there was only one direction, namely eastwards from Petsamo, in which there at least existed the possibility in the foreseeable future of creating a supply route by closing gaps in the roads. On top of that, the construction forces available to the mountain corps were limited. They could only ever work on a single road at a time. This meant that, in hindsight, the mountain divisions would have probably best taken the same route for their advance. With their pack animals, they might have been able to advance for a short time, perhaps 10 or 15 kilometres, into roadless terrain and fight there, but they could not have stayed there all day, let alone push further onwards. If such terrain needed to be traversed, then at least a dirt track would have to be built or perhaps multiple pack animal transport sections would have to be employed. Anyone who demanded greater performance from the mountain divisions and then expressed astonishment at their slow progress to the east of the Titovka demonstrated a poor understanding of the situation and of what the available forces could achieve. We were bitterly disappointed about the lack of roads east of Petsamo. Even if our maps had been more accurate, a fundamentally different approach by the mountain corps than that executed according to the decision of 29 June at 1500 hours would hardly have been possible. The decisive effects of the lack of roads west of the Litsa were the weakening of the penetrative power of the German spearhead, the deceleration in the flow of supplies, and the loss of time demanded by road construction. At any rate, the resources being squandered on the construction of the dirt track east of Luostari could be utilised instead on the road construction east of Parkkina. It might even have become possible in the long term for an entire mountain division to apply maximum pressure against the point of main effort and for the regimental group of the rear mountain division cutting off Rybachy Peninsula to be withdrawn. A day's gain in road construction could have made a big difference for the batteries at the front.

Whilst the mountain corps had been in the process of consolidating its arterial road, the enemy had gained the decisive two or three days he needed to hurl new forces forward via road and sea. He enjoyed aerial superiority at that time, as all of the forces of the Fifth Air Fleet, with the exception of a few fighters and reconnaissance aircraft, had been transferred from Kirkenes further south to support the attack on Salla by the XXXVI Army Corps that was to begin on 1 July.

Nevertheless, even on 1 and 2 July, the advance had not come to a complete stop. Our ground reconnaissance units were still making progress, as were some weak companies here and there. The encounter with the approaching Soviet reinforcements on the Litsa would determine whether the mountain corps would be in a position to take on the mobile defensive forces before Murmansk. Only after that could there be any thought of another offensive. But it was always questions of terrain, supply, and flank protection, rather than preparing for battle, that caused the greatest difficulties.

CHAPTER 9

Meeting Engagements

Map 9

In a telephone conversation on 2 July at 1430 hours, the chief of staff of Mountain Corps Norway had informed the chief of staff of Army Norway that the mistakes that had resulted from the poor knowledge of the layout of the roads meant that an attack over the Litsa River could not be carried out in less than eight days if all of the available forces were to be involved. The mountain corps had nonetheless, in the aforementioned reconnaissance order from the same day at 1800 hours, made it the duty of the mountain divisions, despite all the difficulties, to send several battalions over the Litsa at any points where our reconnaissance had not identified strong enemy forces further east. We wanted to be able to hold the east bank of the river at such locations. What could not be committed to battle or supply was to be used instead for the construction, improvement, or maintenance of New Road (or Russian Road), i.e. the supply road running from Petsamo to the Litsa via the Titovka bridge. A meeting held at that time between the chiefs of staff, the second general staff officers, and the intendants of the mountain corps and mountain divisions resulted in the agreement that the construction and supply troops would need to exert the utmost effort to ensure that the combat units could operate at maximum range from the Titovka Valley. Distribution points along the valley needed to be in place from 6 July, and the supply of ammunition, fuel, and rations had to be safeguarded from that date until 10 July inclusive. The mountain corps could therefore assure

Army Norway in its evening report that it would conduct operations beyond the Litsa as soon as possible after 6 July.

The advance guard of the 137th Mountain Infantry Regiment (the I Battalion) had in the meantime, on 1 July, worked its way from the north-west towards Zapadnaya Litsa, but it had been unable to drive out the security forces there. On the same day at 1915 hours, the II Battalion attacked one or two enemy companies on the slopes of a mountain 3 kilometres south-west of Zapadnaya Litsa. This dominant peak, which we named Herzberg due to its strikingly heart-shaped contour lines on the map, was soon in our hands. The 8th Company of the 137th Mountain Infantry Regiment, reinforced with the 3rd Company of the 82nd Mountain Pioneer Battalion, continued, as the new advance guard, the march upstream along the west bank of the Litsa. The III Battalion of the 137th Mountain Infantry Regiment and the I Battalion of the 138th Mountain Infantry Regiment followed on 2 July and reached the area west of Herzberg before midnight. Light artillery activity flared up on both sides.

German reconnaissance on the morning of 3 July produced an updated picture of the situation. The artillery positions on the north-west coast of Rybachy Peninsula (Pumanki) had seemingly been evacuated. Movements from there towards Eina-Guba on the south coast of the peninsula and then by ship across Motovsky Bay towards the south and south-east had been detected. The mountain corps interpreted this as the withdrawal of excess forces from the peninsula so that they could be used to reinforce the front before Murmansk. An enemy thrust of company strength against a reconnaissance unit of ours near Point 134.2 had already been repelled on the night of 2/3 July, and, at 0900 hours on 3 July, the new advance guard of the 2nd Mountain Division came up against the attack of a Soviet battalion about 3 kilometres north-west of a road bridge over the Litsa (12 kilometres south of Zapadnaya Litsa). This Soviet attack was supported by forces, also of battalion strength, that occupied the hills on the other side of the rapids there (White Water Hill), and by artillery from the south-west (Hill 183.6). The road that led to Murmansk was finally within reach, but for now, given the superiority of the Soviet forces in the vicinity, the advance guard had to fall back to avoid being outflanked. At almost the same time, about 1000 hours, the enemy carried out a successful assault against the rear of the 2nd Company of the 138th Mountain Infantry Regiment. Yet the enemy did not seem to be aware of his success, for he hesitated before pursuing the retreating company. This picture of the situation compelled the mountain corps to accelerate the advance of the 139th Mountain Infantry Regiment and of the III Battalion of the 138th Mountain Infantry Regiment. These forces reached the Titovka bridge by 1700 hours on 3 July.

Meanwhile, the I Battalion of the 137th Mountain Infantry Regiment had taken Zapadnaya Litsa at 1045 hours. The bulk of the battalion had crossed the Litsa just upstream from the mouth of the river and, by 2100 hours, it had occupied the Soviet camp (Litsa Camp) on the south bank of Litsa Bay, 5 kilometres east of Zapadnaya Litsa, without resistance. The 3rd Company of the battalion had advanced some distance along the north bank of the river. Some of its troops had then waded across a shallow stretch of water from a sandbank at 1300 hours; others had crossed with small rafts.

By the end of the day, the 2nd Mountain Division stood along a line connecting Herzberg, Zapadnaya Litsa, and Litsa Camp. It had also established combat outposts south of Herzberg. The 3rd Mountain Division covered the next 3 kilometres to the south-west with the I

View of the mouth of the Litsa River

Battalion of the 138th Mountain Infantry Regiment. The II Battalion of the regiment was advancing straight towards Point 257.4 in order to reinforce the I Battalion as soon as possible. The two mountain divisions were at long last arranged side by side. The command post of the mountain corps had been set up to the south of the Titovka bridge. The construction of the road between Petsamo and Titovka Valley had made considerable progress thanks to the devoted commitment of the workers of 11 RAD units. The beautiful and much warmer summer weather melted the remaining snow in the hollows and dried up some of the marshy areas. The help of the Finnish civilian road construction unit of Savolainen Engineering was certainly noticeable. It had to be explained to those with no knowledge of the tundra that what was meant by 'considerable progress' was that it would now take just a little longer than eight hours for a truck to make the 25-kilometre trip from Parkkina to the Titovka bridge.

General Dietl spent the entire day of 3 July with the leading battalions of both divisions. Worthy of note are several points that arose from his discussions with the divisional commanders as well as from his impressions of the fighting and terrain. The 2nd Mountain Division was not inclined to carry out a frontal assault after the initial manoeuvring battles of that day. The Litsa Valley was muddy, and it was not always possible to see the surrounding terrain properly. There was no field of fire for those who had to move in the lowlands. The dominant peaks were White Water Hill and Hill 183.6, and both were firmly in enemy hands. The mountain division estimated that the enemy possessed a reinforced regiment consisting of gun, howitzer, and anti-aircraft batteries in the vicinity of the Litsa bridge. Major-General Ernst Schlemmer, the commander of the 2nd Mountain Division, put the case for a wide envelopment on the left wing that would advance along a Lapp trail east of Hills 274, 263.5, and 322 in the direction of Ura-Guba. The commander of the mountain corps did not want German forces to go that far forward. He did not wish to risk men and matériel being cut off in the tundra. He preferred that the point of main effort remain in the Litsa Valley, as it was only there that a large formation could be constantly supplied. The fighting of that day had been brief, but fierce, with losses being relatively high. It was clear to General Dietl that an attack through the valley and over the mountains to the east, or around those mountains to strike the bridge defence from the rear, would require powerful forces. Ground reconnaissance units of the 2nd Mountain Division were to explore what was possible in this regard. The possibility of conducting a secondary attack in the direction of Ura-Guba was not to be ruled out. But the next attack could only begin once the units were fully supplied. It was the view of General Dietl that it would be better at this stage to establish a bridgehead rather than attempt to set objectives that were too far away.

A preliminary order was therefore issued at 2310 hours. The mountain corps, on 6 July, was to push towards the south-east along and on the eastern side of the road to Murmansk. It would annihilate the enemy defence of the Litsa bridge and then scout the lake-dotted area 25 kilometres to the south-east of the bridge. Since the 2nd Mountain Division was still responsible for the northern flank, which stretched from Rybachy Peninsula to Litsa Bay, half of its infantry would be unable to partake in the push to the south-east. Its worth in this push would therefore be that of a regimental battle group.

On 4 July, we were rather pleased to learn that more than 150 trucks, mostly serviceable, had been captured in Litsa Camp. For the present moment, though, Litsa Camp and Herzberg needed to be held. Both positions had to defend themselves throughout the day against multiple enemy assaults, with the defence at the camp having to continue well into the night of 4/5 July. Meanwhile, in the area of the 3rd Mountain Division, the I and II Battalions of the 138th Mountain Infantry Regiment closed in on Hill 111.8. They were supplied by the approaching III Battalion, which had taken on a support role.

Reconnaissance units were extremely busy at that time. To the south of Herzberg, one unit discovered the forces that had attacked the mountain the previous day in retreat, so the 137th Mountain Infantry Regiment sent some combat units after them. Another reconnaissance unit encountered a Soviet company in the valley depression south-east of the lake next to Point 110.8. This was a bad sign for the planned push of the 2nd Mountain Division. Finally, increased shipping outside Litsa Bay meant that the left flank along the fjord near Litsa Camp needed to be watched carefully. On top of this threat was a similar one in the vicinity of Petsamo, for the headquarters of Army Norway expressed its concern that evening that a British raid might be launched there to assist Soviet forces.[23] The security group in Petsamo was led by the commander of the 68th Bicycle Battalion, and it was not allowed to be weakened under any circumstances.[24] This was consequently an entire battalion of infantry that could not be used in the push towards Murmansk. Before the front of the 3rd Mountain Division (138th Mountain Infantry Regiment), enemy forces of battalion strength fell back to the south-east. These forces were accompanied by pack animals, the first time we had seen them on the Soviet side. At 2215 hours, the Litsa bridge blew sky high. Except for some combat outposts, the enemy had evacuated the west bank and was awaiting the German attack on the east bank. (This is according to the war diary of the mountain corps, based on the report of the 3rd Mountain Division. However, the records of the 2nd Mountain Division indicate that the demolition of the bridge only took place on 7 July. Given the situation, it is plausible that the combat outpost troops, when they conducted their own withdrawal, set off a second round of explosives to ensure that the bridge was thoroughly destroyed.)

CHAPTER 10

The First Attack over the Litsa River

Map 10

Herzberg provided a rather long-range view of the terrain on either side of the lower Litsa. Hill 314.9 could be seen in the distance, as could the barrier of hills beyond (Hills 322 and 321.9). By 5 July, the peak of Herzberg could be reached by command car at the laborious speed of 10 kilometres per hour along the dirt road that had been made by the 405th Construction Pioneer Battalion. The 2nd Mountain Division had set up its command post there.

The plan of attack foresaw the 3rd Mountain Division on the right and the 2nd Mountain Division on the left. Two battalions from the 3rd Mountain Division (I and II of the 138th Mountain Infantry Regiment) and three from the 2nd Mountain Division (all three of the 137th Mountain Infantry Regiment) would be the first to go into battle. Elements of the III Battalion of the 136th Mountain Infantry Regiment were on their way from Titovka and would be able to reach Litsa Camp by 6 July so that the I Battalion of the 137th Mountain Infantry Regiment would be relieved and thus made available to partake in the attack. All other units were to assist with the supply of the front, provided they were not still making the agonisingly slow march through the tundra, as was the case with the II Battalion of the 139th Mountain Infantry Regiment. It had to be considered that the supply of both combat battalions of the 3rd Mountain Division across the roughly 30-kilometre roadless terrain to the area south of the Litsa bridge could only be achieved if two battalions of the 139th Mountain

Infantry Regiment came to a stop, built a dirt track for the march route, and handed over all of their pack animals, approximately 500 in total, to the 138th Mountain Infantry Regiment. It can be seen, then, that it can be misleading to speak of an attack by two mountain divisions, for neither could advance at full strength.

The I and II Battalions of the 138th Mountain Infantry Regiment were to attack on 6 July. From their assembly positions in the thickly overgrown shrubland 4 kilometres south-west of the Litsa bridge, they would advance eastwards over the river and over two small, albeit prominent, hills to Russian Road, which lay 5 kilometres to the south of the bridge. This first objective was the suspected location of the enemy artillery positions. On the left, the II and III Battalions of the 137th Mountain Infantry Regiment were to cross the river on either side of the Litsa bridge and would seek to carry out the particularly difficult task of taking their initial objectives: White Water Hill and Hill 183.6. In order to ease this frontal attack, the I Battalion of the 137th Mountain Infantry Regiment, already advancing along the east bank of the river near its mouth, was to assemble near Hill 258.3 and then, proceeding along the western slopes of Hill 314.9, was to go over the outlet of Long Lake and execute an envelopment attack against Hill 183.6. The mountain batteries of the 3rd Mountain Division would support the attack that had to plough through the confusion of small shrub-covered hills. For the attack, the mountain division decided to place an operational command post close to the front. The batteries of the 2nd Mountain Division would also provide support from near the banks of the river approximately 4 kilometres to the north-west of the Litsa bridge. The degree to which both battery groups could support the attack would depend upon to what degree they were supplied with ammunition. There were no heavy batteries available for this first attack over the Litsa on 6 July. With the Luftwaffe still committed near Salla, Soviet aircraft were able to observe the movements of our troops unopposed.

Lieutenant-Colonel on the General Staff Rudolf Schmundt, Hitler's chief military adjutant, arrived in a Fieseler Storch early on 6 July for a meeting with General Dietl at the command post of the mountain corps in the vicinity of the Titovka bridge. Schmundt gained an insight into the situation, the plans of the mountain corps, and the difficulties caused by the poor maps and the challenging terrain. He was made aware of the degree to which the forces of the mountain corps were stretched, especially when it came to guarding against the danger from the sea (see footnote 1 in Chapter 9). Rybachy Peninsula had to be covered, but our forces were not strong enough to enter the peninsula and take the coastal batteries there that dominated the entrance to Petsamo Fjord. There were also insufficient forces to man the coastal flank between the Titovka and Litsa Rivers and to combat enemy shipping in Motovsky and Litsa Bays. A telephone conversation between General Dietl and Colonel-General Hans-Jürgen Stumpff produced on the part of the Fifth Air Fleet no more than the vague promise to send aircraft to the mountain corps after the situation in Salla, the area of the southern group of Army Norway, had been resolved. All General Dietl could do was to emphasise most strongly to Lieutenant-Colonel Schmundt that he was severely lacking in mountain infantry units.

In order to be able to follow the flow of events that took place next, between 6 and 10 July, each of the two sectors on the Litsa will be described separately. It is a characteristic of warfare in mountains or in any other kind of impassable terrain that individual actions and movements occur in a widely scattered fashion. This is why it is the mountain infantry battalions that truly bear the brunt of the fighting, and they are organised accordingly. Here, in the tundra, the enemy had split up the mountain corps by defending on the main front and attacking on the northern flank. In addition to the front at the neck of Rybachy Peninsula and that at the Litsa bridge, there was a third along Litsa Bay and another which covered the almost peninsula-like area bounded by the Titovka Valley, Motovsky Bay, Litsa Fjord, and the supply road. This approximately 300-square-kilometre lowland plain comprising several lakes was jokingly named the Duchy of Litsa, or simply the Duchy, by the men of the mountain corps.

On the front by the Litsa bridge, despite the plans for a coordinated attack on 6 July at 1000 hours, an effective thrust did not take place. The 137th Mountain Infantry Regiment was compelled to withdraw its combat outposts to the west bank of the Litsa by 1430 hours, while the 138th Mountain Infantry Regiment experienced such difficulties with the terrain that only elements of its I Battalion were able to cross the river that day. Moreover, a number of our pack animals carrying pneumatic floats were shot by hidden Soviet snipers. Only at 1900 hours did a new united attack by the 2nd Mountain Division begin.

On 6 July at 2300 hours, the evening report stated that the I and II Battalions of the 138th Mountain Infantry Regiment had established a bridgehead that was 1 kilometre in width and 4 kilometres in depth. With this bridgehead extending to the south-east of the bridge, the combat elements of the two battalions had thereby reached the small yet striking hills on the east bank of the Litsa River. The II and III Battalions of the 137th Mountain Infantry Regiment had not succeeded in crossing the river. Heavy artillery fire had rained down on them in their assembly areas and whilst they had been withdrawing the combat outposts. The I Battalion of the 137th Mountain Infantry Regiment had fought its way through particularly hideous marshland to the outlet of Long Lake behind White Water Hill. But it seemed as if the enemy was preparing for a counter-attack. Neither our artillery nor our anti-tank guns had been able to cross the river that day, so all our battalions had gone over to the defensive by nightfall. When the commander of the mountain corps visited the front on the morning of 7 July, he formed the opinion that it would be possible to hold and reinforce what had been gained and to renew the attack shortly thereafter. But heavy enemy counter-attacks were launched at noon, and they lasted the whole day. The II Battalion of the 137th Mountain Infantry Regiment had to move closer to the bridgehead of the 138th Mountain Infantry Regiment to prevent any penetration into the gap that had opened up in between. It was decided that the II Battalion of the 139th Mountain Infantry Regiment had to move into a position behind the bridgehead of the 3rd Mountain Division as quickly as possible, although the terrain meant that this could only be done slowly. The I Battalion of the 137th Mountain Infantry Regiment was trapped in the main defensive area of the enemy to the north-east of Hill 183.6.

On 8 July at approximately 0300 hours, in the pale light and rainy weather, an enemy force of three or four battalions was close to crushing the bridgehead of the 3rd Mountain Division. The mountain batteries of the 2nd Mountain Division, operating at maximum range, supported the 138th Mountain Infantry Regiment to the best of their ability, but they did not manage to relieve the pressure being applied against the bridgehead. The mountain corps therefore decided at 0900 hours to order the withdrawal of forces to a position behind the Litsa. The I Battalion of the 137th Mountain Infantry Regiment was inundated with fire from all sides and was facing defeat, so its elements scattered in different directions. The largest element arrived on the east bank of the river at its lower reaches, and its retreat to the west bank was covered by a brief assault launched by the 2nd Company of the 82nd Mountain Pioneer Battalion. Some elements fled diagonally through the main defensive area of the enemy and made it to the I Battalion of the 138th Mountain Infantry Regiment. Yet another element plunged deeper into enemy territory and then eastwards over the hollows and northern slopes of Hill 322 to the north-east end of Long Lake. Constantly under fire, it fought its way over the saddle between Hills 314.9 and 263.5 and back, exhausted and decimated, to the west bank of the river. The weaponry lost by the shattered battalion, especially machine guns, was not insignificant.

All in all, the result of 8 July was an arduous defence against increasingly powerful enemy attacks. On top of that, the enemy enjoyed aerial superiority. The push by the mountain corps had been conducted without heavy weaponry and with weak artillery support. There had also been a shortage of ammunition and supplies from the outset. It is therefore hardly surprising that the German attack had been repelled. The enemy possessed at least the same strength in infantry as the German side, and his artillery forces were much larger. Standing on the east bank of the Litsa, his positions were well defended and his supplies were secure, so it is perhaps not surprising that he soon decided to continue with his attack. On 8/9 July, he occupied Hill 258.3 with at least one battalion. From Hill 274.0, he threatened the area by the mouth of the Litsa with one or two companies. The 13th Company of the III Battalion of the 136th Mountain Infantry Regiment had just arrived there and was able to defend the area. Given the situation, it had become questionable whether the troops ought to remain in the vicinity of the Litsa bridge. The 137th Mountain Infantry Regiment, without the I Battalion, was therefore withdrawn to the area west of the waterfall which lay 5 kilometres south-south-west of Zapadnaya Litsa, while the 139th Mountain Infantry Regiment, without the II Battalion, was pushed forward to the area south-west of Herzberg.

Staff units secured Herzberg, and a variety of other smaller units plugged the 6-kilometre gap that had opened up between the mountain and the 138th Mountain Infantry Regiment which had in its sector not its own III Battalion but rather the II Battalion of the 139th Mountain Infantry Regiment. The mixing of units continued. The supply train and rear echelon commanders of the mountain divisions made every imaginable effort to ensure that supplies arrived where they needed to be. But there was never enough for the exposed 138th Mountain Infantry Regiment. On 10 July, the units of the 3rd Mountain Division that were committed to the front had a shortage of 700 tonnes of ammunition. The pack animals could carry nothing other than rations. They were worryingly close to complete exhaustion, and the condition of their pack saddles was deteriorating. A warm meal barely ever reached the troops. It was near impossible to make a smokeless fire in the moist birch shrubs. In the hope that the supply situation would improve steadily, even if slowly, with the construction of the road between the Titovka bridge and Herzberg, the mountain corps and the 3rd Mountain Division felt that the bridgehead 4 kilometres south-west of the Litsa bridge might be able to be held.

In the meantime, heavy fighting had been taking place around Litsa Bay, approximately 12 kilometres as the crow flies to the north of the bridgehead. On 6 July at 0630 hours, a destroyer and four other enemy ships had entered the central fjord. Troops landed ashore, although precisely where was not ascertained at that time. Countermeasures were not possible. Heavy batteries such as the 2nd or 3rd Batteries of the 730th Heavy Artillery Battalion may have had excellent range, but they could not yet overcome the route between the Titovka bridge and Herzberg. There were no warplanes in Kirkenes. The Junkers 88 bombers in Banak were unable to take off due to the bad weather there. At around 1000 hours, a rather large ship appeared approximately 3 kilometres to the north-east of Litsa Camp and manoeuvred into the small bay there. It was clear that the enemy planned some landings on the south bank of the Litsa. The first report of what was happening reached the mountain corps at 1715 hours. The 12th Company of the 136th Mountain Infantry Regiment, reinforced with elements of the 11th Company, was attacked by an enemy battalion. At the same time, aerial reconnaissance reported a number of boats going back and forth between the steamship and the land. At 1730 hours, the security forces of the III Battalion of the 136th Mountain Infantry Regiment in Zapadnaya Litsa observed enemy troops moving forward over the hills on the north bank of the bay. In both cases, the enemy landings were repelled. A tremendous explosion could be heard at 1800 hours, and it came to light the next day that it had been caused by enemy forces infiltrating Litsa Camp and blowing up the stock of ammunition there. The shock wave was so strong that the 12th Company of the 136th Mountain Infantry Regiment suffered several casualties. There were a lot of fractures, and many men had been knocked unconscious. However, the 12th Company was rescued when the nearby elements of the 11th Company launched a counter-attack on the camp. After that, those parts of both companies that could still fight set up a new defensive position on the slopes to the west of the destroyed camp. Our delight over the capture of so many motor vehicles had unfortunately been short-lived.

By the evening of 7 July, an enemy battalion was in the area between Zapadnaya Litsa and the important Hill 240.3, and it was advancing on the defensive line near Rybachy Peninsula. This defensive line was held by the III Battalion of the 136th Mountain Infantry Regiment (elements of the 11th, elements of the 12th, and the bulk of the 2nd Companies). The enemy pressure intensified on 8 July when more landings took place. These landings could not be directly observed, as they occurred in a bay (Landing Bay) on the northern bank roughly 9 kilometres north-east of Zapadnaya Litsa. The danger was significant. If the enemy succeeded in taking Hill 240.3, he would be within striking range of the entire rear of the Herzberg area. Our artillery positions, staff headquarters, transloading points, and road construction would all be vulnerable. A short push by the enemy to our sole supply road could have cut off the mountain corps. It had therefore become urgently necessary to carry out a rearward thrust. The enemy strength on both sides of Litsa Bay was estimated at three or four reinforced battalions. According to prisoner-of-war statements, the Soviet landing forces comprised the 8th and 182nd Battalions, independent formations that were not part of any divisional units and that had been hastily thrown together and equipped with light weapons. So as to ward off this danger, the mountain corps sent the III Battalion of the 138th Mountain Infantry Regiment, which had just become available, into battle to the north of Hill 240.3. On 9 July, half an hour after midnight, a platoon of the I Battalion of the 136th Mountain Infantry Regiment arrived at Hill 245.0, which lay in the middle of the Duchy, after having made the journey through the tundra from Titovka. By exploiting all means of transport and without regard for anything that might have broken down, the 2nd and 3rd Batteries of the 730th Heavy Artillery Battalion and the 1st Battery of the 477th Heavy Artillery Battalion were brought into the Herzberg vicinity. They immediately opened fire on targets, whether or not visible, in Landing Bay. They may or may not have hit their targets, but they certainly helped to boost morale. The 2nd Mountain Division was at this time relieved of responsibility for the defensive line near Rybachy Peninsula. This sector henceforth came under the immediate control of the mountain corps.

In a telephone conversation with the chief of staff of Army Norway on 8 July, General Dietl did everything he could to convey a vivid picture of the situation. He made it clear that there could be no thought of continuing with the attack upstream along the Litsa for as long as the pressure against the flank lasted, especially if there were no reserves and no air cover. He needed forces that possessed the strength of one or two regiments to deal with Rybachy Peninsula and the Duchy so that he could finally unite the mountain troops along the primary front. If no progress was being made here or near Salla, then it was worth considering whether a single point of main effort should be formed at just one of these two fronts. Dietl regarded the crisis in the area of the mountain corps to be a temporary one. If the construction of the roads could be completed, if sufficient troops could be allocated to protect the flank against the Soviet landing forces, and if decent support from the Luftwaffe could be provided, he hoped to be able to resume a rapid advance before long. The outcome of the discussion was the promise that a Stuka squadron would be transferred back to Kirkenes, that the 4th Machine-Gun Battalion would be sent immediately to the mountain corps, and that the Finnish 14th Infantry Regiment, consisting of two battalions, would be sent shortly thereafter.

The defensive line to the south of Rybachy Peninsula that was held by half of the III Battalion of the 136th Mountain Infantry Regiment had in the meantime become much stronger thanks to the arrival of the whole of the III Battalion of the 138th Mountain Infantry Regiment. Around Litsa Camp, which had become a no-man's land between the two sides, the enemy enjoyed no further success. The I Battalion of the 137th Mountain Infantry Regiment had managed to regroup and still possessed at least 500 men. Some units of the mountain corps had suffered losses amounting to 15 per cent killed or wounded; for other units it was about 20 per cent. The I Battalion of the 136th Mountain Infantry Regiment could once more be allocated to the 2nd Mountain Division. We could not wait for too long, as that would allow the enemy defence time to intensify. Trusting that the promised reinforcements would arrive and that the temporary pause had lulled the enemy into a false sense of security, the mountain corps decided that the attack ought to be resumed within the next few days. Preparations started at once. This time, the commander of the mountain corps agreed to a powerful lunge to the north-east of Hills 314.9, 322, and 321.9. He now believed that there might not be any other way to dislodge the Soviet defences along the Litsa River. In terms of supply, the greatest difficulties had been overcome. The road between the Titovka bridge and Herzberg had been improved considerably. Only in the immediate vicinity of Herzberg did the road end.

Shortly after the mountain corps had issued its orders on 10 July, which included the details of the planned operations of the 6th Destroyer Flotilla, a great misfortune came to pass. The dispatch rider of the staff of the 136th Mountain Infantry Regiment inadvertently went through the front line and was travelling on the road to Kutovaya on the neck of Rybachy Peninsula. He heard neither the cries nor the warning shots of our posts. By the time he realised his mistake, he was too close to the Soviet lines. He was wounded and taken prisoner. It had to be assumed that the written orders of the mountain corps, which contained all the details of the planned attack, had fallen into enemy hands.

CHAPTER II

The Second Attack over the Litsa River

Map 11

It was not just the loss of the orders for the attack that led to the alteration of the plan. Powerful artillery fire and non-stop reconnaissance on the part of the enemy convinced us that an attack to the south of the Litsa bridge, which was where the 138th Mountain Infantry Regiment had advanced in vain on 6 July, would have no chance of success. Such an attack would have required artillery support to an extent that could not have been achieved. It took until 14 July for extra ammunition to reach the front of the 3rd Mountain Division, and a little more arrived on 16 July. It may be hard to believe that we were only dealing with the supply of six battalions and six mountain batteries. Their supply would have been no problem in most circumstances, but it was a painful process on the Arctic Front. Both divisional headquarters therefore agreed that the point of main effort should be shifted to the front of the 2nd Mountain Division. The forces that were made available for the attack and the groups into which they were organised were as follows:

1. The I and III Battalions of the 139th Mountain Infantry Regiment (Group Windisch) were to be positioned south of the waterfall which lay 5 kilometres north-west of the Litsa bridge.
2. The II and III Battalions of the 137th Mountain Infantry Regiment (Group von Hengl) were to be to the west of the same waterfall. They would be joined later by the I Battalion of the 136th Mountain

Infantry Regiment and the III Battalion of the 138th Mountain Infantry Regiment in the hilly terrain south-east of Zapadnaya Litsa. The last two battalions were already near and to the north of Hill 274.0 on 12 July.

3. The III Battalion of the 136th Mountain Infantry Regiment, with a half company of the 4th Machine-Gun Battalion, would be to the south-west of Litsa Camp and, facing east, would secure the terrain beside the fjord.
4. The I Battalion of the 137th Mountain Infantry Regiment, the 48th Anti-Tank Battalion and the anti-tank company, the 16th Company of the 137th Mountain Infantry Regiment, and the 16th Company of the 138th Mountain Infantry Regiment would secure the Litsa from the bridge to the mouth of the river. The I Battalion of the 137th Mountain Infantry Regiment could also be regarded as a divisional reserve unit.

The divisional command post would remain on Herzberg. The artillery, without the 1st and 2nd Batteries of the 111th Mountain Artillery Regiment, stood in the vicinity to the north-west of Herzberg. The 82nd Mountain Pioneer Battalion was divided between Groups Windisch and von Hengl to support their crossing of the river.

The 3rd Mountain Division left Regimental Group Weiß with the I and II Battalions of the 138th Mountain Infantry Regiment, the II Battalion of the 139th Mountain Infantry Regiment, the 83rd Mountain Pioneer Battalion, and a mountain artillery battalion of the 112th Mountain Artillery Regiment. This battle group was to defend the sector to the south of the Litsa bridge and was also to secure the flank and rear of the attacking forces. It is difficult to assess whether fewer units could have been allocated to Regimental Group Weiß. Its only task was defence and security. It needed enough for that task, but not too much more, for the bulk of our forces needed to be committed to the attack.

The new plan of attack might appear complicated at first glance, but a closer look reveals that it envisaged a logically coordinated series of thrusts, one after the other, from the various assembly areas towards the set objectives. This procedure was not foreign to the mountain troops. It usually involved removing one defence line after another by constantly shifting forward across favourable areas and routes. In mountainous terrain, this could even be done back and forth through the combat zone. The following phases were planned for the coming attack:

1. The III Battalion of the 136th Mountain Infantry Regiment, whilst maintaining a sufficient defence to the east, was to set off on 13 July and take the hill north-east of the small heart-shaped lake (Heart Lake) which was 2 kilometres east of Point 263.5. From there, the battalion was to cover the north-east flank of the 2nd Mountain Division.
2. The I Battalion of the 136th Mountain Infantry Regiment had to take possession of Hill 258.3 on the same day, while the III Battalion of the 138th Mountain Infantry Regiment was to seize Hills 263.5 and 314.9. The battalions would then leave behind small elements to defend the hills, whilst the bulk would make contact with and join Group von Hengl.
3. Group von Hengl would attack from its assembly area on 14 July, covered to the south by an accompanying attack from Group Windisch, and would go around the northern slopes of Hills 258.3 and 314.9, both of which would have fallen into German hands in the meantime. Reaching the area south and west of Heart Lake, it then had to make contact with the I Battalion of the 136th Mountain Infantry Regiment and the III Battalion of the 138th Mountain Infantry Regiment.
4. After that, perhaps on 15 July, it was planned that Group von Hengl, now with four mountain infantry battalions, would advance around the north-east end of Long Lake and proceed towards the south-east so as to conquer Hills 322 and 321.9 from the rear. Most of the mountain batteries of the 2nd Mountain Division were to be positioned in the vicinity of Hill 263.5.
5. Group Windisch, after initially advancing eastwards over the Litsa alongside Group von Hengl, would pivot to the south and carry out an assault beyond the outlet of Long Lake against the enemy position by White Water Hill (Hill 183.6), which lay to the north-east of the Litsa bridge.

6. Should the envelopment wing against Hill 322 be successful, perhaps even by 15 July, the 3rd Mountain Division would send Group Weiß eastwards over the Litsa with Hill 321.9 as the distant objective. Nevertheless, with the advance of Group Windisch receiving priority, it was decided that the command post of the 3rd Mountain Division would be placed behind the 139th Mountain Infantry Regiment.

The commander of Army Norway visited the command post of Mountain Corps Norway on 12 July, and he approved the plan for a strong envelopment attack on the left wing. Between 10 and 13 July, the enemy launched one assault after another in the area of Litsa Camp and to the north of the bay, but we managed to repel them all. The 4th Machine-Gun Battalion, directly under the command of the mountain corps, was to set up a defensive line to the north of Zapadnaya Litsa.

According to our intelligence at noon on 13 July, the enemy possessed two reinforced rifle regiments and a large quantity of artillery before the front of the 3rd Mountain Division, i.e. between the outlet of Long Lake and the east bank of the river at the point opposite the 138th Mountain Infantry Regiment. We could count on the existence of a battalion in the vicinity of Hills 258.3 and 263.5, and further forces of unknown strength could be expected around Hills 322 and 321.9. Judging by the multiple enemy assaults against the area west and south of Litsa Camp, we suspected that he possessed a reinforced regimental group somewhere just to the east of there. Taking reconnaissance and security forces into consideration, the enemy probably had about two divisions in the zone of resistance south of Litsa Bay. To the north of the bay, in the Duchy, the enemy strength was conservatively estimated to be three battalions. Enemy shipping had only decreased slightly since the return of the Stuka squadron. With no fighter defence on the German side, the Soviet Ratas buzzed around and were most troublesome.

Our battalions commenced the advance on 13 July at 1730 hours. The first phase had begun. The III Battalion of the 136th Mountain Infantry Regiment repelled the counter-attacks of the enemy and reached Heart Lake on the morning of 14 July, the I Battalion of the same regiment swept aside light resistance and took Hill 258.3 as early as 2000 hours on 13 July, and the III Battalion of the 138th Mountain Infantry Regiment marched as far as the eastern slopes of Hill 314.9 by the early morning of 14 July.

The second phase was the advance of Groups von Hengl and Windisch over the Litsa on 14 July at 0500 hours. To ensure the security of the crossing of the river, the II Battalion of the 137th Mountain Infantry Regiment had already established a small bridgehead on the previous evening. Group Windisch immediately encountered difficulties due to marshy terrain and enemy resistance on the southern slopes of Hill 258.3. It required the next 24 hours to clear this area and wheel to the south. Meanwhile, the II and III Battalions of the 137th Mountain Infantry Regiment made slow but steady headway. They reached the saddle to the north of Hill 258.3 at 1335 hours, but were not ready to strike downhill from Hill 314.9, in conjunction with the two other mountain infantry battalions of Group von Hengl, until the night of 14/15 July.

The third phase began on 15 July. It had been delayed by 24 hours, but the positions were as planned. Elements of the III Battalion of the 138th Mountain Infantry Regiment had already pressed forward through the narrow gap between Heart Lake and Long Lake on 14 July. A prisoner-of-war statement indicated that there was supposed to be a road that connected Ura-Guba and Zapadnaya Litsa and that this road ran past the eastern side of Hill 322. A path led from Long Lake to the north-east towards Litsa Bay, and it looked as if parts of it could be used by carts and vehicles. Flanking fire would be capable of raining down from all directions into the depression. The markings on a map found on the body of a fallen Soviet captain revealed that an entire regiment surrounded the deep hollow. The assembly area by Heart Lake could only be secured in heavy fighting. The situation was made easier when the hill to the north-east of Heart Lake was taken at noon on 15 July by the III Battalion of the 136th Mountain Infantry Regiment with the assistance of elements of the III Battalion of the 138th Mountain Infantry Regiment. However, the situation worsened again shortly afterwards when further landings took place in Litsa Bay. A multitude of enemy strikes that morning against the defensive line north of Zapadnaya Litsa compelled the mountain corps to reinforce it with the I Battalion of the 137th Mountain Infantry Regiment. This battalion would be placed under the command of the unit already there (the 4th Machine-Gun Battalion). The position in the Duchy from Zapadnaya Litsa to Hill 240.3 remained firm. It even improved in the north, and reconnaissance units were dispatched to sweep the land to the east and north-east. Yet this meant that the 2nd Mountain Division had no more reserves.

The Ura Road began to the south-east of Long Lake, running along the slopes of Hills 321.9 and 322. The four battalions of Group von Hengl reached these slopes in the late evening, whereupon they were hailed with murderous fire from all around. The enemy followed up with a counter-attack. It was obvious that he had significant reinforcements at his disposal. Signal communications to the rear were interrupted for the most part. Fierce fighting continued here on 16 July without pause and without progress. At the neck of Rybachy Peninsula and to the north of Litsa Bay, a short time after 11 small ships had been spotted, numerous enemy troops surged forward.

In the sector of Group Windisch, only the III Battalion of the 139th Mountain Infantry Regiment had finished tracing its curved path to the assembly area north of the outlet of Long Lake. Although the I Battalion of the regiment had already departed the south bank of Round Lake,

Round Lake

which was about 2 kilometres south-west of Hill 263.5, on 15 July at 1500 hours, it was still tied down a little to the south of the western slopes of Hill 314.9. Only gradually did it overcome the undulating marshland. The mountain corps was already considering a continuation of the advance by Regimental Groups Windisch and Weiß under the 3rd Mountain Division. It would be a way of applying much-needed additional pressure against the enemy, especially since it had been necessary to order the withdrawal of Group von Hengl to the eastern slopes of Hill 314.9 at 1630 hours.

The situation on 16 July was dismal. The second attack over the Litsa River had not resulted in a decisive penetration. The battle groups at the front of the bridgehead had to do everything they possibly could to try to hold Hill 314.9. The shrub-covered low ground on either side of Long Lake dampened our initial striking power and resulted in considerable losses. An enormous drain on manpower was the task of carrying the wounded to the rear. A stretcher had to be carried in two shifts, each with four men, over a period of 10 hours through marshland and over hills. Everyone in the vicinity of Herzberg had been alerted and was committed to this task, be they staff officers, rear-echelon troops, or the workers of the three or four RAD units that were in the area. Our ammunition and supplies were almost expended. We could not entertain the idea of continuing operations without the regular flow of supplies. The situation had deteriorated not only for the 2nd Mountain Division but also for the 3rd Mountain Division, where the 139th Mountain Infantry Regiment had relinquished its role as a transportation and supply unit and had been thrown into the fight alongside its sister regiment. The mountain corps did not want to completely abandon the possibility of an attack. On 16 July at 2000 hours, it ordered the continuation of the advance by the 3rd Mountain Division once it had topped up with ammunition. This was at about the same time as a number of enemy counter-attacks got underway near the outlet of Long Lake as well as to the south of the Litsa bridge. Meanwhile, the enemy had carried out an extremely powerful attack at the neck of Rybachy Peninsula. He penetrated the defensive line there at several locations, and it required the utmost effort to resolve the situation. This was only managed due to the fact that the II Battalion of the Finnish 14th Infantry Regiment had just arrived there with the intention of relieving the II Battalion of the 136th Mountain Infantry Regiment and the 67th Bicycle Battalion. The I Battalion of the Finnish regiment had been sent to secure Titovka and the mouth of the river there. By 18 July, it was already committed to the defence against multiple enemy strikes in the centre of the Duchy. The Finnish regiment fought well here and near Rybachy Peninsula, but its striking power in view of its capacity as a home guard unit was naturally limited. It was not equipped for offensive tasks.[25]

It was decided on the evening of 17 July that the attack along the entire front must cease, that the front line must be shortened so that it could be more easily defended, that the units of the mountain corps must be reorganised, that the flow of supplies must be maintained, that the construction of roads must continue, that the flanks must be stabilised, and that the Duchy must be immediately cleared of the enemy forces that had landed there. Even Colonel-General von Falkenhorst agreed that the moment had come to consolidate our position. He could see that the flank to the north of Litsa Bay needed to be taken care of before the offensive could continue. The initial countermeasures there had been too weak and ineffective. The Soviet forces occupied favourable positions in the lake-dotted terrain, which meant that far greater preparations would be required to hurl them back into the sea. Army Norway was of the view that the point of main effort of the enemy defence had been placed before Murmansk. However, it had no additional reserves for the mountain corps. The operation in the region of Salla was not going to be given up. The Finnish III Corps had seemingly discovered a weak point, and a success there was in the making. The discussion between General Dietl and Colonel-General von Falkenhorst ended with the agreement that the I Battalion of the Finnish 14th Infantry Regiment (at that moment in Titovka) could switch places with the 68th Bicycle Battalion (then in Petsamo).

CHAPTER 12

The Operations of the 6th Destroyer Flotilla

Map 12

When war broke out between Germany and the Soviet Union in June 1941, our destroyers *Hans Lody*, *Karl Galster*, *Hermann Schoemann*, *Friedrich Eckoldt*, and *Erich Beitzen* had just rendezvoused in Bergen, Norway. These ships, with the *Hans Lody* as the flotilla leader, constituted the 6th Destroyer Flotilla. After a long period of repair and an extensive change in personnel, the level of training of the crews needed to be brought up to scratch. However, the flotilla soon received an order from the commander of Naval Region Norway, General-Admiral Hermann Boehm. None of the naval forces in Norway, no matter how weak, were to be left unexploited whilst the mountain corps of General Dietl, on the northern wing of the German front, was pushing towards the main strongpoint of the Soviet Northern Fleet. That strongpoint was Kola Bay, where both Murmansk and Polyarnoye Naval Base were located.

Some German ships had already cast anchor in Zapadnaya Litsa Bay in 1939 and 1940. It had been developed as a naval base for Germany as a result of a concession made by the Soviets in the Molotov–Ribbentrop Pact. As Base North, the fjord had served as a supply point for U-boats. Even the *Bremen* had found refuge in Kola Bay for a short time after evading an English blockade on her return voyage. But now, in 1941, this region had transformed into a naval war zone, and the Soviet naval forces were the enemy. The enemy ships we suspected to be in the area consisted of one flotilla leader, eight destroyers, six torpedo boats, 20 submarines, several fast attack craft, and a number of patrol boats and auxiliary vessels. We could expect that they would not just stand idly by while we advanced towards their only major strongpoint which was free of ice all year round. Rather, we could assume that they would be committed to securing the all-important sea lanes, especially between Arkhangelsk and Murmansk, in view of the difficulties of transportation via land. They would also most likely attack German shipping that had to sail around Nordkyn.

The main tasks to be undertaken by the destroyer flotilla were clear. It had to put a stop to the rather active deep-sea fishing in the Barents Sea as well as prevent any English ships from bringing supplies to the Soviets. But the initial priorities for the crews of the destroyers were to become acquainted with the completely new conditions of this geographically and climatically unusual theatre of war and to search the waters for the enemy, whose fighting capability was still largely unknown. Of particular importance for the destroyers was their fuel supply. The only tanker that was available to accompany them was the *Weißenburg*. The operational possibilities for the flotilla would greatly depend on the safety of this tanker. Not to remain unmentioned is the demanding and intricate work that was involved in the maintenance of the machinery. With no shipyards or docks for miles around, it was the experience and expertise of the crews that had to keep the destroyers operational.

Although the flotilla could also rely on the knowledge and help available at local ports, their means were limited. These ports mainly served the needs of coastal defence and small convoys. The vehicles there were mostly obsolete Norwegian types. Many of the ports were so primitive that a great deal of improvisation was required.

Kirkenes was foreseen as the main base from which the operations of the destroyer flotilla would be supported. Naval District Polar Norway, stationed in Tromsø, therefore created a Coastal Command Kirkenes. A naval intelligence officer would be posted in Kirkenes, and the small number of units of the Luftwaffe there were also instructed to provide support. The base in Kirkenes was operationally independent. This was necessary given the frequent interference in telegraph and radio communications with Oslo. The flotilla itself had to obtain a picture of the situation on the Arctic Front. As a small naval unit, the flotilla would not carry out operations in a naval vacuum. Its actions were conducted in conjunction with the army, especially as the objective was one that demanded the collaboration of all branches of the Wehrmacht. That objective was the capture of Murmansk and the occupation of the Murman coast. If possible, this would include gaining control of the White Sea. For the prospective administration of this area, preparations were made in Kirkenes for the creation of a Coastal Command T.

The flotilla established contact with the mountain corps, in particular with General Dietl, shortly after its arrival in Kirkenes. Based on Dietl's experience in Narvik, the commander of the flotilla was able to gain a full understanding of what could possibly be achieved.

The attack of the mountain corps planned for 12/13 July was supposed to coincide with the first action of the destroyers. The enemy had presumably still been unaware of the presence of the flotilla. But after the aforementioned incident in which the orders of the mountain corps fell into enemy hands, the commander of the flotilla decided not to await the redrafted orders. He would lead the destroyers into action as quickly as possible, for it would only be a short time before the Soviets knew that they were in the area.

The following had to be considered at the outset of any action by the flotilla:

1. The uninterrupted day robbed the fast yet vulnerable destroyers of their traditional protection: the darkness (radar was still not reliable enough at that time to render darkness incapable of providing cover). On the other hand, their small numbers could be offset through the element of surprise, above all through the effective employment of torpedoes.
2. Laying mines outside the enemy naval bases, an activity that had been carried out with great success by German destroyers along the English coast in the winter of 1939–40, would only be possible, and reasonable, under cover of darkness. The degree to which this could be done would also depend upon the availability of mines.

3. The primary tasks for the Luftwaffe, which had only a few aircraft based in Kirkenes anyway, were to fight against the Soviet Air Force, to bomb Murmansk, and to support the advance of the mountain corps. Despite the instructions it had been given, and despite its good intentions, the Luftwaffe would probably have little chance to conduct reconnaissance sorties over the sea or protect our naval forces, let alone work in close cooperation with the navy. Yet there could be no doubt that German destroyers operating in the vicinity of Soviet airbases would be attractive targets for Soviet aircraft.
4. The northern flank of the mountain corps ended along the bleak and rocky southern coast of Motovsky Bay, roughly in the area of the former Base North. By sea, Kirkenes was separated from Motovsky Bay by Rybachy Peninsula. The only way to sail into the bay was from the east, going past the coastal batteries that, according to the naval staff handbook of 1939, were positioned not only at the northern entrance of Kola Bay, in Polyarnoye, but also on Rybachy Peninsula. An immediate intervention by the flotilla in this area would simply be impossible, all the more so due to the Soviet destroyers, gunboats, and patrol boats that had occasionally been reported to be there. At best, the flotilla might have been able to execute sporadic assaults in these remote waters at times when the Soviet naval forces had returned to base. However, it still would have been easy enough for the Soviet destroyers to intercept the flotilla on its way back. The Soviet-controlled Rybachy Peninsula was just too much of an obstacle for the German Navy. On top of that, it could be expected that the deep waters just outside Kola Bay, between Rybachy Peninsula and Kildin Island, would either be filled with mines or patrolled by submarines. These waters would also be within range of the enemy coastal batteries. It would not have been worth it to send the destroyer flotilla there.
5. Given the emptiness and inhospitality of the entire region, Murmansk had to be regarded as the decisive centre of supply and communications. By land, it could only be reached via the Murman Railway. Otherwise, supplies had to be delivered to it via sea from the harbours

of the White Sea or, as would most likely soon be the case, from the armaments factories of England. Even if a decisive victory on the Arctic Front did not take place immediately, any disruption of the sea lanes leading to Murmansk would still cause trouble for the Soviet war effort.

6. The destroyer flotilla would be unable to use the harbour in Petsamo. The entrance to the fjord could be seen from Rybachy Peninsula. Any destroyer approaching the fjord would be within range of the batteries on the peninsula. Even so, goods were often conveyed from Kirkenes to Petsamo in small ships, as it allowed the German forces to economise on land transportation. If possible, this was done under cover of darkness or fog, and it was all the better if the Luftwaffe was available at the same time to launch a raid against the batteries on the western coast of Rybachy Peninsula. The coastal guns to be installed around the fjord would only be able to be brought there by sea.
7. In the constant brightness at this time of year, calm weather and good visibility could normally be expected at sea. However, there were some spots where low, thick fog could develop due to the cold polar air and the still relatively warm Gulf Stream.

Without awaiting the new attack by the mountain corps, the flotilla commander, in agreement with the mountain corps and the operational staff of the Luftwaffe, decided on the course of action he would take on 12 and 13 July. The destroyers would sail far to the north to avoid detection by Soviet aerial reconnaissance. They would then split into two groups, one with three destroyers and the other with two. Maintaining a distance of 100 nautical miles from one another, each group would approach and run along the Murman coast. They would reunite after that. Depending on how the situation unfolded, the flotilla would continue towards the north-east so as to sweep the main fishing grounds for Soviet vessels. On the request of the Luftwaffe, the course to be taken by the flotilla was plotted in advance, regardless of whether it might result in an encounter with the enemy. The Luftwaffe could then try to provide support, no matter how meagre.

The first phase of the foray by the flotilla was a success. The western group came across a small convoy heading due east just outside Teriberka. Consisting of tugboats with barges, and escorted by a few patrol boats, the convoy was swiftly destroyed.

After uniting both groups and turning to the north-east, the flotilla was attacked three times by flying boats. It could no longer count on making a surprise appearance in the remote fishing grounds. To avoid the worthless consumption of fuel, a constant concern for the flotilla, it withdrew from action. This proved to be the correct decision, as it was reported later on that the fishing grounds were devoid of enemy ships.

The flotilla entered Tanafjord, which had been chosen as the spot where it could conceal itself, and it soon became clear that not only the supply of fuel but also that of ammunition required urgent attention. In addition to what had been needed to fire back at the flying boats, the expenditure of ammunition in the destruction of the convoy had been alarmingly high, especially since many of the objects on the barges had been small and able to float. The supply quantities that had at first been envisaged would hardly be sufficient in the event of more frequent activity at sea. In contrast, the destroyers remained in good mechanical condition after the three-day operation and would be ready to go into battle again.

The repetition of such an operation along the Murman coast had good prospects. The flotilla would again need to set off from Kirkenes, and, like last time, the mountain corps and the Luftwaffe would need to be kept informed. In the process of sailing back to Kirkenes on 18 and 19 July, the flotilla took the opportunity to carry out a reconnaissance through what was presumed to be the sea lane running from England to Murmansk or Arkhangelsk and through the sea lane, perhaps still in use, that led to the Soviet coal-mining site on Spitzbergen. No contact with the enemy occurred.

There had in the meantime been an increase in the number of enemy vessels in Motovsky Bay, on the northern flank of the mountain corps. They had been shelling the coast and landing troops. The Soviet batteries on Rybachy Peninsula had also been laying down fire. General Dietl was already aware from his discussion with the commander of the flotilla that the destroyers would be unable to intervene in Motovsky Bay and resolve the situation there. The flotilla had better chances of success by carrying out a renewed attack against the Murman coast.

The four destroyers earmarked for this operation had just cast anchor in a tributary fjord near Kirkenes on 22 July when they were attacked by enemy bombers. No damage was done, but it had perhaps become known to the enemy that the flotilla was about to put to sea. Indeed, although a course had been plotted that would again take the flotilla far to the north, the destroyers were twice spotted and attacked by Soviet aircraft while they were at sea. Despite the fact that it had probably been possible to deceive the enemy on both occasions as to the true course of the destroyers, there could be no doubt that all coastal regions would have been alerted. Since the Luftwaffe had been unable to offer support for this operation, the course to be taken by the destroyers could be changed from what had been planned without hesitation. The flotilla sailed due north and, at reduced speed, concealed itself all day long on 23 July in an area with thick fog. Early on 24 July, the flotilla proceeded at full speed and approached the Soviet strongpoint of Yokanga from the north-east. But there were no enemy vessels to be seen in the bay there. The destroyers continued to sail to the north-west, along the coast. They came across a tanker, and it was not long before it was in flames. Continuing on their journey, they successfully deceived reconnaissance aircraft that flew overhead by using the Soviet recognition signal. A seaplane approached the flotilla later on and was destroyed. The sound of guns on the coast opening fire made it clear that the alarm must have been sounded in the meantime. The flotilla therefore withdrew from the coast towards the north. However, the location of the flotilla was now known to the enemy. Squadrons of bombers conducted carpet bombing from high altitudes. This put the flotilla in great danger. The bombers were well out of range of the guns of the destroyers and were difficult to see. Sailing at full speed, the destroyers eventually managed to disappear in thick fog. They returned to Kirkenes with neither damage nor casualties, but the respect of their crews for the capability of the Soviet Air Force had grown immensely.

The end of July was the time when supply transports usually gathered to the south of Novaya Zemlya, on the Kara Sea, to make the trip to the northern coast of Siberia. They would wait for the ice to melt before setting sail along the North Siberian Sea Route. The enemy may have felt reasonably safe in this remote sea territory, but the superiority of the flotilla meant that this was an opportunity to destroy or perhaps even capture several steamships and icebreakers. The latter would certainly be of great value in the winter. It might even have been possible after that for the flotilla to patrol the northern entrance of the White Sea. On 29/30 July, the destroyers set off and sailed further north than they had done before. The enemy remained unaware of their journey. The flotilla was already off Kolguyev Island when it suddenly picked up radio traffic which had evidently been prompted by heavy bombing raids by carrier-based aircraft on Kirkenes and Petsamo, and by German convoys and escort vessels on the way to and from Tromsø. It could be inferred from the alarm that had been raised that this was a case of a major enemy undertaking. There was obviously an English carrier battle group somewhere between the flotilla and its bases in Norway. Even if the defenceless destroyers remained undetected in the constant brightness and current good visibility of the polar weather, there was the very real possibility that the flotilla's tanker, at that time in the vicinity of Kirkenes, might have been destroyed. If that were the case, the only way in which the destroyers could refuel would be to return to base.

No radio message was sent to the destroyer flotilla. This reinforced the fear that there had been extensive damage. After a short time of waiting in vain, the commander of the flotilla decided on the evening of 30 July to turn back and steer towards Vardø and then along the coast. The destroyers would protect any convoy vessels that might still be underway, after which, if there was no further news, they would return to Tromsø to refuel. Radio silence had to be carefully maintained for the time being anyway.

The destroyers proceeded at full speed in the brightness of the midnight sun and reached the convoy route the next morning. It was ascertained later on that they had actually gone past the British carrier battle group just outside its radius of visibility to the south. It was fortunate that the enemy had no airworthy aircraft at that moment. He was therefore unable to conduct any reconnaissance sorties, and this enabled the destroyers to make it safely to the Norwegian coast. The overwhelming superiority of the enemy forces would have proved deadly for the flotilla had a confrontation taken place. The carrier battle group consisted of two aircraft carriers, two heavy cruisers, and eight destroyers! As it turned out, the air attack on Kirkenes on 30 July had been a failure for the English. Out of approximately 40 aircraft (Westland Lysanders and Fairey Battles), only a small handful returned. There was little damage on the German side. By the time this news reached the flotilla, it had already completed most of the return trip with the intention of helping friendly convoys along the coast. German reconnaissance aircraft flew overhead at about the same time and made the mistake of reporting that they had sighted an enemy flotilla. Some nerve-racking time went by until the situation was clarified for the Luftwaffe.

At any rate, this attack by carrier-based aircraft on Kirkenes had to be regarded as a sign that England was on the point of establishing, and of being able to protect, a supply route to the Soviet Union. The enemy had correctly identified Kirkenes as the primary base of supplies for the German Arctic Front. Neither along Norwegian National Road 50 nor along the Finnish Arctic Ocean Highway could sufficient quantities of goods be brought. An attack on Kirkenes itself would be more effective than one on the shipping route leading there. The bottleneck in the flow of supplies that Kirkenes represented was caused neither by the number of supply ships nor by the lack of security forces. Rather, it was the meagreness of the pier installations in Kirkenes that was the problem. There were berths for no more than two steamships, and it took a long time for goods to be unloaded and carried away on trucks.

The English enemy had at least been convinced of the preparedness of the German defensive forces in Kirkenes. He could expect that convoy traffic would be fiercely protected. By the same token, stronger English forces might return to these waters and thereby increase the danger to German transports. Given the importance of these transports for the Arctic Front, the destroyers had to withdraw from the offensive operations they had been conducting so far and instead serve most urgently as escort vessels.

Nevertheless, it seemed to Naval Region Norway that an attempt ought to be made to carry out an operation in Kola Bay and Motovsky

Bay. There had been repeated reports about the threat to the northern wing of the mountain corps from the sea, and the conclusion had been reached that, in view of the overall situation, any chance that might arise to render assistance to the army should be exploited. Such an operation was no doubt risky due to the coastal fortifications that, according to the naval staff handbook, surrounded the bay. On top of that, it was not known to what degree those waters were infested with mines or submarines. Amidst daylight and good visibility, a surprise attack could be ruled out.

So as to be less conspicuous near the coast and ensure adequate manoeuvrability, three destroyers were selected to carry out the operation. In the early morning hours of Sunday 10 August, despite all probability, the destroyers sailed full speed ahead towards Kola Bay in a manner that was almost reminiscent of a cavalry charge and succeeded in taking a gunboat by surprise. After a brief engagement, barely 10 kilometres from the coast, the gunboat was sunk. The destroyers then conducted a reconnaissance of Kola Bay and Motovsky Bay, but, even though visibility was good, no further enemy vessels were found. The destroyers waited for half an hour, but to no avail. Given the proximity of the barren coast with its threatening fortifications, the order was given to create a smokescreen and to make a zigzag withdrawal. The Soviet coastal commander must have been waiting for the destroyers to edge a little closer to the fortifications, but he now gave permission to fire at will. From Kildin Island, from the entrance of Kola Bay, and from Rybachy Peninsula, a multitude of batteries opened fire simultaneously. Four heavy batteries in particular proved to be quite a challenge to avoid. As had been indicated by the naval staff handbook, it was indeed quite a powerfully armed gauntlet that the destroyers had to run. They sailed at top speed and were rapidly increasing the distance that lay between them and the coast. The destroyers were still for some time within the 38-kilometre range of the heavy batteries, but the only thing at which they could fire back was the occasional flying boat that approached them. Those flying boats managed to direct a group of Soviet warplanes, which were in the process of carrying out a surprise raid from the clouds in the area of Vardø, towards the destroyers. A bomb narrowly missed the *Beitzen*, although the shockwave damaged some auxiliary machinery. There were insufficient means on board to repair the damage, so it would be necessary to send the destroyer back to the Fatherland.

The remaining destroyers needed time for maintenance, so they sailed to Narvik for this purpose. Because the *Schoemann* required extensive work, she too returned to a shipyard in the Fatherland.

A number of U-boats had arrived in Kirkenes in the meantime, and they soon set off to patrol the Barents Sea and the Murman coast. They confirmed much of what had been observed up to that time, conducted a reconnaissance of enemy waters, and succeeded in sinking four steamships. Other than that, they found very few worthwhile targets.

In consideration of the ever-more-urgent need for replacements and supplies on the Arctic Front in the course of August, the three destroyers that were still in the area were mainly committed to escorting the all-important convoys. On 30 August, a convoy made up of four troop transports and escorted by two destroyers and several submarine chasers left Tromsø. The convoy was off Loppa Island, between Tromsø and Hammerfest, when it was confronted by the British submarine *Trident*, which sank the ships *Donau II* and *Bahia Laura*. Those on board the two ships included replacements for the 137th and 138th Mountain Infantry Regiments as well as for the 68th Bicycle Battalion. Most of them were able to be rescued, thanks in part to the energetic assistance of the Norwegian steamship *Midnatsol*. The personnel of the 2nd Company of the 214th Pioneer Battalion and those of the 702nd Veterinary Company also escaped with their lives. However, 200 horses and lots of equipment were lost. In addition to that, the ore transport *Ostpreußen* was sunk. The British submarine escaped unharmed despite all the depth charges that were dropped.

The couple of transports that had survived arrived in Kirkenes two days later. The difficulties involved in convoy protection had become quite clear. In contrast to the rear lines of communication, the supply routes that ran along the coast were directly exposed to the sea. A daring and decisive enemy could easily choose at which point along the extensive route he would like to attack. In spite of the relatively strong escort, the presence of the British submarine near Loppa Island had only been noticed the moment it had launched its torpedoes. At long range, the submarine detectors on the submarine chasers and destroyers could not easily distinguish a submarine from the rocks of the mountainous seafloor of the Norwegian coast. The numerous skerries also interfered with the performance of the detectors. Lying in wait in the Atlantic, enemy submarines enjoyed a great advantage. German submarines patrolling that large ocean had to make every effort to try to locate the enemy first. Enemy submarines could be anywhere, but German convoys had to take almost exactly the same route through the skerries. Even in the absence of skerries, each convoy, usually only weakly defended, had to stay near the coast to enable help to arrive quickly in the event of an emergency and to minimise the time it would take for the already slow trip to reach its destination.

Faster vessels like passenger ships and refrigerator ships originally had no escort. They would have otherwise had to match the low speed of their escort vessels. But they now had the destroyers assigned to protect them. Hospital ships were also escorted by the destroyers, for their safety could by no means be guaranteed by respect for international law. With the presence of the destroyers, the usual convoy route was no longer used. The new route was further out to sea. The vital personnel transports occasionally used this new route when escorted by the destroyers. They were able to cover the distance quickly and considerably more safely, rather like what had been done during the occupation of Trondheim and Narvik in April 1940. Transports carrying matériel continued to use the old convoy route.

In the meantime, English transports had started delivering supplies to the Soviet Union. As had been predicted, this dramatically increased the danger to our own convoys, especially when the enemy escort vessels were on their way back to base and were less bound to the empty transports. As these escort vessels consisted mostly of cruisers and destroyers, our comparatively weakly defended convoys were almost completely helpless.

At noon on 3 September, a British formation of two aircraft carriers, two cruisers, and three destroyers had been spotted by the Luftwaffe 250 nautical miles north-east of Nordkapp. This enemy caused the Norwegian docks and coal-mining facilities on Spitzbergen to go up in flames on

5 September. Before daybreak on 6 September, at approximately 0300 hours, two British light cruisers and a group of destroyers steered towards Nordkyn and came across the first convoy, protected by the artillery training ship *Bremse* and a few small vessels, that was carrying the forces of the 6th Mountain Division. The *Bremse* drew the enemy away from the convoy, but she was soon destroyed and most of her crew were lost. The transports *Trautenfels* and *Barcelona* escaped to Honningsvåg. Bad weather meant that the Luftwaffe was unable to intervene.

On 11 September, British fighters (Hurricanes) with British nationality markings appeared on the Arctic Front for the first time. They had possibly been brought there by the two aircraft carriers. On 12 September, long-range reconnaissance aircraft sighted a formation of three cruisers and three destroyers near the coast of Kola Peninsula. These ships were obviously not of Soviet origin. On 12/13 September, the freighter *Ottar Yarl* and the steamship *Richard With* were sunk to the north of Tanafjord. At about the same time, Soviet fast attack craft appeared in Jarfjorden, 25 kilometres east of Kirkenes. It can therefore be understood why there was growing concern about sending supplies by sea.

While a number of minesweepers had been sent to Kirkenes in an attempt to better protect the German convoys, the destroyer *Lody*, unfortunately, had to sail back to Germany in September for extensive repair and maintenance. In October, the destroyer *Eckoldt* was rendezvousing with a convoy when she rammed into the roadstead in Tromsø. One of her engine rooms filled with water, so she too had to return to the Fatherland. In November, the *Galster*, which had covered 32,000 nautical miles without ever visiting a shipyard, was the last to return to Germany for an overhaul.

The new naval operations staff, Naval Region North Sea, arrived in Kirkenes on the escort vessel *Tanga* at the beginning of December. All the destroyers, U-boats, and fast attack craft that were employed in the Barents Sea would come under its command.

The 8th Destroyer Flotilla had also been transferred to Kirkenes in December, and it had its first encounter with Soviet naval forces on 12 December near the entrance of the White Sea. A Soviet destroyer was severely damaged and probably sunk. Several mines had been delivered in the meantime, and they were laid along the Murman coast in the darkness of the polar night. Operations were also carried out later against convoy shipping from America.

From a naval standpoint, the Barents Sea had been of ever-increasing importance since the outbreak of war with the Soviet Union. The seizure of Murmansk and the occupation of the Murman coast would have practically resolved the situation in the Arctic theatre of war and would have put a stop to transports bringing supplies to the Soviet Union. Yet this did not happen. Although losses for Allied convoys were high, essential supplies continued to flow in large quantities from the West to the Soviet Union. German naval and aerial forces constantly had to be committed to this struggle, but there was simply not enough to be able to overwhelm the enemy or to exert a decisive influence on him.

The operations of the German Navy, and especially of the 6th Destroyer Flotilla, have been depicted here chronologically in order to demonstrate the relationship between the war at sea and the events on the Arctic Front in 1941. It has been shown that the German naval forces were unable to directly influence how events unfolded on the coastal flank of Mountain Corps Norway. This meant that the mountain corps was on its own in dealing with the enemy forces that had landed on the banks of Litsa Bay and Motovsky Bay.

CHAPTER 13

Mopping up the Duchy

Map 13

In the fighting on the flank north-east of Zapadnaya Litsa, in the so-called Duchy, the enemy had been applying constant pressure since the middle of July against the defensive line held by the 4th Machine-Gun Battalion and the weak I Battalion of the 137th Mountain Infantry Regiment. His assaults against this line were carried out at the same time as those against the Litsa front and against the defensive line near Rybachy Peninsula. The initiative had clearly been held by the enemy since 16 July. Not a single day nor a single bright night went by without multiple attacks being carried out, be they of platoon or regimental strength, and they were always supported by artillery, aircraft, and ships. The enemy's heavy mortars inflicted several casualties on the defenders. We could ill afford such losses after the two failed attempts to attack over the Litsa River. The now almost daily fog that would set in between midnight and the early morning in the bays, valleys, and lakes was of great benefit to the enemy. If he had concentrated his forces against a single point like the Litsa bridgehead instead of carrying out so many scattered attacks on a daily basis, it is highly probable that the front of the 2nd Mountain Division would have been unable to hold out given its significant losses during July. The 137th Mountain Infantry Regiment alone had lost 1,367 men in a period of two weeks. The battalions of the other mountain infantry regiments each lost an average of 200 soldiers.

The enemy attacks in the Duchy were almost always in the direction of the supply road of the mountain corps. Even Titovka lay within the striking range of the enemy. He carried out reconnaissance missions throughout the region and tried to prise open the wings of each front. Security detachments at Cape Pikshuyev (a place with a lighthouse, a former small observatory, and a lot of driftwood) reported Soviet attempts to make a landing. It was high time that this situation be cleared up. Even if we were to assume that we were dealing with nothing more than a regiment of three battalions, an extra day could have been enough time for the enemy to double his strength. With the arrival of the 14th Machine-Gun Battalion near Rybachy Peninsula on 26 July, the regimental staff and the II Battalion of the 136th Mountain Infantry Regiment could finally be released. With all nearby units placed under his command, the commander of this regiment, Lieutenant-Colonel Hofmeister, was to carry out the mopping-up operation from 26 July. The operation would henceforth be named after this commander. The description that follows on how the operation unfolded is based upon the report written by the quartermaster of the mountain corps on 7 August 1941.[26]

Operation *Hofmeister* is a prime example of a small but difficult mountain operation with a limited objective. Valuable lessons can be drawn from it with regard to preparation, timing, commitment of forces, supply, and execution. The following forces were placed under the command of Lieutenant-Colonel Hofmeister for the operation:

- Staff of the 136th Mountain Infantry Regiment with a bicycle platoon, a signal communication platoon, and military band troops (for telephone communications or stretcher bearing)
- Elements of the 136th Light Mountain Infantry Column
- Elements of the 16th Anti-Tank Company of the 136th Mountain Infantry Regiment (for carrying supplies)
- 68th Bicycle Battalion with the 1st Company of the 67th Bicycle Battalion subordinated to it
- I Battalion of the 137th Mountain Infantry Regiment
- II Battalion of the 136th Mountain Infantry Regiment

- 4th Machine-Gun Battalion
- Finnish Tiitola Border Guard Company
- 1st Battery of the 730th Heavy Artillery Battalion (10.5cm Skoda M.35 guns)
- 4th Battery of the 111th Mountain Artillery Regiment (7.5cm Skoda M.15 guns)
- 1st Battery of the 112th Mountain Artillery Regiment (7.5cm Skoda M.15 guns)
- Staff of the 498th Army Coastal Artillery Battalion with the 580th Army Coastal Battery (French 10.5cm guns) and the 9th Battery of the 111th Mountain Artillery Regiment (Norwegian 10.5cm guns)
- A casualty clearing station from the 67th Mountain Medical Company of the 2nd Mountain Division
- 22nd Pack Train (disembarked in Kirkenes on 31 July)
- Unit K 3/373 of the RAD (for carrying supplies)
- Unit K 6/376 of the RAD (for carrying supplies)

Additional assistance was to be provided by the following:

- 2nd and 3rd Batteries of the 730th Heavy Artillery Battalion from the vicinity of Herzberg
- 999th Army Coastal Battery (field guns) of the 504th Army Coastal Artillery Battalion, based in Titovka
- Flank and rear security detachments on the south bank of Titovka Bay from the 2nd Company of the 67th Bicycle Battalion
- Supply Headquarters North[27]
- Luftwaffe forces in accordance with special operational orders, in particular the flight of Lieutenant Hauschild of the 1st High-Wing Monoplane Squadron of the 32nd Reconnaissance Group

Extensive ground reconnaissance had already been conducted by Lieutenant-Colonel Hofmeister, his subordinate commanders, and the artillery a number of days before the commencement of the operation. This was accompanied by the aerial reconnaissance of Flight Hauschild. Titovka was to be the main base from which the operation would be carried out. While the 4th Machine-Gun Battalion had to continue to hold its defensive line, it was planned that the enemy there would be dislodged by an advance that would have gone through the northern chain of lakes and whose main emphasis would be on the left wing. The point at which the advance would pivot would be in the sector of the I Battalion of the 137th Mountain Infantry Regiment. This battalion was to emerge from the strip of land north-west of Hill 262.2. To its left would be the 68th Bicycle Battalion and then the II Battalion of the 136th Mountain Infantry Regiment. The bicycle battalion, at that time guarding the coastal flank against enemy landings, was to be relieved by half of a heavy machine-gun platoon of the Finnish Tiitola Border Guard Company. One or two Soviet companies landed near and to the south of Pikshuyev in the meantime, but the Finns managed to throw them back into the sea.

There were no roads in the Duchy. Supplies had to be carried in multiple stages. So that the supply route could be secured, the 68th Bicycle Battalion moved forward to Hill 245, 5 kilometres south-east of Titovka. Most of the soldiers earmarked for the operation then returned to Titovka without their equipment and, from 28 July, began to carry ammunition and rations back to their units with the help of the RAD

Looking towards Motovsky Bay from Cape Pikshuyev. In the background is Rybachy Peninsula

units as well as of the troops that had specifically been assigned the task of carrying supplies. This process lasted three days. On 31 July, the troops, if they had not already done so, moved into their assembly areas. The primary role of the RAD units during the fighting would be to bring the wounded to the rear areas.

The route from Titovka to Hill 245 could be covered in two-and-a-half hours by troops burdened with supplies. For the group on the left wing, the journey took an additional three hours. Reloading points and reserve depots were therefore placed near the front. Considerable difficulties arose from the demand for telephone cable. Even with the cable provided by the 463rd Corps Signal Battalion as well as by the 67th Mountain Signal Battalion of the 2nd Mountain Division, there was not quite enough to cover the full distances in the Duchy. The beginning of the attack was postponed from the originally planned 1 August to the night of 1/2 August 1941. We were confident that the operation would be a success.

The first step was for the left wing to take possession of Hill 177.3. This hill lay to the east of and was partly surrounded by a lake, so it would be easily defensible. The 68th Bicycle Battalion approached the hill according to plan and swiftly drove out the weak enemy forces there. However, the left pincer in the form of the II Battalion of the 136th Mountain Infantry Regiment failed to appear. It had been delayed due to the difficulties presented by the terrain. It had originally been envisioned that the infantry battalion would go around *in front of* the bicycle battalion on Hill 177.3 and would then head south along the series of small hilltops that led to Hill 262.2. After that, it would have taken the eastern side of this hill in one stroke. So as not to lose any time, the regimental commander decided that the bicycle battalion, which he had just joined, could continue with its advance over Hills 187.9, 178.4, and 227.4. The enemy could then be cut off from his landing bay as soon as possible. The II Battalion of the 136th Mountain Infantry Regiment would therefore go around *behind* the 68th Bicycle Battalion. The I Battalion of the 137th Mountain Infantry Regiment could then start its attack from the strip of land it occupied between the lakes 3 kilometres north-west of Hill 262.2. Once the II Battalion of the 136th Mountain Infantry Regiment had gone past, the I Battalion of the 137th

Mountain Infantry Regiment could pivot towards the summit of the hill. The fighting proved to be particularly fierce before this hill could be reached. In order to relieve the mountain infantry battalions and apply greater pressure against the enemy, the 4th Machine-Gun Battalion went over to the attack along the bay. Many a soldier fell in this attack. The 68th Bicycle Battalion did not manage to reach Litsa Bay in one go, for the enemy forces on Hill 227.4 were particularly stubborn. The bicycle battalion regrouped on the night of 2/3 August and executed a new attack from the valley that ran from the north-west to the south-east, parallel to the range of hills it had traversed the first time, towards the landing bay. It arrived there opposite Aspatkin Island. Nevertheless, the enemy was able to evacuate several troops on this night of 2/3 August. There was little that the Luftwaffe could do against all the small ships in Litsa Bay and Motovsky Bay. At any rate, the enemy lost hundreds of men in the Duchy and abandoned much matériel that we could make use of. By 4 August, we had annihilated the equivalent of a battalion and had taken possession of the entire region. Some of our forces on the south bank of Litsa Bay had been able to support our efforts around Hill 262.2, but they had to keep an eye on the main front line and not stray more than 2 kilometres away from it.

Operation *Hofmeister* had been executed quickly and decisively. It was a tremendous success thanks to the superiority of the German soldier in swift movement and the exemplary preparation of supplies so far from roads. It had certainly helped that there had been enough time to make such preparations.

The supply centre was now shifted to Herzberg so as to shorten our supply routes. The small reserve depots in the Duchy had been exhausted. The headquarters and the II Battalion of the 136th Mountain Infantry Regiment, as well as the I Battalion of the 137th Mountain Infantry Regiment, were no longer needed in a defensive role along Litsa Bay and could therefore be reallocated, after their long absence, to the 2nd Mountain Division. Many of the auxiliary troops returned to their original units or to their former tasks. The mountain batteries and the 22nd Pack Train remained. Assuming command of all the forces in the Duchy was the oldest officer there, Lieutenant-Colonel Braun, who was the commander of the 4th Machine-Gun Battalion. Alongside the group of Lieutenant-Colonel Saul (14th Machine-Gun Battalion) at the neck of Rybachy Peninsula, Group Braun was placed directly under the command of the mountain corps.[28]

It had been disadvantageous that the 4th Machine-Gun Battalion and the 68th Bicycle Battalion had lacked pack animals. Had the 22nd Pack Train not arrived in good time and been available to take care of the off-road supply of both battalions, then the battalions themselves would have had to carry their own supplies. The machine-gun battalion would have thereby lost at least one-third of its striking power; for the bicycle battalion, it would have been as much as a half.

On 5 August at 2000 hours, Lieutenant-Colonel Hofmeister reported that the Duchy had been cleared. Our losses had been bearable. Much of the enemy's equipment had fallen into our hands. The effect our success had on the enemy could soon be perceived. His attacks against the 2nd Mountain Division diminished, and he also regrouped his forces. In particular, we noticed that he staggered his artillery further to the south in the area of the 3rd Mountain Division (i.e. before the 138th Mountain Infantry Regiment). It appeared as if he was shifting his focus back to the bridgehead in the expectation that a new German attack over the Litsa River would shortly take place. His position was such that it could be defended easily.

It ought not to remain unmentioned that the German submarines *U-63* and *U-81* had indirectly contributed to our success in the first few days of August. In the waters near Murmansk, they had stopped large transport ships from bringing more troops to the Duchy.

CHAPTER 14

The Last Days of Summer

Maps 14 and 15

At the end of May, after the ice on the major rivers has begun to melt and the stormy weather has started to subside, the winter in the Arctic Circle draws to a close. June is the month in which spring really appears. The sun remains high in the sky and melts what is left of the snow on the hilltops. The month of July is like the middle of summer and can be characterised by astonishingly high temperatures. The summer weather can last well into August, but it can also fade away quite early on. The night frost can set in at any point from the middle of the month. From the beginning of September, one can start to speak of a genuine night that lasts for hours. Aspen and mountain ash trees are resplendent in brownish yellow, and the red colours of the wilting dwarf birches stand out amidst the light green of the moss that grows over the tundra. At the time of the equinox, it is possible for the bleak coastal cliffs to be covered with the first layer of snow, or it might be the case that the weather becomes bitingly cold and wet due to the arrival of wind and rain. The winter then reigns from October until the middle of May. The subarctic summer is too short for the winter to be forgotten. Provisions for winter cannot be neglected for even a brief moment.

The failure of the first couple of attacks over the Litsa River in July 1941 meant that we were running short of time. The OKW and the headquarters of each of Army Norway and Mountain Corps Norway remained committed to the offensive against Murmansk for the time being, despite the fact that the first month of the war against the Soviet Union had not resulted in a penetrative success for any of the three corps in North Finland. The additional forces that had been allocated to the Arctic Front – the Finnish 14th Infantry Regiment (two battalions), the 4th Machine-Gun Battalion, the 14th Machine-Gun Battalion, and the 223rd Bicycle Battalion – enabled the mountain corps to stabilise the flank and to hold the front. Also, the arrival of some personnel replacement battalions had compensated somewhat for the losses of the mountain corps. But the relatively high daily casualties, especially those of the 2nd Mountain Division in its defence of the bridgehead, meant that the units of the mountain corps could never quite reach full strength. The best time for the resumption of the offensive would therefore be just after the arrival of as many reinforcements as possible. With the approval of the OKW, Army Norway decided that the reinforced 388th Infantry Regiment (with the I Battalion of the 214th Artillery Regiment, the 2nd Company of the 214th Pioneer Battalion, and a cart section) would be detached from the 214th Infantry Division and sent, along with the 9th SS Infantry Regiment, from South Norway to the Arctic Front. These regiments would be transported by sea and would then stand ready in Kirkenes. General Dietl was not particularly enthusiastic about this decision. He foresaw that these units, neither of which were made up of mountain troops, could only be of limited use in a third attack over the Litsa. Both regiments were without combat experience and were neither equipped nor trained for warfare in the mountainous tundra. The OKW therefore agreed to substantially strengthen the mountain corps with the 6th Mountain Division, which had just left Greece and was being refreshed in Semmering, Austria. Although this mountain division would be unable to partake in the new attack, it could still make use of and build upon any early success. It was then planned that, with the onset of winter, the 6th Mountain Division would relieve one, if not both, of the 2nd and 3rd Mountain Divisions at the front. The 6th Mountain Division departed Semmering on 23 August, and it was hoped that it would arrive in Petsamo between 5 and 20 September. However, the mountain corps could not await the assembly of the 6th Mountain Division before the commencement of the new attack. The first week of September was the latest point at which this attack could be carried out, and we still wanted to exploit any chance of a breakthrough in 1941.

For longer than he had ever done before, the commander of the mountain corps cast his gaze over the terrain that would lead towards Murmansk. An optimistic appraisal of the upcoming operation might envision the decisive defeat of the enemy forces before Murmansk and the absence of any appreciable resistance being put up between Litsa Bay and Kola Bay after that. However, the 60 kilometres of terrain that would have to be covered offered many possibilities for enemy resistance. The first bulwark was the current Soviet position behind the Litsa River. The second was that of the chain of lakes stretching from Ara-Guba Bay towards the south-south-west. There were several hills between those lakes (300–301.9 and 237.9–220) as well as behind them (305–281–269). The third obstacle to be overcome was the Ura River with the large hills to its east (354–370.6–256.2–347.7). The low mountain range of the final 15 kilometres to Kola Bay offered the enemy a deep defensive zone. The bay was between 2 and 4 kilometres in width, and the opposite bank, peppered with batteries in concrete emplacements, was where the city of Murmansk lay. On the left flank was the sea fortress of Polyarnoye. To the right, the impressive Tuloma River flowed into the bay. The bay was 60 kilometres in length, so that could be added to the 60-kilometre sea flank that would be created by an advance from the Litsa River to Kola Bay. Enemy forces could land anywhere, so it was not hard to imagine, even with the aid of the road that ran nonstop between the Litsa River and Kola Bay, that considerable German forces would be tied down to the defence of these 120 kilometres. It could be expected that the enemy would mobilise everything that was available on Kola Peninsula. He would send reinforcements via Arkhangelsk and via Soroka (Belomorsk), with the Murman Railway having been extended to the latter only just that year.[29] He would fully exploit the approximately 14 airfields that lay on the eastern side of and further inland from Kola Bay, and he would continue to do so even after German forces reached the bay. The Soviet Arctic Fleet would still have bases in Teriberka and in other coastal harbours, and would thus be able to continue carrying out one attack after another from the sea against the flank of the mountain corps. Finally, rather than relinquishing Rybachy Peninsula, as we had anticipated in June, the enemy would hold on to it as a strong position from which a counter-attack could be launched. Alongside these operational and tactical considerations, there was one which was no less important, and that was the question of what the mountain corps ought to do if the Kandalaksha–Kola stretch of the railway line did not fall into our hands. Even if it did, what if it was damaged beyond repair, or what if its 250-kilometre length could not be adequately protected? Was the mountain corps supposed to stay in Murmansk permanently? Could it be safely supplied by sea if Polyarnoye was cut off? Would it be supplied by land from Petsamo, even though the roads near the front had not yet been made ready for winter?

So far, the question of supply had only been important up to the Litsa. There had been no major problems in this regard, but this was because the Allies had not yet made a major effort to completely put a stop to the flow of German supplies over the North Sea, the Atlantic, and the Barents Sea. The increasing success of the U-boats and the Luftwaffe against enemy shipping in 1941 and 1942 also played a role. However, the mountain corps must have followed the events in the Arctic Ocean in August and September 1941 with some concern. There had been rumours of enemy plans for a large-scale landing at the beginning of July, but these had not been taken seriously. What did hold our attention, though, were the operations of enemy naval forces. They could at any time bring American convoys to Soviet waters, or they could just as easily attack German convoys.

The units of the 6th Mountain Division were supposed to be transported in multiple waves in the following fashion: by rail through Germany, by sea to Oslo, by rail to Trondheim, by sea to Kirkenes, and on foot to the front. On 16 September, Army Norway informed the mountain corps that this would no longer be possible. One regimental group of the division disembarked in Billefjord Harbour, which was south of Honningsvåg in Porsangerfjord, and had to march approximately 500 kilometres from there to the front. Other elements of the division arrived in Nordreisa and had to march about 700 kilometres to Petsamo. The remaining elements had partially arrived in Tromsø but then had to return to Trondheim. From there, they travelled by rail to Oslo and were transported over the Baltic Sea to Finnish ports. Trains hauled by the wood-burning Finnish locomotives then took them to Rovaniemi, and from there the troops covered the 530-kilometre distance along the Arctic Ocean Highway, on foot, to Petsamo. The advance officer of the division had reported to the headquarters of the mountain corps on 1 September that the bulk of the divisional units, thanks to the circuitous route, would only be able to assemble to the south of Petsamo at the beginning of October.[30] Not only would the 6th Mountain Division be unable to take part in the third attack over the Litsa; it would also be too late to help maintain the momentum of the attack.

It is difficult to say whether and to what extent General Dietl was daunted by the many factors that had to be considered for this campaign, not to mention the many things that were unknown about it. He was not a pessimist, but he was fully aware of the importance of the question of supply for this theatre of war. He was very conscientious in his studies of how to continue operations on the Arctic Front, and he particularly concerned himself with the tactics that would best be employed when carrying out an attack over the Litsa. He would hike as much as 30 kilometres up and down the front almost every second day. His companions on these trips were not always the same, for few could maintain his pace. With unit commanders and ordnance specialists by his side, he personally visited every single important spot in the combat zone. On 11 August, Lieutenant-General Walter Warlimont of the OKW arrived at the Arctic Front for detailed discussions and to gain an impression as to the nature of the region along the Litsa River. The chief of the operations staff of the OKW himself, General of Artillery Alfred Jodl, and the army liaison officer to the commander of the Luftwaffe, Lieutenant-General Rudolf Konrad, visited the Litsa front on 5 September for the same purpose.[31] On 18 August, the headquarters staff of Army Norway and Mountain Corps Norway met to discuss the situation. General Dietl provided a detailed report to the commander of Army Norway in Rovaniemi on 22 August. The Arctic Front was being taken seriously by everyone. There were many difficulties to be overcome, and there were varying opinions amongst the field commanders and headquarters staffs, but the consensus was that the overall situation was not entirely unfavourable. Despite the unexpected degree of enemy resistance and armament potential, our offensive spirit could not be allowed to wane. The point of main effort of Army Norway would now lie with the mountain corps. The attack over the Litsa was to be renewed. With the help of the 388th Infantry Regiment and the 9th SS Infantry Regiment, the enemy there was to be annihilated. He would be brought to his knees not by a frontal attack but by a double envelopment. One pincer would strike from the eastern front of the bridgehead and the other would advance behind Hills 322 and 321.9. The two pincers would then link along New Road, a recently discovered connection between Ura Road and Russian Road. The jump-off positions for the pincers were 20 kilometres away from one another. Each attack group would encounter enemy fortifications after advancing approximately 5 kilometres. These would be north-east of Knyrk-Lubol Lake and south-east of Long Lake. It would then be necessary to push through a zone that was roughly 10 kilometres in depth. We could hardly count on our attack coming as a surprise to the enemy. He had been making defensive preparations for some time, and he always had a lot of aircraft flying overhead. Army Norway contemplated the idea of sending the 6th Mountain Division along the Luttojoki in the hope that it would find a road along which to advance.[32] However, the more likely result would be the creation of a new front which would be filled with marshland and lakes, and whose supply lines would be extremely long. Other considerations were not to be neglected. If the third attack over the Litsa River failed, we still wanted to be able to hold the existing front line after that. A permanent post had not yet been found to the west of the river. A retreat behind the Titovka would have made it impossible to supply the position at the neck of Rybachy Peninsula and would have robbed the defence of the nickel mines of Kolosjoki of the room for manoeuvre it needed. There was so much that was dependent on being rapid in movement and relentless in attack. Other factors were, as always, the weather and terrain. The road from Petsamo to Herzberg via the Titovka Valley had been improved in July and August. It could be used by motor vehicles without problem for the first 25 kilometres and to some degree for the final 35.[33] Even though some cart roads and pack animal paths had been prepared beyond Herzberg, there were still 15 kilometres of wilderness to be overcome to reach the assembly area of the 3rd Mountain Division. We had to take care not to allow ourselves to succumb to the wishful thought that it would only require two or three days to gain access to Russian Road. It was the mountain infantry battalions alone that would bear the brunt of the deep thrusts into enemy territory. The infantry units would only be able to manage small attacks in the rough, off-road terrain, while the Luftwaffe had announced that, from the beginning of October, the bulk of its units would have to be transferred to the south due to the climate.

The commencement of the attack was set for 8 September. The bothersome sea wind drove lashing rain from the low-lying clouds, the troops froze in their drenched clothing and canvas tents, and the condition of the roads deteriorated in the marshy depressions. The field kitchens could barely find brushwood within a radius of several kilometres that was suitable for giving off heat, and lighting a fire in this terrain was unthinkable due to the thick, white smoke that would be able to be seen all around.

At the end of his visit to the front on 5 September, General Jodl had remarked that the decision as to what would happen after the attack had been carried out would be made by the Führer and the supreme command. The mountain corps would need to provide its assessment of the situation when that time came, and it would then be determined whether the attack ought to continue in the direction of Murmansk, whether the territory that had been gained ought to be held, or whether, so long as the enemy forces before the mountain corps had been destroyed, the territory that had been gained ought to be abandoned. Jodl himself was of the view that a push towards Murmansk would only be worthy of consideration if it were also possible for Kandalaksha to be taken, for German forces would in that case be in complete possession of the Murman Railway.[34]

CHAPTER 15

The Third Attack over the Litsa River

Map 15

According to the plan for the attack, the forces of the mountain corps were to assemble and advance as follows:

1. The 3rd Mountain Division was divided into a main group on the right wing and a secondary group on the left. These groups were to make themselves ready on the west bank of the Litsa River. The former would be 12 kilometres and the latter 3 kilometres to the south-west of the blown-up bridge. The movement of the units into position and the delivery of supplies to the units would take place along the lengthy, newly created pack animal road from the area of Hill 168.9. Before that point, the road that had been used was one that led from Herzberg and that had been built by some of the forces of the division and by the 405th Construction Pioneer Battalion, but it was barely suitable for motor vehicles.
    (a) The main group would consist of the reinforced 138th Mountain Infantry Regiment (Klatt), the reinforced 139th Mountain Infantry Regiment (Windisch), and the 83rd Mountain Pioneer Battalion. This group was to strike over the Litsa as far as the strip of land between Knyrk-Lubol Lake and Knyrk Lake and would then cover its flanks whilst advancing along New Road towards Hill 321.9.

(b) The secondary group would be the reinforced 388th Infantry Regiment. It was to advance at the same time as the main group over the Litsa on a narrow front and was to take the small hills approximately 4 kilometres to the south of the Litsa bridge. It would then seize Russian Road to the east of there and would prepare for a further attack towards the north-east so as to encircle the enemy position on and around Hill 185.6 from the south. If necessary, it might also need to advance towards Hills 321.9 and 322.

2. The 2nd Mountain Division would assign to the 55th Anti-Tank Battalion and the 4th Machine-Gun Battalion the role of defending the entire western part of the bridgehead (i.e. between the third waterfall upstream from the mouth of the river and Hills 258.3 and 274.0). In the eastern part of the bridgehead, three attack groups would stand ready from left to right as follows:
   (a) Group Hofmeister would consist of two attack groups.
      (i) On the left wing, to the west of Litsa Camp, would be the III Battalion of the 136th Mountain Infantry Regiment, the 1st Company of the 82nd Mountain Pioneer Battalion, and the 9th SS Infantry Regiment without its I Battalion. The III Battalion of the mountain infantry regiment was to set off before the SS formation and take the mountain (Fjordberg) immediately to the east of Litsa Camp. The battalion would then pivot to the south and attack towards the hills that lay to the south-south-east. It was planned that the battalion would unite here with the II Battalion of the 136th Mountain Infantry Regiment, which would be approaching from the other direction. The III Battalion of the SS regiment would proceed after the III Battalion of the mountain infantry regiment out of Litsa Camp and would take possession of Hill 173.7 and the range of hills to its east. It was then to cover the east flank of the division up to Litsa Bay. The II Battalion of the SS regiment had to seize some smaller, but still important, hills to the south-south-east of Litsa Camp. If these hills were not occupied, the movements for the second

phase of the attack would not be able to be carried out. Once these hills were taken, the bulk of the II Battalion would help the III Battalion of the SS regiment in covering the flank to the east.

(ii) To the south of Litsa Camp would be the II Battalion of the 136th Mountain Infantry Regiment. It was intended that this battalion, along with the III Battalion of the same regiment after its arrival from Fjordberg, would sweep through and secure the range of hills south of Hill 173.7, thereby shielding the east flank of the division inland from Litsa Bay up to the valley that extended towards the north-east of Long Lake (Lopatkina Trail). The bulk of the regiment would then veer to the south-west and take the hill that rose out of the depression between Heart Lake and Long Lake (Hill 200).

(b) Group von Hengl would start to the north of Hill 274.0 with the 137th Mountain Infantry Regiment, the I Battalion of the 136th Mountain Infantry Regiment, and the 82nd Mountain Pioneer Battalion minus its 1st Company. With four-and-a-half mountain battalions, this would be the main attack group of the 2nd Mountain Division. After Group Hofmeister had secured the east flank and the land up to the Lopatkina Trail, Group von Hengl would follow the II and III Battalions of the 136th Mountain Infantry Regiment over Hill 200 and conduct the main thrust through the already familiar marshy lowlands north-east of Long Lake in the direction of the range of hills east of Ura Road (the Ura Hills). Afterwards, Group von Hengl was to strike towards Hills 322 and 321.9 from the north-east (i.e. from the rear) with the intention of linking up with the 3rd Mountain Division.

The fighting in the area of the 2nd Mountain Division proved to be quite dramatic from the very first day. After the rather trouble-free capture of Fjordberg by the III Battalion of the 136th Mountain Infantry Regiment, the 9th SS Infantry Regiment, with tremendous force, stormed the hills it had been assigned against the moderate resistance of a weak enemy who, contrary to all expectations, had been taken by surprise. The III Battalion of the SS regiment reached the mountain top 2 kilometres east of Hill 173.7 on 8 September at 1700 hours. It had entered what seemed to be a deep zone of Soviet resistance and was immediately subjected to multiple heavy counter-attacks. The inexperienced companies of the battalion were in a state of shock and fled back to Hill 173.7, with some elements retreating even further. Nevertheless, the regimental commander managed to maintain order, organising the units of the regiment and rapidly pushing forward elements of his II Battalion so as to secure the southern slopes of Hill 173.7 against all enemy attacks. In order to prevent a new crisis from arising, the division sent the I Battalion of the 137th Mountain Infantry Regiment to occupy the area between the northern slopes of the hill and Litsa Bay on the night of 8/9 September. This was only a temporary task for the battalion, and it was pulled out on the morning of 9 September. The III Battalion of the SS regiment had quickly reassembled and was soon back in action. To its south, the larger part of the II Battalion of the SS regiment had been unable to gain more ground.

The 136th Mountain Infantry Regiment had in the meantime been heading towards the hills 2 kilometres south of Hill 173.7. It succeeded in taking possession of those hills at noon. At the same time, the 82nd

By Heart Lake

Mountain Pioneer Battalion approached the small hill north of Heart Lake from the north and north-east. Group von Hengl departed behind Group Hofmeister. The latter did not make any progress on this day in its advance on Hill 200. By the end of the first day of the attack, it was clear that the enemy had been caught unawares. His disorderly artillery fire revealed that he could not ascertain the direction of advance of the German forces.

The morning of 9 September went by with the relocation of artillery and heavy weaponry and the movement of the troops into new attack positions. From 1500 hours, the 136th Mountain Infantry Regiment executed a number of attacks towards the southern slopes of the contested Hill 200. These attacks did not manage to punch through. Immediately to the north-west of Group Hofmeister, the 82nd Mountain Pioneer Battalion endeavoured to create an opening through the range of hills between the lakes. The entire II Battalion of the 9th SS Infantry Regiment was now in action alongside the III Battalion of the same regiment. A visit by the commander of the mountain corps helped to raise the spirits of the men of this regiment.

The attack of Group von Hengl was to begin on 10 September. Unfortunately, there were increasing signs that the enemy was reinforcing his front in the area of the 2nd Mountain Division. Destroyers in the outer parts of the bay certainly indicated that more enemy troops were landing. A series of counter-attacks were then executed by the 205th Rifle Regiment. We had assumed that this unit had been lying quietly near Lopatkina. Our forces had thrust into the midst of the 52nd Rifle Division. Enemy counter-attacks had been relentless since the afternoon of 8 September. Moreover, these counter-attacks were systematic and were of greater than battalion strength. The enemy soon withdrew his front line a little to the east, which was a welcome development for the mountain corps, although it meant that our main thrust to the south would require constant flank cover. He conducted relief attacks in the Litsa Valley as well as at the neck of Rybachy Peninsula as part of an overall effort to put up resistance to our advance. Throughout the day on 11 September, we neither gained nor lost territory.

On 12 September, after heavy fighting, Group von Hengl reached the northern slopes of the Ura Hills by 1300 hours. There was no further success on that day despite the help of our Stukas. Confronted by non-stop counter-attacks from the east, south-east, and south, our front line had to be brought back to Hill 200 on the night of 13 September. A defensive rather than offensive position had to be established here.

Even if the push to the south had yet to succeed, it would at least be possible to consolidate the bridgehead. The 2nd Mountain Division therefore regrouped and assigned Lieutenant-Colonel Kräutler the task of taking Hills 263.5 and 314.9 on 15 September. For this purpose, the units placed at his disposal were the III Battalion of the 137th Mountain Infantry Regiment, the II Battalion of the 136th Mountain Infantry Regiment, and the 82nd Mountain Pioneer Battalion. The assault began at 0400 hours. Hill 263.5 was occupied by 1100 hours, and so was the mighty Hill 314.9 in the course of the afternoon. The last of these two hills would be of great importance for artillery observation for the division, and indeed for the entire mountain corps. No less significant was the fact that our seizure of this hill deprived the enemy of that very same artillery observation. The Soviet III Battalion of the 58th Rifle Regiment had been defeated. 400 men were taken prisoner and a large quantity of matériel fell into our hands. The two hills were immediately absorbed into the bridgehead defensive zone, and Group Kräutler was disbanded. Both mountain infantry battalions were then sent to the rear as reserve units. But to the east, south-east, and south, against the echeloned fortifications and natural obstacles to the south of Long Lake, it would not be so easy to straighten out the front line with the forces that were available there.

Unlike the 2nd Mountain Division, the 3rd Mountain Division did not run aground in a zone of resistance characterised by defensive positions amidst rocky terrain. It instead pushed the limits of the overtaxed supply units, traversing difficult ground with neither roads nor bridges. Any work that needed to be done to make the journey easier had to be carried out by the troops themselves. There had been some initial success due to the fact that the enemy had been taken by surprise, and it was hoped that this could be exploited to such an extent that perhaps the strip of land between Knyrk-Lubol Lake and Knyrk Lake could be reached as soon as the second day of the attack. The lack of enemy resistance at the beginning of the German attack would have allowed this. But the strength of the Soviet defence became greater with each passing day. Enemy activity also increased against the flanks and rear of the 3rd Mountain Division. In recognition of the significant danger posed by the German pincer movement, the enemy had sent a freshly activated division from Polyarnoye to put a stop to it. The Soviet division executed its counter-attack with perfection, and the mountain infantry, by this point completely drained, were unable to hold out against it.

The advance of the 3rd Mountain Division began on 8 September at 0350 hours when the leading mountain infantry battalions of the main group crossed the Litsa and encountered only weak enemy security forces. Approximately 2 kilometres east of the river, near Tafelberg, was where enemy resistance became more stubborn. His counter-attacks were quite powerful and difficult to overcome. By the evening, the I and II Battalions of the 138th Mountain Infantry Regiment stood before a fully developed enemy position 2 kilometres south of the strip of land between Knyrk Lake and Knyrk-Lubol Lake, while the II Battalion of the 139th Mountain Infantry Regiment, advancing to the north-west of Knyrk-Lubol Lake, made about the same amount of progress and found itself amidst a minefield. Between the lakes and on the other side of the minefield, a line of bunkers had been constructed out of stone and wood. The 7 kilometres of territory that had been gained on this day through marshes and bushes and rocks was an impressive achievement.

Such movements through impassable terrain can lead to a vulnerable position when the time comes to relocate heavy weaponry and bring forward supplies of ammunition, fodder, and rations. That moment had now arrived, and it was made worse by the fierce fighting and nonstop rain. Army Norway repeatedly criticised the slowness of the operation. Only the enemy combat outposts could be driven back on 9 September, and they retreated to the strip of land between the lakes. The troops edged their way forward in the next few days and kept a lookout for the best attacking possibilities. The 139th Mountain Infantry Regiment managed to push forward systematically to the hills immediately to the west of the northern end of Knyrk-Lubol Lake, a position that would be important for artillery observation. Unfortunately, the range of hills in enemy territory provided a good view of our movements. The enemy would also have been aware of the presence of the four mountain batteries on either side of the southern end of Knyrk-Lubol Lake from the moment they opened fire. These were the batteries that had been given to the main group of the 3rd Mountain Division (i.e. the 1st, 2nd, 4th, and 5th Batteries, equipped with Skoda M.15 mountain guns, of the I Battalion of the 112th Mountain Artillery Regiment). All the counter-attacks that the enemy conducted on these few days were crushed. He had sent several tanks to the front via Russian Road, but our troops succeeded in disabling most of them.

The supplies that the troops had set off with lasted until 13 September (i.e. four days). This was done because it was barely possible for the most urgent daily requirements of matériel to be brought to the front on a daily basis. It took a pack animal two days to make the journey from the final reloading point to the area just behind the line of battle, and it had to be accompanied by another animal which carried the fodder for itself and for its companion (mules are roughage eaters!). That meant an efficiency of only 50 per cent in the use of the supply trains. It was less than that when it came to supplying the artillery. The delivery of its ammunition caused the greatest difficulty. One pack animal could carry 12 shells. The experienced battery commander saw to it that every mountain cannoneer carried in his backpack a single round for the mountain guns. This ensured that the batteries near Knyrk-Lubol Lake had enough ammunition for approximately two days. The mountain infantry regiments experienced more difficulties. They were particularly low on rations throughout the offensive. Understandably, despite the tremendous effort of the men, such a circumstance could not help the operation to proceed swiftly. It must have been a bitter feeling for our front-line troops to look through their binoculars and see enemy trucks driving right up to the combat zone via Russian Road or New Road. This was in stark contrast to the dreadful state of our supply lines.

Nonetheless, there were some notable successes on 14 September. The 138th Mountain Infantry Regiment advanced 2 kilometres through the strip of land between the two lakes. The 139th Mountain Infantry Regiment seized the fortified positions to the north-west of there, and some elements even reached Russian Road. Control of that road was soon handed over to the 138th Mountain Infantry Regiment. On 15 and 16 September, the Carinthians of the 3rd Mountain Division pushed forward towards the hills of the enemy position 4 kilometres south of the Litsa bridge. Our troops had assaulted this position in vain during the second attack over the Litsa, and they now fought tooth and nail for this blood-sodden ground one more time. They finally managed to take the position after multiple attempts on 16 and 17 September. Stukas had provided valuable assistance, as had the corps batteries guided by an artillery liaison command post. The regiment, with its front facing east, held on to the positions that had been reached on Russian Road, but the men and their animals were utterly exhausted. The supply route had become 20–25 kilometres in length, and, on the second day of the attack, a footbridge had already been laid across the point at which it crossed the river (the Litsa talon). Both the 138th Mountain Infantry Regiment and the mountain batteries needed to be supplied along this route. The 139th Mountain Infantry Regiment was examining the possibility of a shortcut for its supply route that would go directly to the west through the area of the 388th Infantry Regiment, but this had yet to be prepared. There were still enemy forces holding out in the vicinity of the Litsa bridge. As this bridge still needed to be rebuilt, there could be no thought at this stage of fully opening Russian Road. On top of that, the road could not be used safely until the dominant Hills 321.9 and 322 had been occupied. The enemy hurled into battle the 69th and 114th Rifle Regiments, and their concentrated counter-attacks were carried out in conjunction with the assault of an enemy unit of approximately regimental strength against the southern flank of the 3rd Mountain Division, putting our supply lines and artillery positions in great danger. Our batteries had to ward off multiple raids, for the widely stretched-out security lines of the III Battalion of the 138th Mountain Infantry Regiment to the east of the Litsa and of the I Battalion of the 9th SS Infantry Regiment to the west of the river were unable to prevent every single infiltration by the enemy. Bad weather made aerial support impossible. Snowstorms had set in from 18 September. The divisional commander therefore requested at 1000 hours on 19 September that a withdrawal be made to a position behind the Litsa River. General Dietl granted this request. Step by step and in an orderly fashion, the retreat over the river took place over the next few days approximately 4–7 kilometres to the south-west of the blown-up Litsa bridge.

The secondary group (the reinforced 388th Infantry Regiment) had commenced its attack on 8 September at the same time as the main group of the 3rd Mountain Division. It had soon crossed the Litsa. Concentrated under the commander of the 112th Mountain Artillery Regiment were the batteries of the I Battalion of the 214th Artillery Regiment, the 3rd and 6th Batteries of the 112th Mountain Artillery Regiment (mountain howitzers that, even when drawn by two animals, had been unable to follow the main group), and the 1st Battery of the 730th Heavy Artillery Battalion (its guns brought to the front one by one and with great difficulty). These batteries inundated the enemy with their fire. However, the inexperienced troops, despite their momentum, shortly suffered heavy casualties in the middle of the main defensive area of the enemy. These troops were without climbing boots and were unaccustomed to the rugged terrain, the hidden snipers, the fire from enemy bunkers, and the confusion caused by counter-attacks and close combat. So as to prevent their complete destruction, the I and II Battalions of the infantry regiment were withdrawn behind the Litsa on 9 September and merged into a single battalion. The regiment then assigned its III Battalion and the security forces that were downstream (the 233rd Bicycle Battalion and the 48th Anti-Tank Battalion) the responsibility for the defence of the 12-kilometre stretch of river in the sector of the 3rd Mountain Division. On 10 September, the III Battalion of the 388th Infantry Regiment was already committed to the protection of the southern flank to the west of the Litsa. It was relieved on 16 September by the I Battalion of the 9th SS Infantry Regiment (from the reserve of the mountain corps). In an attack that had lasted only one day, the casualties of the two battalions of the 388th Infantry Regiment that had taken part accounted for 22 officers and 434 men.

The ferocity of the fighting can be comprehended from the casualties suffered by the mountain corps in the period between 1 and 10 September. The total was 2,005 (399 fallen, 1,375 wounded, and 231 missing), of which 84 were officers (23 fallen, 56 wounded, and five missing). In a letter to the chief of the operations staff of the OKW, General Jodl, on 23 September 1941, General Dietl made a list of the casualties:[35]

Since 8 September
 959 fallen, including 33 officers
 3,447 wounded, including 83 officers
 220 missing, including five officers
Since the beginning of the campaign on 29 June
 2,211 fallen, including 68 officers
 7,854 wounded, including 202 officers
 425 missing, including 10 officers

On 18 September, at the airfield in Luostari, the chief of staff of Army Norway had given the commander of the mountain corps an overview of the situation in Lapland. The forces of the army had been unsuccessful in reaching the objectives that had been assigned. While the objective in the south had not yet been given up, the complete blockade at sea at that time along the coast of North Norway required the cessation of the operations of the mountain corps in the direction of Murmansk. The German Navy found itself unable to improve the situation, and it would still take a few weeks for the 6th Mountain Division to fully assemble. Once the 6th Mountain Division was ready, it would maintain a defensive line throughout the winter, whilst the 2nd and 3rd Mountain Divisions could spend that time in East Finnmark, Petsamo, or central Lapland.

In the abovementioned letter, General Dietl described the condition of both of the Austrian mountain divisions. His words were moving, but also objective and without exaggeration. He requested that they be transferred to another theatre of war after having spent so much time fighting in the Arctic.

CHAPTER 16

The Reasons for Failure

Map 1

There are a number of reasons for the failure of the three attacks over the Litsa River, and thereby for the failure of the offensive against Murmansk in 1941.

Although the supreme command may have been aware of the geopolitical importance of Murmansk when designating it as an operational objective, its conception of the military-geographical conditions of a combat zone between Petsamo and Kola Bay was incomplete, or perhaps even non-existent. It expected from the mountain corps the fulfilment of a task whose ability to be carried out had not been carefully considered. The first question that should have been addressed was whether it was even necessary to take Murmansk in a direct manner. It may have been desirable from the point of view of naval strategy, but what was more important in the first instance was the prevention of supplies being delivered to the city via the Arctic Ocean and the Murman Railway. While the navy would have had to deal with the sea route, it was the ground forces that would have been responsible for taking care of the rail route. Putting a stop to rail traffic was far more urgent than the occupation of the city or of its harbour. If, however, we were to remain intent on the seizure of Murmansk, the next question that would have required consideration was whether the city would have best been approached from Petsamo or from the south. Either plan would have been audacious and difficult to carry out. Doing both simultaneously would have been impossible. Not only would there have been insufficient time; it would have also split up our meagre forces and made operations in the roadless tundra against a heavily fortified enemy utterly hopeless. The route from Petsamo was shorter, but an advance via Kandalaksha would have been more likely to secure success. The problem, then, lay in the choice of the main focus of the Kola operation. An advance towards the Murman Railway from Salla towards Kandalaksha certainly would have been difficult over the wooded mountains, rocky slopes, and significant obstacles. Nevertheless, if the railway line could have been seized, it would have become easier to supply the advancing forces and to properly prepare them for winter. This direction of advance could therefore have been regarded as relatively favourable. An accompanying attack via Kiestinki in the direction of Louhi could only have served the purpose of tying down a few enemy forces. The enemy would have held the advantage in the event of such an accompanying attack, for he would have been able to access the front there via a short branch line and also via road, the distance of which was around 50 kilometres. The German–Finnish side would have been at a great disadvantage, for the distance to the front would have been 300 kilometres and the sole available route would have been a bad and only partially constructed road. A long, pencil-thin thrust might have been able to touch the Murman Railway, but it was probably best that this idea be shelved. The wilderness there provided good protection, and a few reconnaissance and security forces would have been enough to set up a defensive position against any Soviet attack forces. The divisions employed there would have stood us in good stead for the future. Had the accompanying attack been carried out, the main advance towards Kandalaksha would have been lacking in penetrative power. The enemy would have been capable of sending reinforcements rapidly from the north and south, while we would have only been able to do the same at a slow pace and with tremendous effort. As a consequence, an energetic advance on Kandalaksha, which would have been earmarked as the point of departure for further operations against Murmansk, would have required considerable strength from the outset. A no-less-energetic advance by the Finns towards the railway junction in Soroka (Belomorsk) would have also been necessary.[36] This was where, coming from Murmansk, one line of the Murman Railway led through East Karelia and another led to Arkhangelsk. The capture of Soroka would have cut the railway and provided cover for the German southern flank. It would have also aided the operations of the Finns between Lakes Ladoga and Onega. However, we could not expect that the Finns would pay particular attention to and commit their main forces in the direction of the White Sea for as long as they still had to secure the Svir and the area to the south of Lake Ladoga. Marshal Mannerheim regarded an operation in the direction of Soroka as the correct course of action. The only forces upon which he could potentially draw, though, were those in the area of the Karelian Isthmus, and there was no way that could happen in 1941. Leningrad was in that area, and it was the plan of the OKW that the German and Finnish forces would meet on the eastern side of Lake Ladoga. Yet it was also the plan of the OKW that the advance of the German forces in Lapland towards the Murman Railway be accompanied by the Finns. This meant the fragmentation of the relatively meagre forces in the vast area between the Baltic Sea and the Arctic Ocean.[37]

It would have obviously been quite complex to plan an offensive from Finnish Lapland against the Murman Railway, but if this problem is looked at without any concern for East Karelia or Leningrad, there would still be the question of where to place the point of main effort. A discussion of the ideal organisation of forces can only be theoretical. What we really needed were far more forces than were available. Maintaining a defensive position along most of the front, it might have been possible for an attack group to force its way through to Kandalaksha reasonably quickly. Such an attack group ought to have comprised two or three mountain divisions, the two divisions of the Finnish III Corps, and, for flank protection in the second phase of the attack, two infantry divisions. It goes without saying that this attack would have needed the support of artillery and pioneer formations, including road construction troops. Whether the OKW would have refused to make these forces available for such an attack group is difficult to assess. The belief that may have prevailed in the OKW that the Arctic Front was a secondary theatre of war was probably what led to the German forces in Lapland having to get by with varied forces from Norway, but this ignored the fact that there were some very important objectives to be reached and that actually reaching them would be exceptionally difficult.

General Dietl, in the previously mentioned letter that he wrote to the chief of the operations staff of the OKW on 23 September 1941, had expressed his opinion on the lack of an adequate point of main effort: 'The tragedy of the operation I led in the tundra is that there were always too few forces available for the rather demanding fighting there. Army Norway had failed to create a real point of main effort, which meant that we were unable to carry out an attack with local superiority. As a result, despite unprecedented sacrifice and tremendous effort, we were denied final victory.'[38] Attributing blame to Army Norway alone, however, does not seem to be just. The supreme command would have weighed up competing demands and possibilities, and it would have been responsible for the degree to which it equipped Army Norway. Waldemar Erfurth discussed the chopping and changing of the OKW in his article, 'Das Problem der Murmanbahn', in issue 6 of *Wehrwissenschaftliche Rundschau.* On 7 July, after the fall of Salla, the OKW ordered that the German and Finnish forces continue their attack with reduced forces. On 2 August, it ordered that there be points of main effort on both wings near Salla and that the Murman Railway was to be cut in two in the vicinity of Louhi. On 5 August, after it seemed that the fall of Leningrad was a foregone conclusion, the OKW ordered that a Finnish division be sent from there to reinforce Mountain Corps Norway. On 20 August, the OKW directed that it remained the objective of Army Norway to take Murmansk. On 23 August, the OKW ordered that Murmansk had to be cut off from the south in 1941 and that this was to be achieved with the continuation of the attack in the direction of Kandalaksha. On 14 October, the OKW ordered that the offensive was to be brought to a halt. On 1 November, it ordered that a renewed attack in the direction of Kandalaksha would be carried out with the participation of the Finns.

That the ideas laid out at the beginning of this chapter would not have been far-fetched is proven by a meeting that took place on 15 October in Inari between the chief of staff of Army Norway on the one hand and the commander of the mountain corps and the chief of staff of the mountain corps on the other. Also present were the army adjutant to the Führer, Major Gerhard Engel, as well as the senior quartermaster of Army Norway and the quartermaster of Mountain Corps Norway. Major Engel had brought with him the new directive from the Führer. It ordered the cessation of all attacks in North Finland, but nonetheless foresaw the need for a winter operation. Until then, it would be the task of the mountain corps to hold on to the ground that had been taken and to protect the nickel mines. Army Norway started to think about the winter operation and was of the view that the point of main effort would need to be applied against Kandalaksha. For this purpose, it wanted to concentrate the 163rd Infantry Division (currently near the Svir River), the 169th Infantry Division (Salla), the 3rd Mountain Division (to be detached from the mountain corps), and the 7th Mountain Division. After this concentrated attack group commenced its advance, Mountain Corps Norway would set off in the direction of Murmansk with the 2nd, 5th, and 6th Mountain Divisions. This operation would possibly be conducted in conjunction with an advance along the Luttojoki River, perhaps by a reinforced mountain infantry regiment, and would conclude with the seizure of Rybachy Peninsula. Another possibility was that the attack on Kandalaksha would be accompanied by an advance of an entire mountain division along the Luttojoki, while the attack on the Litsa front would only begin once the offensive against Kandalaksha and Ristikent had made an impact. It was envisioned that this operation might commence at the beginning of March 1942. Whether the operation could be brought to a conclusion before the thaw set in at the beginning of May would depend upon the rapidity with which progress was made. The commander of the mountain corps made it clear to the commander of Army Norway that such a plan would require that the bulk of the officers and their men involved in the attack, whether it be in the direction of Murmansk or in the direction of Kandalaksha, had mastered skiing and been trained to a level that would enable them to fight in the vast winter terrain. All the attacking divisions would have to be so equipped to the last man that they would be able to cope with the subarctic conditions. The supply lines would need to be able to reach every single front-line unit, even if off-road and over snow and ice. If there was a heavy snowfall or if a long-range assault was launched, the flow of supplies would still have to be maintained. Such preconditions could not yet be met. It was still the case that only some of the men of the 2nd and 3rd Mountain Divisions were adept at skiing, and the training that the replacement troops had received before their arrival was not any better. General Dietl had a lot more to say, but Major-General Buschenhagen, who was the chief of staff of Army Norway, emphasised the purely informatory nature of the meeting. He said that little more could be done and that such preconditions might never be fully met.

From the third day of the advance of Mountain Corps Norway, the Soviets always had the lead in being ready for action. They had roads that led directly to the Litsa River, whereas the mountain corps had to build its own roads. The Soviets could quickly bring reserves to the front along the Murman Railway or by sea, but the reinforcements of the mountain corps had to travel 600 kilometres on foot, by motor vehicle, or along an unpredictable sea route. On top of all of that, the numerical superiority of the enemy, despite the low quality of his equipment and training, was just far too overwhelming.

What was also beyond doubt was the naval and aerial superiority of the enemy. He dominated the coastal areas and held the initiative for a long time with his landing operations. The neck of Rybachy Peninsula and the Duchy deprived the front of perhaps those very forces which could have given penetrative power to any of the three attacks over the Litsa. Our concern for the supply road tied down a number of highly valuable mountain infantry battalions in the rear area. If the forces of the Luftwaffe that had been allocated to the Arctic Front at the beginning of the war in the East remained in that area at all times, the mountain corps probably would have had no grounds for complaint. The difference between the will to do something and the means to carry it out is highlighted most dramatically by the way in which it was demanded of the Fifth Air Fleet that it, with only a small handful of squadrons, should alternately support two combat fronts that lay approximately 400 kilometres away from one another. What is more, the air fleet often had to try to give priority to the operational air war during its presence in Kirkenes.

The core of the Soviet units was composed of tough and acclimatised soldiers, mostly Siberian, who fought with determination. Russia had a tradition of being able to put up a strong defence, and it was no different on this occasion. It was hard to crush the resistance of the enemy, and the terrain made our advance all the more difficult. Heavy artillery guns were unavailable. While they could have increased our striking power, they would in any case have been troublesome to deploy. There was always a shortage of mountain infantry formations from the moment we reached the Litsa. It would have been necessary from the outset to ensure that there were sufficient special forces for flank protection in the north and south. Even all headquarters troops would have needed their own climbing boots, wood-frame pack carriers, carts, pack animals, packsaddles, transportable weapons, and small field kitchens, as well as separate infantry gun platoons, pioneer platoons, and signal communication platoons, if they were to be usefully employed as mountain troops. If these troops were fighting on the same battlefield, then they ought to have been provided with the same equipment. The number of pack animals allocated to the mountain corps probably could have been increased by 500 or 1,000 without overtaxing the supply of fodder, as it could be expected that some animals would be lost in the course of the campaign. The situation would have been better if there had been a mountain supply column battalion at the disposal of the mountain corps, as had been the case in 1940. This battalion would have needed to be made up of several pack trains and cart sections.

If we had been more aware of the state of the roads in the sector of the mountain corps, we could have had a greater number of construction and supply troops, and thereby more construction equipment and supplies, assigned to us. At the very least, we could have better rationalised the use of what was available. One or two construction brigades with lots of trucks (especially dump trucks), bulldozers, loaders, graders, steamrollers, and other equipment might have been able to extend the supply road of the mountain corps all the way to the Soviet road network in only a few days. Something that we particularly lacked was any possibility of being supplied from the air. A single squadron could have covered the short distance from Kirkenes to the front and could have played a particularly important role in eliminating the difficulties we encountered in the vicinity of the Litsa.

There may have been differences of opinion on tactical matters, but storming the enemy positions around Hills 314.9, 322, and 321.9 could hardly be avoided. They were key positions for the Litsa front and for an attack from the west against Murmansk. The enemy was always fully aware of this.

CHAPTER 17

Landslide and Relief

Maps 4–6

At 1645 hours on 28 September, the chief of staff of the mountain corps received a radio message at the command post by the Titovka bridge:

> Landslide on either side of the Parkkina bridge caused by bombs at 1600 hours. About 800 by 500 metres of riverbed have disappeared. Bridge and all telephone lines destroyed. Quartermaster, Mountain Corps Norway.

What this brief message referred to was the effect of bombs that had been dropped from the air. The Soviet pilot who was responsible had probably never dreamed of being able to cause so much damage. Great harm had been done to the mountain corps by something that had been incredibly unlikely. It could be regarded a blessing in disguise that this incident did not take place eight or more days later. It requires close attention here because the consequences determined the measures of the mountain corps for weeks to come and took precedence over the defensive fighting at the front. This landslide also revealed a particular characteristic of this theatre of war.

Scandinavia emerged from the sea after the Ice Age with the receding of the enormous Fennoscandian ice sheet. This process continues to take place most clearly at the northern end of the Gulf of Bothnia, where the land is rising at the geographically rapid speed of 1cm per year. But even the coast along the Arctic Ocean and in West Norway once lay deep under the continental ice, and traces of these prehistoric circumstances remain to this day in some places on the mountain slopes. In some of the fjords and at the lower reaches of the rivers, the geological rise exposed layers of silt and wet, grey clay that were often several metres high. Rivers gradually cut paths for themselves through these layers. Such a terrace, about 8 metres high, ran along the length of the lower Petsamonjoki roughly from Luostari to the mouth of the river. The layers of soil there could generally take a load. Even the Arctic Ocean Highway was situated on the left bank of the river. Hills of sediment would have occasionally formed along the river and would have shaped it into bends and loops. The terrace was covered with birch brushwood and bushes, overgrown with moss, and filled with sandy dunes. There were also lots of boulders in the valley which would have been shaped by erosion or brought there through glacial motion. The silt had maintained its moisture and was therefore lacking stability. The higher the land rose and the lower the river was, the more probable landslides were. It was into this marshy higher ground of the Petsamonjoki Valley, several hundred metres south-east of the emergency bridge in Parkkina, that 250kg bombs from three or four Soviet bombers fell at 1600 hours on 28 September. As had been the case so often before, the bridge had been the objective of the bombing raid. The bombs struck the ground relatively close to one another. The clay soil between the bomb craters gave way. The rock faces, suddenly without a supporting structure, broke off. The neighbouring layers of silt and clay surged into the gap that had opened up with all their might. The entire 500-metre width of the terrace, nearly reaching the rocks at the foot of the mountain, was sliced away from the east bank, causing a chain reaction that continued almost 1,100 metres upstream along the valley. About 8 metres in height, the terrace slid at an angle over the lower layers of wet earth in one, virtually noiseless movement to the bottom of the valley and onto the riverbed. The Petsamonjoki, which in the vicinity of Parkkina was at least the size of the Isar in Munich, flooded the west bank, the water rushing as if it had been tipped out of a giant bucket. The tidal wave tore the west bank to shreds and swept away the telegraph lines. Some of the water ran as far as the Arctic Ocean Highway and left behind a lot of puddles. Fortunately, no damage to the road was done. Even the handful of Finnish houses which lay between Parkkina and Luostari escaped unharmed. The camps, reloading points, and barracks in the area were on the western side of the highway, so they too suffered no damage. The sight of the rubble was mind-boggling. The bushes and brushwood that had once been on the hillside were now carried along, in their autumnal blaze of colour, by trickling water at the rate of approximately half a metre per second towards the valley. A large part of the imposing river that had flowed through the land there was gone. That moment of astonishment could not last long. The realisation that the only bridge over the river had vanished aroused great consternation. The debris of the bridge was found later on by the edge of the fjord. This bridge had been 90 metres in length. At this narrow point, there was now a muddy tangle made up of chunks of earth of various sizes, rocks, crevices, and pieces of trees and shrubs. All the gaps and depths in this maze of rubble had soon filled up with water. A glance was enough to recognise that there was no chance of rebuilding the bridge there.

The quartermaster was on the spot and took the following measures at once:

> A radio message has been sent to the leadership of the mountain corps. Contact has been made with the commander of the 6th Mountain Division, who is currently in Luostari, and he has been requested that he come with his second general staff officer to the spot where the bridge had been. Measures have been put in place for traffic regulation on the Arctic Ocean Highway along the stretch where the landslide occurred. The size of the landslide upstream has been established and an investigation of the state of the now dammed river is being carried out. Bushes and brushwood from the hillside have been observed being washed downstream between the bridge site and the fjord. Orders have been issued for the repair of the telephone lines on the west bank. A telephone station is being set up for communications with the front, and an assembly point for vehicle traffic on the east bank has been decided upon. The commander of Army Norway has been informed of the situation over the telephone by a signal officer in Luostari. All units in the Petsamo Valley have been alerted, and measures have been taken to equip them with entrenching tools. A reconnaissance of the dammed area is being conducted so as to find the best way to create a water channel and to build an emergency footbridge over the chunks of earth to the east bank. A review is being done to determine how best to organise the reloading points on either side of the river and how best to carry supplies across the footbridge. The supply situation at the front is being ascertained, especially the current availability of rations and fodder for the combat units east of the Petsamonjoki.

Major-General Ferdinand Schörner, the commander of the 6th Mountain Division, arrived at the site of the catastrophe at about 1700 hours. Recognising that the supply and relief of the front was greatly endangered, and fully aware that winter was not too far away, he immediately made all of the forces of his division available for the resolution of the situation. The 91st Mountain Pioneer Battalion was given the task of building a new bridge and reconnecting the two banks. The battalion was supported by the pioneer staff officer of the mountain corps and by the leader of the 33rd Military Geology Unit from Army Norway command post in Finland, both of whom arrived at the site early on 29 September. The alerted units, headquarters staff, security troops, and supply troops from the vicinity of Petsamo worked the whole night through, guided by the pioneer troops, to create drainage channels and to build a footbridge, suitable for two-way traffic, over the chunks of earth and rubble. Preparations were made to organise a unit for carrying supplies across the footbridge such that there would be 100 men per two-hour shift.

Reloading points were improvised on both banks for rations, fodder, ammunition, fuel (in barrels and canisters), and, most urgently, building material (for field fortifications and shelters). The supply officers of the front-line divisions were given control of all motor traffic to the east of Petsamo. For the time being, a stop had been put to shifting troops back and forth between Petsamo and the front. The telephone network was operational again early on 29 September, and a new permanent field telephone line was being constructed near the Arctic Ocean Highway. The commander of the mountain corps and the commander of Army Norway came to discuss the situation with the commander of the 6th

Emergency footbridge over the landslide near Parkkina on 28 September 1941

Mountain Division as well as with the staff officers at the site. Also present was the German military attaché in Stockholm, Lieutenant-General Bruno von Uthmann, who was at that time on a visit to the mountain corps.

The landslide debris had in the meantime been piling up 1 kilometre downstream from the former bridge site (Map 6). This was at a point almost 500 metres before the widening into the fjord. The Petsamonjoki flows around the eastern side of a large gravel ridge there and turns again to the north about 200 metres later. Ala Luostari, formerly a monastery, lies on this ridge. Its bell pavilion is as significant a landmark in Petsamo as is the Arctic Ocean Highway. The river widens gradually into the fjord. The water flows on either side of an island as it goes past the village of Parkkina, bends to the east around a large sand terrace (where there would later be a military cemetery), and rapidly enters the inner fjord, where it is already 900 metres in width. The colour of the water in the bay had now become light grey. The tides influenced the water level upstream beyond the island, and, in two days, they had spread the greyish colour over the entire bay south of Trifona. An artificial lake started to form 1.5 kilometres upstream from the former bridge site. Fortunately, given the depth of the river there, the valley did not flood. From the evening of 29 September, the river began to flow over the landslide debris more and more. The water soon carved the channels that had been traced by the pioneer troops into substantial arms of the river. There was no rainfall for the next few days, so none of the larger chunks of earth were carried downstream. We were concerned that the water pressure might send the debris hurtling down the river, but this did not materialise. Supplies were carried across the river systematically. The units that had been the first on the scene were able to be relieved by some of the supply units from the front. On the whole, it was thanks to the efforts of the men who carried the supplies of rations, ammunition, and other necessities on their backs that 120–150 tonnes were able to be taken across the river on a daily basis. Alarmingly, the required quantity of fodder for the roughly 7,000 horses at the front could not be supplied. The construction of a new 8-tonne emergency bridge was of the utmost priority.

The result of the investigation into bridge construction by the 6th Mountain Division and into matériel procurement and supply possibilities by the quartermaster led to the following decisions by the mountain corps on 30 September:

1. The new bridge must be built from Parkkina over the sandbank at the upper reaches of the fjord (Parkkinansaari). The access routes go over layers of sand and offer no difficulty. The tidal range, with the ice from the bay in winter, will loosen the supports of the bridge and cause them to rise, but there is nothing that can be done to counteract this. For the construction of a new bridge upstream from the landslide, it is necessary that a mountain on the east bank be bypassed with several kilometres of completely new road.[39] The new bridge will be 650 metres in length.
2. There will have to be some delay to the delivery of supplies for winter so that the wood that is needed for bridge construction can be collected. This wood will come from three places:
   (a) From the sawmill that belongs to the mountain corps in Nellimö, on the shore of Lake Inari. The transport distance is 200 kilometres.
   (b) Small quantities of lightweight wood from Kirkenes can be brought by sea to Petsamo immediately.
   (c) Wood can also be obtained from the stock of mine props at the nickel mines of Kolosjoki. The mountain corps will compensate for this later on by acquiring 25,000 tree trunks from the sawmill next to Lake Inari. The OKW will have to be notified of this. The area of the mountain corps must be given priority.
3. The supply units of the currently available elements of the 6th Mountain Division, roughly a regimental group, are to be mobilised, as are some of the troops of the mountain corps and of the auxiliary units of the Luftwaffe. Army Norway will also provide support. The 477th Corps Supply Service is to organise the transportation of the wood from Nellimö.
4. Fuel is to be rationed more sparingly. Much of the current stock of fuel must be devoted to bridge construction, and there is the very real danger of a shortage in the near future. The sea route is already endangered, and there will, on top of that, be inevitable delays in the flow of supplies to the front while the bridge is being built. Front-line rations must be reduced for the time being. Any horse-drawn vehicles that are not urgently needed at the front are to be diverted to Parkkina.[40]

5. Completion of the new Prinz Eugen Bridge is intended for the evening of 10 October. Until then, the relief of any units at the front must be postponed. The front-line elements of the 3rd Mountain Division will be withdrawn in the meantime to a predetermined defensive position for the winter. The plans that have been made for the alignment of the winter defensive position and for the build-up of supplies for the winter will be adhered to.

By the beginning of October, detailed plans had been made for the relief of the front-line units. The 3rd Mountain Division was to go to South Lappland, while the 2nd Mountain Division would be sent to the Kirkenes–Svanvik–Luostari area. The 6th Mountain Division was to take over responsibility for the entire front, consolidating its strongpoints and withholding strong reserves for a flexible defence. This division would be reinforced with the 388th Infantry Regiment, the 14th Machine-Gun Battalion, the 68th Bicycle Battalion, elements of the 730th Heavy Artillery Battalion, the 405th Construction Pioneer Battalion, and various supply troops. It would also have at its disposal the army coastal artillery that was at that time in Titovka and by the mouth of the Litsa. The rest of the I Battalion of the Finnish 14th Infantry Regiment, the 9th SS Infantry Regiment, and the 1st Company of the 40th Panzer Battalion had already been recalled by Army Norway. The withdrawal of the RAD units could be expected. Further units soon had to leave the Arctic Front: the 4th Machine-Gun Battalion on 23 October, the 233rd Bicycle Battalion on 19 November, and, at the request of the mountain corps, the I Battalion of the 214th Artillery Regiment on 21 November. The I Battalion of the 5th Flak Regiment was swapped over with the II Battalion of the 46th Flak Regiment in November and December. Both Finnish border guard companies in Petsamo were assigned to the Ivalo Battalion. The 55th Mountain Carrier Battalion was sent to the front in the middle of October. At the end of the month, Army Norway assigned to the mountain corps a battalion headquarters, a motor maintenance repair shop platoon, and four transport companies from Transport Group Speer of the National Socialist Motor Corps. They were supposed to offer a transport capacity of 720 tonnes, but this figure dropped swiftly to 150 tonnes. The motor vehicles had been sent from the beautifully warm autumn weather in Germany at the beginning of October, but their water-filled radiators were already damaged by the extreme cold by the time they arrived in the Finnish harbour of Oulu. Around 70 per cent of the entire vehicle fleet had therefore begun their service in Lapland with radiator and engine block damage.

The relief of the units at the front was scheduled to take place the day after the completion of the Prinz Eugen Bridge. This bridge was to open to traffic on 8 October. The long columns could now roll forward, carrying the supplies that had been held up for so long and that were so urgently needed at the front. The sky was overcast. A strong north-westerly wind whistled over the fjord, and the snowstorm that had developed by the evening across the Arctic Front did not bode well. The winter had arrived quite unexpectedly. The storm lasted for 50 hours. Any attempt at movement was futile. The supply road was covered in snow before long. It had no snow fence, and there were no snowploughs in the area. Everything possible was mobilised to clear the snow. Tractors were soon in action, and the RAD units worked with devotion. Meanwhile, the efforts of the commander of the mountain corps ensured the maintenance of traffic discipline. The bad weather resulted not only in further delays to the relief and supply of the units at the front but also in a number of losses. Men went missing, drivers were suffocated by gases in snow-covered motor vehicles, and the troops of the poorly equipped 388th Infantry Regiment suffered frostbite. Losses of animals were also considerable, especially the horses of the 388th Infantry Regiment (from Norway) and the I Battalion of the 214th Artillery Regiment. About 1,400 horses died from exhaustion in the freezing temperatures of that October. The old pack animals and the middleweight draught horses of the 2nd and 3rd Mountain Divisions, slightly run-down yet hardened, held out well. The small Greek mules of the recently arrived 6th Mountain Division, on the other hand, survived the change of climate in only the rarest of cases.

The positional warfare at the front ebbed and flowed. The enemy pursued the withdrawal of the 3rd Mountain Division carefully but systematically. Our forces in the bridgehead over the Litsa and along the defensive line at the neck of Rybachy Peninsula were able to repel all enemy attacks. It was a pleasant surprise when, on 27 September, the enemy mistakenly launched a bombing raid against his own positions on Hills 321.9 and 322. The main focal points were now Hill 314.9, east of the Litsa, and Mustatunturi Mountain, near Rybachy Peninsula. The opinion that the headquarters of Army Norway had expressed on 9 October to the effect that the enemy might decide to disengage seemed to be quite unlikely in reality, for he continued to carry out one attack after another. His efforts were supported by naval artillery. There was a great deal of activity on our flanks. On 25 October, the enemy tried in vain to conduct a raid against the command post of General Dietl.

The advance officer of the 3rd Mountain Division had departed for Rovaniemi on 29 September. The 6th Mountain Division assumed responsibility for the sector of the 3rd Mountain Division (west of the Litsa) at noon on 25 October and for the sector of the 2nd Mountain Division (the bridgehead) on 28 October. Herzberg became the command post of the 6th Mountain Division. On 1 November, the 3rd Mountain Division was detached from the mountain corps and placed directly under the command of Army Norway.

It is not without interest that here, for the first time, the question arose as to whether the relief of divisions in the far north could be carried out by simply exchanging personnel. It was clear to those in positions of leadership that the process of relieving entire units would last for months and would entail risks. Major on the General Staff von Zawadski from the General Army Office of the OKH and Captain on the General Staff Popp from the OKW arrived in Parkkina on 28 October to discuss this matter. The differences in the composition of the mountain divisions immediately came up. The mountain corps wanted the artillery arm of every mountain division to be equipped with six batteries of the GebG 36 mountain gun and three batteries of the leFH 18 light howitzer. It also wanted, as far as possible, for each mountain division to have a battalion of the sFH 18 heavy howitzer. It requested that the supply troops of each mountain division on the Arctic Front be given one mountain carrier battalion, four pack trains, five light motor transport columns, and one fuel and lubricant supply column. The remaining elements of the mountain divisions could maintain their usual composition. Such an exchange of personnel did not happen. The way in which events on the Eastern Front had unfolded meant that none of the other mountain divisions could be released.

CHAPTER 18

Positional Warfare, Strongpoints, and the Line of Security

Maps 16 and 17

After the failure of the offensive over the Litsa River and the shift of the mountain corps to the defensive, the question arose as to what would be the most suitable defensive position. It was necessary to keep the enemy far enough away from our flank along Litsa Bay and from our artillery observation posts. This meant that the front-line would have to run inland from Hill 173.7 and, most importantly, would have to lie to the east of the dominant Hill 314.9. The position of the 3rd Mountain Division by the Litsa talon would have to be abandoned immediately due to the difficulty of the supply situation there. But even the area to the south of the blown-up Litsa bridge remained too exposed. The front line of the 3rd Mountain Division needed to be shortened most urgently. Because of this, the mountain corps saw to it that a preliminary reconnaissance was carried out as soon as possible to determine where the new position of the mountain division should be. The retreat of the division to this new position would need to be covered by rearguards and combat outposts along the Litsa and by scouting and security units on the southern flank to the west of the river.

Soviet strength on about 20 September was estimated at roughly four divisions. One of these was the 114th Rifle Division with three regiments somewhere between Litsa Bay and Long Lake. Another was the 52nd Rifle Division with three regiments between Hills 322–321.9 and, going past the bridge site, the strip of land near Knyrk-Lubol Lake.

Yet another was the 58th Rifle Division with two regiments, which we assumed was advancing from Ura Road over New Road. There were also forces of approximately regimental strength approaching from the south against the rear and the deep flank of the 3rd Mountain Division. A border guard formation or a unit of the 114th Rifle Regiment appeared to be active in the vicinity of Motovsky, for we had spotted a number of pack animals there. According to statements obtained from prisoners we had taken, the Soviet forces there had specifically been given the task of carrying out raids and long-range reconnaissance missions on the right wing of the 3rd Mountain Division. Before the front at the neck of Rybachy Peninsula, the enemy was estimated to have a reinforced infantry regiment, one or two machine-gun battalions, and a special unit. He retained naval and aerial superiority. Despite the willingness of the Luftwaffe to provide support, its numerical weakness meant that it would barely be able to make a difference. English aircraft were in the vicinity of Murmansk. Their precise strength was not known, but they probably amounted to no more than one or two groups.

In view of the strength of the enemy, we were concerned that he would be able to go over to the offensive and fully exploit our weakness. However, it was probably the case that his losses had also been so heavy that he was unwilling to take decisive action. He cautiously followed our retreat, conducted extensive reconnaissance, set up only defensive positions on any ground he gained, and adopted, as he had in August both here and at the neck of Rybachy Peninsula, the tactic of multiple small assaults, usually of company or battalion strength.

The 6th Mountain Division, or at least those elements of the division that had thus far arrived in the Petsamo–Luostari area, had been placed under the command of the mountain corps on 21 September. The III Battalion of the 143rd Mountain Infantry Regiment, with the 3rd Company of the 91st Mountain Pioneer Battalion and the 91st Replacement Training Battalion, had temporarily been withheld by Army Norway, but they were made available to the mountain corps before long. The order of Army Norway on 21 September, which reached the headquarters of the mountain corps on 23 September, required that the mountain corps immediately make preparations to spend the winter in a position near the Litsa River with strongpoints that would enable the lines of communication to the rear to be protected. The first point emphasised in this order was that the permanent defence would lie in the area of the Litsa, by which was meant the maintenance of the bridgehead on the east bank and the protection of the flank on the west bank. The second point emphasised the system of strongpoints as the tactical means whereby the defence would be conducted. Rather than having a rigid front line that would extend through the terrain, the main line of resistance would be made up of a series of small fortifications and combat posts. Such a system was consistent with what had been learnt from mountain warfare in the past. Logical preconditions for the maintenance of a chain of strongpoints would be to construct the strongpoints themselves and to plan for the frequent relief of the outpost troops. In addition, each sector would need its own reserves. Centrally organised reserves, even if larger, would be of less use, for they would be slower to respond to any local crisis. Only the reinforced 6th Mountain Division was earmarked for the Arctic Front. This meant that the entire winter defensive position would have to get by on six mountain infantry battalions. With these facts in mind, the mountain corps sought out the best locations for the winter position. The 6th Mountain Division itself was involved in the reconnaissance work. General Dietl particularly valued the experience of the Finns, for which reason he had a long discussion with Colonel Willamo on 23 September. There was great concern as to how, at the beginning of winter, new positions, troop shelters, depots, command posts, and so on could be constructed rapidly in previously unprepared lines. The first priority was to set up the positions in such a way that would, at least to some degree, protect the men and horses from the wet and cold. They would need brick bunkers, makeshift heaters (the material for which might not always be the best), Finnish millboard tents, Norwegian canvas tents, and things like that. Although Army Norway was preparing the delivery of temporary barracks, it was unlikely that they would arrive before December.

On 28 September, the mountain corps approved the locations that had been recommended for the winter position. There had been no doubt whatsoever as to where those locations would be in the area of the 2nd

Mountain Division. Map 16 shows where the strongpoints were placed. They are numbered here in accordance with the designations used by the 2nd Mountain Division, i.e. combat strongpoints (K) between the Litsa and the fjord. Taking into account our combat experience in this area, additional work was carried out in these locations as necessary so that they could function effectively as zones of resistance. K2 and K3 were the central combat strongpoints of the bridgehead. K1a, K1b, and K2a protected the bridgehead against any approach from the Litsa Valley. The chain of combat strongpoints from K4 to K9 would defend the bridgehead against attack from the east and against any outflanking movement from the fjord. Hill 314.9 in particular would prove to be a location of fierce fighting throughout the winter. This fighting would be tiring as well as costly in terms of men and matériel. The enemy approached the hill from Long Lake and ensconced himself on its steep south-eastern slopes. He sat just below the plateau, and the fighting there could only really be carried out with hand grenades. On just that one hill, tens of thousands of hand grenades must have been used in the course of the winter. The steadfastness of the mountain infantry troops on the hill in the long polar night deserves the highest praise. The almost uninterrupted assault by the enemy on Hill 314.9 commenced on 13 October. This was at about the same time as the enemy started to apply constant pressure against Mustatunturi Mountain at the neck of Rybachy Peninsula.

There were fewer mountain strongpoints to the west of the river. What was employed for the defensive position there was a mixture of strongpoints, trenches, minefields, and other obstacles. A significant stretch of the right wing was covered by the large and variform lake 7 kilometres to the south-west of Herzberg. From there, the defensive chain wrapped around the southern and south-eastern slopes of Hill 240, a spot that was most important for artillery observation, and then extended to the north-east towards the river, reaching it at a point near a hill named Loreley. A strongpoint in the middle of some marshy terrain to the east of this hill was where the sector of the 2nd Mountain Division began. There was also a flank strongpoint that was placed far to the west so that communications could be maintained with the intermediate strongpoints in the direction of Titovka Valley and in the vicinity of Lake Chapr.

The entire defensive position was divided into three battalion sectors: the front to the west of the Litsa, the front between the Litsa and Heart Lake, and the front between Heart Lake and the fjord. Each sector would have a battalion at the front and another battalion in the rear. The defence to the north of Litsa Bay was also limited to strongpoints for the winter. If we wanted to be able to spot and repel landing operations from the fjord into the Duchy, we had to establish a series of staggered outposts along the fjord roughly opposite where K9 lay. Hills 227.4 and 172.3 overlooked Landing Bay and were therefore chosen as combat posts, while smaller positions were set up on either side of these hills. To the rear, a battalion headquarters with reserve forces formed an obstacle line between the lakes approximately 5 kilometres to the north of Zapadnaya Litsa.

On 2 October, the mountain corps was reorganised for the purpose of repositioning its forces. Any troops that were not going to occupy the strongpoints would remain in the rear.

So that the defensive position could be effectively maintained in the middle of winter, the vast area of tundra between the Finnish border and the Litsa River had to be given constant attention. The winter, especially in the period from February until April, was the better time for military movements by the enemy. One of the most important tasks of the mountain corps was the protection of the nickel mines and the smeltery in Kolosjoki, which required that measures be taken to prevent the incursion of enemy forces in the region between the Litsa and Motovsky. The lakes had frozen over, and the marshy areas had solidified. Soviet ski patrol troops, winter-mobile reconnaissance troops, assault squads, and, later on, even so-called reindeer ski brigades patrolled this region. Soviet patrols were generally less of a threat in the summer, but it was still necessary to be on the alert. Indeed, on 28 July, the mountain corps received an advance warning of a planned enemy raid. A deserter appeared on the supply road and testified that he had come from a reconnaissance company near Point 289.6, which was 11 kilometres to the south of the Titovka bridge. The task of the company was to conduct a raid against a German headquarters that the enemy presumed was in the vicinity of the bridge. It was reassuring in a situation such as this that there were no good roads in the southern area of the mountain corps. However, the old Lapp trails could still be of considerable use to the enemy. That the threat of enemy raiding parties was not a product of our imagination was abruptly proven for the first time on 30 October when a lone armoured car was attacked on the supply road at a point approximately 3 kilometres west of the Titovka Valley (at the 21-kilometre mark):

> The commander of the 91st Replacement Training Battalion and three of his men were driving to the front at about 0700 hours. They were not accompanied by any other motor vehicles. A sheaf of machine-gun fire wounded the driver and probably the commander himself. As they abandoned their car, they were captured by enemy patrol troops who had been lying in wait. The patrol troops secured the wounded on sleds and then withdrew immediately. Their retreat was covered by a strong rearguard in the hills approximately 500 metres to the south of the road. So quickly did this raiding party withdraw over the Titovka and to the south-east that any attempt to pursue it was in vain. A Fieseler Storch air observer reported in the afternoon that the raiding party was already halfway between the Titovka and Litsa Rivers, several kilometres to the south-west of Hill 350.

In order to better respond to such brazenness and to ward off the danger to the aerodrome in Luostari and the nickel mines in Kolosjoki, a mountain infantry regiment of the relieved 2nd Mountain Division was sent from Luostari to establish a line of security on the eastern side of the Titovka which ran parallel to the Finno-Soviet frontier. The regiment was to ensure that there was always one reinforced mountain infantry battalion holding this line. The new strongpoints that would make up this line in the middle of nowhere had to be set up from scratch. They would at first be temporary structures, but would eventually become fixed combat posts, bunkers, supply positions, and so on. The Tyroleans of the 2nd Mountain Division gave the strongpoints along this roughly 20-kilometre line of security names from their homeland, among which were Zuckerhütl (Hill 323.3), Rabenkopf (Hill 287.1), Ortler, Venediger (Hill 373.1), Katschberg (Hill 297.4), Wendelstein, and Hochriß (Hill 255.8). Between this line and the Finnish outposts along the Lutto sector were contact patrol troops from both sides. The hollows and valleys through which the new line of security ran did at least possess more vegetation than did many other areas on the Arctic Front, but our troops had to be vigilant. The actions carried out from the strongpoints there placed high demands on the skiing ability, the physical endurance, and the combat training of the mountain infantry. Anyone who was separated from their unit or who was wounded, be it amidst a snowstorm or in combat, was usually lost. Aerial observation would be impossible until February or March. This line of security would become a perfect example of how to wage a war of movement in bushes and mountains in the middle of winter.

There was no change in the situation near Rybachy Peninsula. Occupying the defensive line there for the winter would be the 388th Infantry Regiment and the 14th Machine-Gun Battalion. There would always be two battalions along the line itself and then two relief battalions a little to the rear. Some elements of these forces also had to cover the area to the south-east of the mouth of the Titovka against any landing attempts by the enemy. The Finnish soldiers who had originally been there were gradually withdrawn. The guns of the platoon of the Tähtelä Battery that had been brought by a motorboat to Cape Pikshuyev in the late summer could no longer be taken back due to the fact that the very same boat had been lost in the meantime. The guns, though buried in the snow on 28 October, were later found and taken away by the Soviets. The small observatory there was burned down during an enemy landing operation on 8 November. Neither at Cape Pikshuyev nor near Titovka nor at the neck of Rybachy Peninsula could any active defence be put up against the patrol activity of enemy motorboats. All that could be done was observation with eyes and ears. Soviet landing forces repeatedly attacked the first and second lines of our positions from behind, with varying degrees of success. The commander of Army Norway visited the position by Mustatunturi Mountain on 22 October and was convinced of its decisive importance for the front at the neck of Rybachy Peninsula. The shift of the command post of the mountain corps from the Titovka bridge back to Parkkina between 29 October and 4 November seemed to signify that full responsibility for the combat zone had been handed over to the 6th Mountain Division.

In the wake of the raid of 30 October on the supply road, the mountain corps decided that every company, battery, and similarly sized supply unit would be accompanied by an anti-partisan platoon which would constantly have to be on the alert. Such platoons had their first success as early as 5–7 November, pursuing Soviet raiding parties on the southern flank and henceforth contributing significantly to the improvement of the security of the front.

The instructions from the OKH that reached Captains on the General Staff Obermeier and Sauerbruch at the headquarters of the mountain corps on 11 November stated that a report was to be made to the operational section outlining how the troops would be able to cope with positional warfare in the winter. Although they were aware that there was still much to be done by the mountain corps, they could be confident that the troops would be able to master the situation.

CHAPTER 19

On the Luttojoki River

Map 18

It will be recalled that the Finnish Ivalo Border Guard Battalion had been given the task at the beginning of the campaign of crossing the Luttojoki and advancing as far as possible to the east beyond the Finno-Soviet frontier whilst also ensuring that its supplies continued to flow in an orderly fashion. The battalion was then to conduct a reconnaissance of and secure the Lutto-Songelsky area.

The valley of the Luttojoki runs from Lapland to Kola, although much of it has the character of a pathless wilderness of woods, marshland, and lakes dotted with a handful of Lapp villages and a small number of Finnish ranger settlements. As the troops moved along the river and past the rapids, they could have been forgiven for imagining that they were on an expedition of exploration of Mato Grosso in the Brazilian Amazon rainforest, or perhaps of the Congo Basin from the time of Henry Morton Stanley. There was barely any economic exploitation of the primeval forest. The only way in which Finland is able to benefit from the forests to the north of the watershed in the middle of Lapland is to raft the wood along the Paatsjoki to Kirkenes, from where it can then be exported. There is no way in which the wood can be transported to the south.

The Luttojoki flows over the border into the Tuloma, the outflow of which is Kola Bay. The Finns had no roads beside the Luttojoki that led to the border. Regarded from the point of view of the enemy, Ristikent

Cottages in the vicinity of Inari

could be approached by road, but the 50 kilometres from there to the village of Lutto (Luttokylä) had to be covered mostly by water and partly by path on the north bank of the river. On the Finnish side, the 80 kilometres between the frontier and Raja Joseppi were lacking in roads. Any route in the Lutto Valley would encounter difficulties. Between Nautsi and Talvikylä was a 35-kilometre path which was converted into a road in the following months.

The regular border guard troops in the province of Lapland were organised into companies and, on occasion, would be concentrated into a whole battalion in Ivalo. The troops were native Finns from the forests who had been familiar with the country, the climate, the night, the woods, and the marsh since childhood. They were proficient skiers, and their puukko knives were handy tools. Their tenacity, endurance, resourcefulness, and self-assurance distinguished them from all others. These troops would barely say a word when on patrol. They kept their eyes peeled, nodded at one another, pointed silently, and understood one another like the trappers in the novels of Karl May. Going on a reconnaissance mission with them was an instructive experience. It should not be overlooked, though, that standing opposite the Finnish border guard troops was a similar, yet numerically superior and constantly active organisation of Soviet border troops whose men were no less familiar with the land.

The commander of the Ivalo battalion wanted, as far as possible, to resolve the task that he had been assigned with a rapid offensive. The supply was the main brake that essentially bound him to the frontier. The battalion commenced its advance on 29 June with one company heading in the direction of the unimportant Russian settlement of Songelsky and the rest going towards Luttokylä. The occupation of this village was expected to result in control of the Lapp trail that crossed the Luttojoki there. But the battalion seemed to go missing on 30 June and 1 July. A Fieseler Storch reconnaissance aircraft spotted four Finnish soldiers in Songelsky, and, on 2 July, the German pilot managed to land near Luttokylä, where the pioneer company of the battalion was located. Spoken communication was impossible, but, by making signs and pointing at maps, the pilot soon understood that the position of the bulk of the battalion was 3 kilometres to the south of the village. In the next few days, Finnish assault squads patrolled as far as the area of Ristikent. On 7 July, they cut off the lines of communication to the village and forced the enemy border troops to retreat to their strongpoint. The enemy conducted air raids against Luttokylä, and especially against the battalion camp there, in an attempt to relieve the pressure on his forces. Then, on 27 July, the battalion reported that a much stronger enemy battalion was advancing westwards from Ristikent. In the course of the next two weeks, the Finnish battalion fought cautiously against the Soviet one, withdrew towards the border, and established a defensive position. The mountain corps had to see to it on a number of occasions that sea rescue aircraft were sent from Kirkenes to evacuate the severely wounded. These aircraft did so by landing on and taking off from a lake situated very close to the front. The corps intendant, with the intention of resolving the supply situation, flew to the area of the Ivalo battalion, but his Storch was damaged upon landing. It was soon sighted and destroyed by Soviet aircraft, and the intendant had to make a three-day journey along the river to return via Ivalo. In a series of skilfully executed attacks, the Finns destroyed the enemy outposts and captured much matériel. The village of Lutto was at one stage cut off by the enemy, but this made no impression on the Finns. They simply requested aerial reconnaissance in such cases, and they even asked for aerial deliveries from time to time. The battalion was surrounded by the Soviets on 4 August, but it decisively broke through the ring of encirclement and withdrew behind the border at the confluence of the Akkajoki with the Luttojoki. It almost wiped out an enemy battalion in the process. Luttokylä and Songelsky had to be yielded to the enemy. From that point on, there was an increase in reconnaissance, scouting, and security measures. The fighting evolved in a manner typical of forest warfare. Finnish operations always involved raids conducted deep into enemy territory. For example, the Finns destroyed an enemy supply depot near Vuolle Lake on 19 September and an enemy company to the east of the Ainvaara on 23 September.

With the onset of winter, the Finnish battalion required reinforcements to be able to relieve its units and to continue to conduct reconnaissance and pursuit. The commander of the battalion therefore requested during a meeting with the commander of the mountain corps in Ivalo on 16 October that he be given both border guard companies in Petsamo (Tiitola and Turi). This request was granted and was carried out step by step from 23 October. The boundary between the Ivalo battalion and the security front of the 2nd Mountain Division was determined. There were reports of 10cm of snow as early as 23 October, and the ice layers on the lakes had a thickness of between 10cm and 15cm. Winter warfare along the border sector had begun. The enemy, whose strength was estimated at two or three battalions, conducted operations mainly from Songelsky and Luttokylä. He had pack animals. The border guard strongpoints marked on Map 18 are incomplete, as there are no precise records of them today. Talvikylä, Luttoköngäs, Alksoaivi, Ainvaara, Vilgesjaur, Lounakoski, Huuttvaara, Lounavaara, and Karnsjaur were positions that were frequently referred to in daily reports in 1941.

It was important for the assault squads as they fought in the forests of the wintry taiga that they pay attention to the ski tracks that tended to remain in the snow for a long time. The Finnish defenders laid control tracks around their strongpoints and checked them irregularly but frequently for unfamiliar tracks. If any were discovered, they were examined to determine how fresh they were. An assault squad might then set off in pursuit. This was not simply a case of chasing after the enemy. His raiding parties had particularly capable cross-country skiers who could quickly return to their units with, quite often, the intention of ambushing the pursuer. This required that the Finns possess almost a sixth sense to ascertain whether or not there existed the possibility of a trap. They would carefully take into account the terrain, the age of the tracks, the time of day, the suspected strength of the enemy, the combined or separate movements of the enemy, and the general circumstances in order to make their assessment. If a piece of terrain arose suspicion, the pursuer sought to bring his main forces sufficiently at a distance from the enemy tracks into the flank and rear of the enemy unit, cutting off its probable route of retreat and occupying the spot where its temporary camp was likely to be found. A seemingly deserted outpost could potentially be an enemy strongpoint, but it was also often the case that such abandoned locations had been mined with malicious intent. Enemy strongpoints typically consisted of several combat posts, bunkers, wire entanglements, and minefields. If the Finns decided to attack one of them, they would always approach from multiple sides, sometimes simultaneously, sometimes in a staggered fashion, with or without a diversionary manoeuvre, and never according to a rigid plan. During the withdrawal from such an operation, all efforts had to be put towards getting out of enemy territory as quickly as possible and shaking off any pursuers. It was then that the cross-country skills of the Finns proved to be advantageous. Tirelessly and all day long, they would cut down enemy units like trees into smaller chunks and then encircle them. Isolated in the snow and forests and marshlands of Karelia and Lapland, these chunks would be swiftly annihilated. It was for the employment of these motti tactics in the Winter War and in World War II that the Finns became renowned throughout the world.

The mountain corps was closely united with the Finnish border guard troops under its command in a shared struggle. The German and Finnish soldiers were brothers-in-arms. When General Dietl was awarded the Order of the White Rose of Finland by Lieutenant-General Hugo Österman on behalf of Marshal Mannerheim, he regarded this highest honour as an expression of the true friendship between both armies.

CHAPTER 20

The Supply of Mountain Corps Norway

Maps 1 and 19

Before 1940, the various services of the Wehrmacht had given little attention to the supply of large bodies of troops outside Central Europe. It was probable that the supreme command had not thought much about it either, even by the time it ordered the occupation of North Norway and the operation against Murmansk. It was envisaged that the merchantmen that had to collect the ore from Narvik would be able to carry supplies on their way to North Norway. The shipping of ore had become constant, but the situation required that the merchantmen sail through the skerries for as long as possible, that the navy provide escorts, and that the Luftwaffe conduct reconnaissance. Otherwise, it did not seem as if there would be any major difficulties. The supreme command hoped that the stationing of troops in Norway would be peaceful and that, afterwards, the capture of Murmansk would be executed rapidly. The supply of the Arctic Front exhibited and exacerbated the same problems as those that existed in North Norway. These problems were associated with Finland and Lapland, with the system of roads and railways, and with the stance of the nations who owned those roads and railways. The supply situation cannot be regarded in isolation, and a proper analysis should restrict neither the time period nor the geographical area under consideration. It is not enough to focus just on the second half of 1941 or just on the area east of the Paatsjoki, the river which flowed along the Finno-Norwegian border. Before the conditions at the front and their effects can be investigated, it is necessary to understand the supply command, the traffic and transportation system, the dependency of delivery efficiency on the type of goods and their destination, the supply procedure, and the dangers posed by the enemy and the climate.

The Allies were always adept at planning for matériel requirements across seas and continents. They had been thinking for a long time about how to supply armies that were at war across long distances, but the various German headquarters in Scandinavia, especially those of the army, only began to develop these ideas from 1940. The unprecedented rapidity with which the events of the war had unfolded meant that the military leadership suddenly had to change its conception of the scope of space, time, and security. The distances involved were now much greater than they had been in the immediate proximity to the Fatherland. Our calculations in Central Europe were precise, but those for Scandinavia were less so. Deadlines tended to represent desired rather than strict time limits. Great demands were placed on the improvisational abilities of every level of command, be it Army Norway or a company. There was already much discussion about the diverse nature of a land that had been fought for and occupied and that was now our friend. The security zone of the mountain corps in the first half of 1941 covered an area that was approximately 1,200 kilometres in length and 100 kilometres in width. In the second half of the year, the operational area of the mountain corps, including its rear combat zone, was about the size of Bavaria. It was unfortunate that the extent of command of the mountain corps overlapped with that of the High Command of North Norway in East Finnmark (the 702nd Security Division). The best solution was found at the beginning of 1942 when a boundary was established between Army Norway and the newly created Army Lapland which ran along the meridian going through Nordkyn. Because the Ivalo battalion came under the command of the mountain corps, the 68th parallel north was decided on as the boundary with the rear area of the army (specifically, the 525th Army Rear Area Command). In the Finnish zone, the German Army was a welcome guest; on Norwegian ground, however, territorial and political questions had to be sorted out with the territorial commissariat in Kirkenes, the outlying station of the Reich

Commissariat for the Occupied Norwegian Territories. So ineffective was the civilian occupation regime that it was the Wehrmacht that provided essential support for the civilian population. Many Norwegians worked in the ironworks and ore mines in Kirkenes, some worked in the fishing industry, and others were able to find much sought-after work with the German supply administration. Lapland, however, was a vacuum. Almost without exception, the very small number of Finnish industries there were in need of the few workers that were available. And there were only a few hundred prisoners of war who could be put to work. In the autumn of 1941, the mountain corps had to request that 3,000 prisoners be sent from Germany. The total number of prisoners that Army Lapland received in this way in the year of 1942 was more than 8,000.[41] At the beginning, the lack of technologically advanced industries or trades, aside from the handful of fishing organisations, meant that anything that needed to be repaired, no matter how small, had to be sent to the Fatherland or to South Norway. It would then take several months for the matériel to come back, if it did at all. Such a procedure took up space on our transports. It was unprofitable and could not be maintained. From the autumn of 1941, and increasingly in 1942, the army created its own supply installations in Lapland. There was no need to do this in most of the other theatres of war, where it was usually possible to exploit the land in the rear areas. The lack of a civilisation or population in Lapland also meant that there was an extensive lack of rear-area communications to begin with.

No other difficulties in the area of supply were so wide-ranging, persistent, or significant as those that were associated with the traffic and transportation system. Good cooperation with the transport officers, the Reich Commissariat for Ocean Shipping (from the autumn of 1942), the harbour masters, the pioneer troops, and the construction troops was of the utmost importance for the quartermasters of the mountain divisions and mountain corps. If we were to accompany some supplies on their entire journey from production in the factory to use at the front, we would be able to get a good idea of the complexity of supply in Scandinavia and especially on the Arctic Front. In order to raise awareness of this complexity, the mountain corps recorded the journey of a bundle of hay from a mountain farmer in the Fatherland to the final pack animal position on the Litsa in a series of images which were sent to relevant superiors and headquarters in Germany. In a similar manner, the senior quartermaster of Army Lapland conducted a supply map exercise in 1942 for the purpose of informing senior authorities in the Fatherland about the problems of supplying raw materials, especially metals. The map exercise revealed that there was always the serious threat of 'back to zero', the sinking of the transport ship after a journey of about 2,000 nautical miles and shortly before it had reached its objective. It strongly highlighted the dependency of the supply in this theatre of war on long-distance transportation.

Mountain Corps Norway was completely dependent on the flow of supplies across the North Sea, the Atlantic Ocean, and the Barents Sea. Its supply harbour was in Kirkenes. Ships would never go directly to Petsamo (Liinahamari or Trifona), but they might have sometime sailed there from Kirkenes according to the situation and what was needed. The supply across Finland was an emergency route and will be discussed later. The armies in Norway and Finnish Lapland had been placed immediately under the command of the OKW. Although the quartermaster general of the OKH remained in charge of the supply of matériel and was responsible for quantities and allocations, the Supply and Transport Office of the Wehrmacht in Scandinavia, which was directly under the command of the OKW, was responsible for the transportation of the goods.[42] Supplies were generally transported by rail from their production areas to Hamburg. But there was always the possibility that a supply train might not arrive there. For this reason, supplies were sourced from different locations. Rations and fodder might have been brought from western Germany, for example, while other supplies might have come from production areas in the eastern provinces. If goods needed to be transported by sea from the eastern provinces to Hamburg, then it was usually the ships in Stettin that were fitted out for the task. Supply ships from Hamburg or Stettin were escorted from Germany to South Norway (Kristiansand, in the area of Naval District Southern Norway). The next leg of their journey was from Kristiansand to Bergen (Naval District Central Norway) and then from Bergen to Trondheim (Naval

District Northern Norway). The strait between Shetland and Bergen and the skerry-free waters around the peninsula of Stadlandet were dangerous spots for English attacks from sea and air. Convoys sometimes had to sail from harbour to harbour; at other times, they went to Trondheim or Narvik or Tromsø in one go. It was best if convoys could be made up of fast ships. Tromsø (Naval District Polar Norway) was always the assembly point for the continuation of the journey to Kirkenes. Near Lopphavet, west of Hammerfest, and from Honningsvåg to Kirkenes, the route veered out into the open sea. It was there, on either side of Nordkapp, that most ships were sunk in 1941. Not only English but also Soviet naval units conducted operations there. Throughout most of the war, the Norwegian resistance radioed details of the coastal movements of German ships to the enemy. Very few resistance members along the 19,000 kilometres of coast were apprehended. There were some cases where it was possible to reduce the dependency on supplies from the Fatherland by making use of Norwegian resources. Most of the barracks of the various branches of the Wehrmacht in Norway were produced in the south of the country. Trøndelag had a surplus of straw and hay. These goods would be brought by rail to the harbours in Oslo or Trondheim. They would be loaded onto supply ships or freighters and then taken to Kirkenes.

Narvik was of particular significance. It had been the main transshipment port of the mountain corps in 1940. The goods arrived there by sea or by rail from Sweden. The goods that were taken through Sweden were mostly for civil use, although there would often be ammunition as well. They would have entered Sweden in Trelleborg via the train ferry that sailed from Sassnitz on Rügen Island in Germany. The rail journey through Sweden then went directly to Narvik. On top of that, Army Norway had been given permission, and the currency, to purchase barracks, timber, plywood tents, canvas tents (with heating), and hospital beds in Sweden in 1940 and 1941. While the army often had to exercise restraint due to overpricing, the Luftwaffe had more freedom in this regard because its needs were seen as more urgent. At any rate, the mountain corps enjoyed priority over other army formations in view of the earlier onset of winter in the north. Acquisition and allocation in Norway came under the control of the senior quartermaster who, after the creation of Army Lapland in January 1942, was responsible for both Army Lapland and Army Norway. As the senior quartermaster of the outlying post of the OKH in Scandinavia (Norway from 1945), he reported to the quartermaster general of the German Army.[43] He worked in close cooperation with the Wehrmacht transport officer in Oslo, Norway, and the outlying post there, with the transport officer of the military attaché in Stockholm, Sweden, with the German transport authorities in Helsinki, Finland, and with the Supply and Transport Office of the Wehrmacht in Scandinavia. Once its goods had arrived, initially in Narvik and later in Kirkenes, the mountain corps was responsible for its distribution. The supply ships could only partly dock in the small ports of the isolated towns. Many were unable to find a suitable pier, while others lay a short distance offshore. The delays that resulted from unloading just a small number of ships at a time in multiple harbours could not be tolerated for long. The small harbours were therefore expanded in 1942 and 1943 with the help of Organisation Todt. There was no wood to be sourced in North Norway, and even South Norway generally did not have big enough trees. Tree trunks that were 20–25 metres in length had to be brought all the way from Salzburg, making the journey on the flatbeds of the German Reich Railway and on the decks of large freighters to Balsfjord, Lyngen, Alta, Hamnbukt, Ifjord, and so on. In Narvik and Kirkenes, the supply services of the mountain corps or of the mountain divisions had so-called distribution fleets at their disposal. These consisted of fishing cutters, each with a displacement of up to 500 tonnes, that had been chartered by the German Navy. A transport headquarters (later the outlying post of the Wehrmacht Transport Office in Norway) and a supply headquarters were established in Narvik in 1941 and were given the task of assisting the mountain corps. From Kirkenes, the distribution fleet supplied all the small harbours in Varanger Fjord and on the northern coast of Varangar Peninsula, especially where the army coastal batteries were inaccessible by land.

For the convoy to Petsamo, the mountain corps, depending on the shipload, had to make its request to Coastal Command Kirkenes for escort vessels. In the eternally bright summer, an engagement with the enemy could not be avoided as the ships sailed closer to Petsamo. The entire one-hour stretch between Peuravuono and Petsamo Fjords was within firing range of the heavy batteries on Rybachy Peninsula. Such an operation therefore required the following forces: minesweepers for clearing the sea route, escort vessels (outpost patrol boats, submarine chasers, fast attack craft, and so on) for defending against Soviet submarines and fast attack craft from Pumanki, smoke-releasing aircraft for concealing the convoy, bombers for attacking the Soviet batteries on the west coast of Rybachy Peninsula, and fighter escorts for our bombers and ships. It is not surprising that many small aerial and naval battles could take place whenever one of these trips was made. The navy repeatedly requested of the army that it eliminate the batteries on the peninsula. Between 2 and 22 November 1941, an operational study for the seizure of the peninsula was developed and revised and then submitted to the OKW. Yet Operation *Wiesengrund* could never be carried out, as the extra reinforced mountain division it would have needed was unable to be provided. In the course of the year of 1943, the mountain corps constructed a road that led directly from Petsamo to Tårnet, by Iarfjord, which was itself connected by road to Kirkenes. This shortened the supply route by land so significantly that more trucks could be used to bring supplies to the front. Goods could thereby be stockpiled in Petsamo during the winter, under cover of darkness, for the months of the midnight sun.

Not all problems were solved once the supply ships arrived at their destination harbours. The great dangers posed by the enemy at sea were over, but there would then be the renewed danger from the air to be faced, especially in Kirkenes and Petsamo. Our defences were nevertheless strong enough to make it difficult for enemy aircraft to strike their targets. There was relatively little damage that resulted from the approximately 500 air raids launched by the enemy up to October 1944. Although ships of all sizes could dock beside the quay installations in both harbours, only the ore shipping quay (Siberia Quay) in Kirkenes had fixed cranes. The hospital ships *Berlin* or *Stuttgart* sometimes occupied this quay for a long time. Anywhere else, it was the cargo handling gear on the ships themselves that had to do the unloading. There were difficulties from time to time for some of the small ships which had needed fixed cranes in Germany for the loading of goods. If there were more ships than piers at a harbour, then some of the ships would have to wait near shore until a quay was available. In order to save time, the waiting ships would be partly unloaded by transferring supplies to smaller ships, barges, sloops, naval tank landing craft, and so on. The supplies would then be taken to shore outside the main quay installations. The sea transportation authorities understandably insisted on the shortest possible unloading times, for the cargo space on the ships was urgently needed. The navy was just as keen for goods to be unloaded quickly. It was reluctant to let its escort vessels remain for long in Kirkenes, where they were vulnerable to air attacks. And the escort crews would barely have a chance to rest, for there would often be more waves of supply ships waiting to be escorted from Honningsvåg or Tromsø. The capacity of a harbour, though, depended not only on quay installations and cranes but also primarily on how smoothly the process of transloading goods could be carried out. Storage areas, parking spaces for vehicles, distances between storage areas and the harbour, the performance of the columns, and the number and goodwill of workers were all important in this regard. The improvement of the transloading process occurred gradually. It was with a feeling of great pride when, in 1942, the day arrived on which the daily performance exceeded 1,000 tonnes for the first time. The depots of the mountain corps for rations, fodder, clothing, and sheltering equipment lay in Bjørnevatn, 12 kilometres away from the harbour. It was time-consuming to get the goods there, but necessary for their easy distribution. Closer to the quays were the ammunition depots on open-air ground and fuel depots in remote corners of the harbour. There were also depots nearby with replacement parts and instruments for motor vehicles. The Luftwaffe had its entire pool of supplies in the vicinity of the airbase in Kirkenes, about 4–6 kilometres to the west of the town, while the navy kept its supplies on an island in the bay on which the harbour lay. But the performance in the transloading of goods depended on yet more than what has been described thus far. Small stowage on a number of ships, incorrect procedures for storage at many harbours, imprecise address details on individual packages, missing or inadequate bills of lading, barracks parts without numbers, grenades and cartridges mixed up with foreign grades of ammunition, and things like that frequently caused delays.[44] It was often the case that supply ships might arrive with only a part of the load that they had been supposed to carry or that they had conveyed light but bulky goods like roughage at the expense of heavy but essential supplies like ammunition, equipment, and vehicles. Coal and cement would almost always be made ready for transportation, but care had to be taken to ensure that they were isolated from other supplies. Our horses would be harmed, for example, if their fodder was contaminated by coal and cement dust. Ships carrying fodder often departed from a harbour rolling from side to side, their decks with full loads rising high over the waterline. Costly errors often occurred with the way in which some loads were put on board ships. For example, rolls of roofing felt would be damaged if supplies of ammunition had been placed on top of them, while the prisoners of war of the Kirkenes work crew had to wade ankle-deep through puree right at the bottom of a ship if heavy goods had been heaving about on top of jars of jam in rough waters all the way from Hamburg. With shortages in Germany, it was not long before seaworthy packaging could no longer be guaranteed. After the first few months, with a lot having taken place and many supplies having been delivered, there were soon several men amongst the mountain infantry who had become competent dockers.

Yet even the experts of the Reich Commissariat for Ocean Shipping could not have done anything to boost the efficiency in the harbours if the troops had not already organised transloading operations with the involvement of various command elements of the Wehrmacht, with the utilisation of a permanent fleet of motor vehicles, with the employment of workers, with the construction of workshops, and with the establishment of telegraph and telephone installations. Major van der Upvich in particular served meritoriously as the leader of the Wehrmacht transloading headquarters in Kirkenes and later of the transloading control headquarters under the senior quartermaster of the outlying post of the OKH in Scandinavia. The success was due to the prioritisation of efficient haulage methods and basic economic principles over purely military characteristics. The various Wehrmacht transloading headquarters came under the control of the local territorial commanders. This only applied for the harbours in Scandinavia to begin with, but, by the end of the war, it also applied for the harbours on the Baltic Sea. In the area of Kirkenes and Petsamo, the responsible territorial commander was General Dietl, the commander of the mountain corps. In Germany, the transloading of goods destined for the mountain corps came under the control of the Supply and Transport Office of the Wehrmacht in Scandinavia. Military police units would sometimes be assigned to each of the Wehrmacht transloading headquarters. In addition to the establishment of transloading headquarters, supply transportation specialists (senior quartermasters or quartermasters of supply transportation) were assigned to Army Norway, Army Lapland, and Mountain Corps Norway. These specialists managed the flow of supplies to the Arctic Front, their wall maps displaying the positions and loads of all the ships and trains along the supply route.

After the goods had been unloaded from the ships and taken to the storage depots or the next transloading points, it was then possible for the troops to be supplied. Either the motorised supply trains or the units positioned close to the storage sites would be given the task of collecting the supplies, so this usually meant any troops that were stationed in Kirkenes. The 477th Corps Supply Service could only occasionally provide support to individual units in bringing supplies to the front, for its main responsibility was the urgent transportation by land of whatever goods the mountain corps might be lacking. For a long time, two of its three light motor transport columns were devoted to the delivery of supplies for road construction. In the vicinity of Petsamo, especially on either side of the Arctic Ocean Highway between Luostari and Parkkina, there soon came into being several supply depots for rations and a number of special camps for chilled cargo and potatoes, for ammunition and equipment, for construction material, and for wood and coal. Smaller quantities of supplies, in particular the valuable equipment for medical services, veterinary services, motor vehicles, and signal communications, were taken to the appropriate workshops, hospital companies, or veterinary companies, from where they would then be issued. The hospital, veterinary, bakery, butcher, and army postal service facilities of the mountain divisions remained behind in the Petsamo Valley. In contrast, the clearing stations of the mountain hospital companies, the horse collection stations of the mountain veterinary companies, the distribution points of the divisional supply services (ammunition and equipment), and the divisional ration supply offices, including those of Supply Headquarters North, were closer to the front. Once the front line was in more or less a static position, these supply services were able to establish more permanent installations. Deserving of mention are the shellproof and bombproof operational and unit bunkers of the mountain hospital companies that stood south-east of Mustatunturi Mountain near Rybachy Peninsula, by the steep slopes of the south bank of the fjord opposite Zapadnaya Litsa, and behind the right sector of the position 5 kilometres south-west of Herzberg. These bunkers were manned by groups of surgeons who, thanks to their close proximity to the front, saved the lives of many soldiers of a regimental group that had suffered heavy casualties in the winter defensive fighting. Also deserving of mention is a special unit that was available only to the mountain corps. In winter, it was often easier, and gentler, for the wounded to be carried in special sleds over frozen lakes as well as along roads to the rear. For this purpose, the mountain corps had been assigned the sole dog sled column of the German Army. There were 10 Nansen sleds, each with a driver and each drawn by nine dogs (a leader and four pairs). With another nine dogs in reserve, there were a total of 99 dogs, most of them Samoyeds. This unit was trained by Technical Sergeant Aspegrin, a Swedish volunteer, and performed its assigned task with excellence in the wintry tundra.

The supplies for the mountain corps and mountain divisions, including vehicle components, had to be collected from the transloading camps in Petsamo. These came from the distribution points to the supply positions near the front. Many horse-drawn vehicles were employed for this task. The combat troops picked up their supplies here with carts and reloaded them as required onto pack animals. Positions that were far away and that could not easily undertake the task of picking up the supplies they needed had to rely on the 55th Mountain Carrier Battalion. This was primarily the case for the position near Rybachy Peninsula. Empty goods, which had to be collected and handled carefully, were returned in the same way to the supply camps and depots. Each carrier and supply section would ordinarily be loaded in such a way that they would be able to make one trip within 24 hours. Many of the supply routes were exposed to enemy attacks. There were sometimes heavy losses as a result. In situations where there was increased demand for certain supplies, like hand grenades during the heavy fighting on Hill 314.9, additional carriers and pack animals had to be assigned by the leadership of the mountain corps.

If and when necessary, from 1941 onwards, supplies could also be sent to Mountain Corps Norway via Finland, albeit on a smaller scale. This route was useful if emergency supplies were needed for a critical situation or if special goods were urgently required for some purpose. It was probably of greater importance for the Luftwaffe, with its technical supplies, than for the army. When supplies were sent along this route, the matériel that had been requested would be transported by sea from Stettin or Danzig to harbours in South Finland and then by rail, hauled by broad-gauge, wood-burning, old Russian-built locomotives, to Rovaniemi. The supplies would then be taken by the motor vehicles of the 463rd Army Supply Service along the Arctic Ocean Highway to Petsamo, Kirkenes, Ivalo, or elsewhere. The ability to make use of the harbours in South Finland depended on the climate. The ships went to Oulu or even Kemi in summer.[45] Once the ice set in along the coast of the Gulf of Bothnia from December, the harbours further to the south had to be utilised. Turku remained open most of the time. From the end of April until the beginning of June, the harbours further north could be used again. For those supplies that could not be permitted to be held up, especially rations, transloading camps had to be positioned by the harbours in Turku, Rauma-Mäntyluoto, Pori (for Luftwaffe supplies), Vaasa, Kokkola, Oulu, and Kemi (which had facilities for cold storage). All these harbours were connected to the railway network. An 8,000-tonne potato cellar was built in the vicinity of Kauppi. There were freezing facilities there as well as an underground railway siding. Much special material could also be transported to Rovaniemi by rail from South Finland, from the southern part of the province of Lapland, from Sweden, or from Germany via Sweden. Such material included snowblowers, graders, special steel, replacement parts, fuel tanks, machinery, and washing trucks and trailers.[46] This material would often be accompanied by the letter post, and it would all then be taken along the Arctic Ocean Highway to the mountain corps. In 1941, it would take approximately 14–20 days for these supplies to be transported from the Fatherland to Petsamo. After that, it took about eight to 12 days. Purchasing in Finland by the German military was only allowed with the permission of the liaison staff at the Finnish war ministry or at its outlying post in Rovaniemi. Germany generally provided raw materials to Finland as payment in return, so certain quotas had to be maintained. Items that were in high demand, like timber and round wood (from the area south of the watershed in Lapland), barracks of all sorts, high-fibre fodder, reindeer hides (stretcher material for the evacuation of the wounded, with seven hides needed per stretcher), and paper bags for charcoal, had to be incorporated into the yearly German–Finnish trade agreement.

A particular problem was supplying the troops with fresh potatoes. Frost comes to North Finland at the time when potatoes are dug up in Germany. The Supply and Transport Office of the Wehrmacht in Scandinavia therefore had to see to it that the earliest autumn potatoes were rapidly shipped to the front. They had to be escorted all the way and the transloading points had to be run smoothly. Army Norway and Mountain Corps Norway awaited the potato fleet with extra supply trains and special loading units. By September, the potato cellars at every post had been prepared by the troops. In this way, the supply for the period from October until January could almost always be guaranteed without problems. After that period, either frozen potatoes or, from Denmark, dried potatoes were supplied, for these were not so easily ruined by low temperatures whilst being transported.

The considerable stockpiling of supplies for the German troops in Finland that had been ordered by the OKW in 1942 raised a few eyebrows.[47] The troops had mainly lived from hand to mouth in 1941. The naval blockade in the autumn months along the coast of North Norway created a dangerous situation. Not only the Gulf of Bothnia but also the Gulf of Finland remained frozen for several months in the winter of 1941–42. Ice even blocked the German Baltic ports for three months, so there existed the very real danger that the supply of Army Norway via the Baltic Sea and of Mountain Corps Norway via the ice-free harbours of the Arctic Ocean would be delayed. Army Norway could not let such handicaps increase the danger. In early 1942, it had been possible with the utmost effort to maintain the supply of rations and fodder needed in South Lapland by transporting it by rail from South Norway to Rovaniemi via Sweden. There could be no certainty, though, whether the stance of Sweden would remain so friendly. The orders of the OKW came in response to the experiences of Army Norway regarding the security of its supplies, even though such stockpiling would be quite demanding in terms of supply maintenance, transport capacity, and workload. From 1942, efforts were made to ensure that, by 31 December, the mountain corps would have at its disposal all of the goods it would require for a period of nine to 12 months and that the other two corps under Army Lapland would have enough for a period of seven months. For those other two corps, provisions had to be made for the time during which the northern part of the Baltic Sea freezes over (i.e. between December and June), so an additional month of supplies was preferable for them. It could be expected that losses would result from any setback or withdrawal. In accordance with Führer Directive No. 50, preparations were made from the autumn of 1943 for conducting a retreat and carrying out a scorched earth policy.

There were some particular transportation problems that arose that still need to be mentioned. Barracks, due to their multitude and bulkiness, could only be brought to the mountain corps by sea despite the fact that many of the parts had been manufactured in Finland. It required the greatest effort on the part of the Supply and Transport Office of the Wehrmacht in Scandinavia to obtain from the Reich Commissariat for Ocean Shipping, on only a few occasions, the freighters needed for the time-consuming journey of 3,000 nautical miles, all the way around Scandinavia, from Oulu to Kirkenes. Another problem was chilled cargo, which could not be supplied without being properly stored and transported. Refrigerator ships belonged to the navy, and they remained under the control of the navy in the Scandinavian theatre. Nevertheless, the navy willingly placed them at the disposal of the senior quartermaster in Scandinavia for the purpose of supplying the army. The subsistence supply experts at the Cold Weather Duty Station North advised the army administrative authorities in Norway and Finland on the creation of storage areas, the construction of refrigerated storage buildings, and the procurement from Denmark of refrigerator units.

Even the transportation of the wounded required the involvement of all branches of the Wehrmacht. The motor ambulance platoons were responsible for bringing the wounded from the front to the field hospitals. Light and heavy casualties were taken from Petsamo to Kirkenes by sea with the small hospital ship *Alexander von Humboldt*, and there was of course always the risk of Soviet artillery fire or torpedo attacks. Those unable to be healed in the divisional field hospitals or in the corps convalescent unit would then have to be transported to the Fatherland for treatment. One of the large hospital ships, *Berlin* or *Stuttgart*, would be responsible for such transportation, and they had on board all of the facilities that could be found in a base hospital. After being topped up with fuel, the hospital ship would be conducted by the navy to Germany. Only rarely would the wounded of the mountain corps be evacuated along the Arctic Ocean Highway to the base hospital in Kemi or from there with hospital trains through Sweden to Germany. In exceptional cases (e.g. brain, eye, or spinal injuries), the wounded were taken away by air. With such an abundance of lakes in the area, waterborne aircraft usually served well as ambulance vehicles.

Fresh horses always came from South Norway. Each horse was examined there for its suitability before being mobilised. The beautiful and docile Fjord or Vestland horses, generally dun horses, were much welcomed by the mountain corps. They were suitable both as pack animals and as carthorses. Their performance almost exceeded that of the breeds brought by the mountain corps (Carpathian ponies, Bosnian ponies, Međimurje horses, Haflinger horses, and northern Italian mules). Another complicated matter was the supply of fuel for heating, not only for the mountain corps but also for those who needed it in its territorial zone, including the civil population. Brushwood for the field kitchens could still be found in the surrounding terrain in 1941, but, from the winter onwards, the wood that was required all had to be supplied. It had already been necessary in the summer to send assault squads southwards to collect wood. Practically nothing could be procured in the woodless

Varanger region. What was worse, the quantity of fuel consumed in the supply of wood was enormous. The coal from Spitzbergen that had previously been so accessible was unable to be supplied after early 1941 due to the cessation of shipping there. So it was that 167,000 tonnes of coal from Germany had to be delivered to the area of the mountain corps each year from 1942. This figure does not include the coal that was needed by the navy and the merchant marine. German industry did not even use half that amount.

Something that particularly helped with the supply of the Litsa front was the construction of the cable railway that had been proposed as early as 24 October 1941. In 1942, the mountain corps received so many components that had been taken from an old Austrian cable railway that it was possible in its reassembly to establish a continuous connection that ran through 12 motor stations between the southern outskirts of Parkkina, in the vicinity of the bell tower, and the area of the medical strongpoint on the south bank of Litsa Fjord. It was 55 kilometres in length, enabled the delivery of supplies to several depots along the way, and its longest stretches went over the Petsamonjoki and the mouth of the Litsa. Only two or three times during the entire war was the cable damaged by a lucky hit from the eager fire of enemy artillery. Transportation buckets were suspended from the cable, each of which could carry, for example, a bale of hay or straw, a sack of oats together with a box of ammunition, some wood for the construction of field fortifications, two sacks of coal, or even a wounded man wrapped in layers of fur. A pioneer company was responsible for the operation of the cable railway. The significant advantage of the cable railway was that it was unaffected by snowstorms, whereas the road might be blocked for days on end. At no point whatsoever did this valuable piece of equipment experience a technical failure, even though many of its parts had been used in World War I.

A railway line across North Norway or from Rovaniemi along the Arctic Ocean Highway would have been of real use as a German counterpart to the Murman Railway, but any ideas of such a line remained hypothetical. Reich Minister Fritz Todt visited the mountain corps on 25 and 26 September 1941 and, accompanied by Colonel on the General

Staff von Mirow, conducted a reconnaissance of the terrain. The result was a final rejection of the idea of a railway line.

In the autumn of 1941, the wintertime security of the supply road to the front was the most urgent concern for the quartermaster of the mountain corps. If the three attacks over the Litsa, the response to the landslide, the early onset of winter, and the relief of the divisions had consumed a great deal of material and had made the supply of wood for snow fences and snowplough stations impossible, it was now up to the mountain corps and the 6th Mountain Division to make up for this despite the already accumulated snowdrifts and frozen ground. Major-General Schörner's statement that 'the Arctic is nothing' inspired the troops to overcome the difficulties they encountered on the road. The one single advantage of the late construction of snow fences was that it was possible to quickly gain a sense of the wind direction. Snow fences in the Arctic Circle had quite different dimensions to those in East Prussia. The posts were made of strong tree trunks that were 3 metres in height and approximately 10cm in diameter. They and the horizontal planks that connected them were sourced from the area of Lake Inari. These planks were placed higher in the winter so as to accommodate the larger snowfall. For stretches of road with whirling snowstorms, several snow fences were arranged one behind the other at different angles. Those that were in front lay approximately 20 metres away from the road.

For the clearance of snow, the mountain corps was allocated the 602nd Snow Removal Battalion in January 1942. It was far too late for the pre-winter period, but it could still be of use in the middle of winter. The battalion had three companies under its command, each organised into snow removal platoons and snowblower platoons. Each snow removal platoon had between four and six snowploughs of different types mounted on powerful all-terrain trucks, while each snowblower platoon possessed two or three 14-tonne snowblowers that could be wheeled, half-track, diesel-driven, or petrol-driven vehicles. These snow-clearance vehicles were ordinarily able to keep the supply road open, even when there was snowfall. After a snowstorm, though, the road might be covered, or the walls of snow might have become too high. The construction troops and the snowblowers would then need to combine their efforts.

The former would break up the walls of snow and shovel them into the road whilst the latter would drive alongside, working their way through the piled-up snow and discharging it 15–20 metres leeward through their impellers. Snowploughs cleared up the remaining snow afterwards. This procedure had been developed in North Norway. The snowblower crews had at first been trained at the snowblower assembly plant in Paris and then on the Grossglockner High Alpine Road in Austria. Additional construction work of the kind that was necessary in North Norway, like road embankments, road tunnels, or avalanche barriers, did not need to be carried out to the east of Petsamo thanks to the cable railway. Responsible for the winter road clearance between the Petsamonjoki and the Litsa were two snow removal companies together with a pioneer battalion or a construction pioneer battalion or, later on, a prisoner-of-war construction battalion.

The land around Petsamo offered nothing other than rocks and bits of wood. From shoelaces to bales of hay, and nails to barracks, everything had to be brought from the distant south. Supplies of all kinds were therefore in high demand. There were many dangers and difficulties. And after the landslide of 28 September, there would on several occasions be more bad news for the mountain corps before the end of the year. In the last few days of September and again on 10 October, a Soviet submarine infiltrated the harbour in Liinahamari. Its torpedoes were well aimed, but fortunately they were duds. On 30 September, the coastal batteries on Rybachy Peninsula laid down barrage fire before the entrance of Petsamo Fjord for the first time.[48] It became clear on 1 October that the RAD would be withdrawn sooner or later. Clothing was of considerable concern. The clothing of the troops had become rather worn out in the months leading up to winter, and there were also some essential items missing for those units that stood on the Arctic Front for the first time. What was most disastrous, though, was when a fire occurred in the clothing depot of the mountain corps in Kirkenes. A considerable portion of the almost 5,000 sets of white camouflage suits had been lost only a day or two before they were to be issued. The 25,000 tree trunks that had to be given to the nickel mines of Kolosjoki by the sawmill next to Lake Inari have already been mentioned. In the sawmill of the mountain corps in

Nellimö, production stagnated due to a shortage of replacement parts. Much of the old equipment there was of Russian origin. A supply ship with roofing felt and building material had been sunk off the Norwegian coast. Three smaller tankers were heading for Kirkenes shortly afterwards, but they too were sunk. The presence of a British fleet consisting of an aircraft carrier, a cruiser, and two destroyers in the waters off Spitzbergen on 20 October prevented German convoys from sailing from Tromsø to Kirkenes. On 25 November at 0430 hours, Soviet warships (one cruiser and two destroyers) bombarded Vardø and laid mines. On 21 December, German forces awaited what they expected would be a new British naval raid against Lofoten. On 25 December, enemy warships appeared not only before Stamsund and Hammerfest but also outside Bergen, where a commando raid put a coastal battery out of action.[49] It was expected that the enemy might try to establish strongpoints on the skerries. It is of interest in this regard that a Soviet deserter on the Litsa front had stated, on 23 December, that he had learnt from the political commissar in his unit that English landings had been scheduled to take place within the next few days. On 28 December, in the vicinity of the Ritter von Hengl Bridge, a mudflow on the south bank of the Litsa buried the road which ran from the mouth of the river to Litsa Camp.[50] Soviet attacks against the bridgehead continued unabated. Advent and Yuletide were therefore as much a period of concern on the Arctic Front as they were on the Eastern Front between Lake Ladoga and the Black Sea.

Despite some shortages, the problems of supply had not so much to do with the non-existence of certain goods like ammunition, rations, clothing, replacement parts, or building material. Rather, for the most part, the problem was bringing those goods safely to the front. The specifics of individual areas of supply, be it something like the types of barracks that needed to be procured or the detailed testing of equipment that had to be carried out, cannot be investigated here. The equipment of the mountain troops was always of good quality. But a word will be said about the supply of fuel, as it was of the utmost importance for most kinds of movement and construction. It had been one of the main points of conversation during the meeting in Inari on 15 October between Army Norway and Mountain Corps Norway. The daily consumption of fuel by the mountain corps in December 1941 was 50 cubic metres. That meant approximately 1,500 cubic metres per month, although it had increased to 2,500 cubic metres per month by 1943. On 28 December, the day of the mudflow, the rations at the disposal of the mountain corps was enough for eight days, and it was considerably more when it came to bread and oats. There was a shortage of roughage, but what there was would still last for as long as 14 days. However, the fuel that was available would last no longer than five days. If the supply to the mountain corps by sea stopped for whatever reason, Army Norway believed that it would be able to deliver 50 cubic metres of fuel per day. Such a commitment would be costly. The daily transport by the army supply service of 50 cubic metres of fuel from Rovaniemi to Kirkenes or Petsamo would require a transport capacity of at least 150 tonnes and would itself use up about 4 cubic metres of fuel. How would it be possible to economise? Could the Luftwaffe or the navy be expected to reduce their usage of fuel? Could we do away with warming up the engines of our vehicles? Could we make greater use of horse-drawn vehicles? Yet this would have just restricted our ability to carry out important projects like constructing snow fences and barracks. Also, our stockpile of supplies would have been reduced. We could ill afford to curtail transloading operations, supplies to the front, the construction of field fortifications, or snow removal. Every soldier, above all our drivers, was made aware of the situation. The discipline of the men of the mountain corps helped a great deal in this crisis, and it was only just before our fuel had been depleted that a tanker arrived with more.

The endurance and combat morale of the soldiers at the front, the undauntedness of all road and construction services, the hard work of the supply troops, and the objective rationality and calmness of the headquarters staff enabled the secure transition from the offensive to the defensive on the Arctic Front by the end of 1941.

On 15 January 1942, General of Mountain Troops Eduard Dietl became the commander of the German forces in Finland. Colonel-General von Falkenhorst returned with his chief of staff and other headquarters staff to Army Norway. The command post in Finland became the headquarters of the newly created Army Lapland, which would be renamed the

Twentieth Mountain Army on 22 June 1942. Mountain Corps Norway came under the command of the recently promoted General Schörner, the 2nd Mountain Division under Colonel Ritter von Hengl, and the 6th Mountain Division under Major-General Philipp. The 3rd Mountain Division, without the reinforced 139th Mountain Infantry Regiment, departed from Finland.

The Arctic Front in the year of 1941 is inextricably linked with the name of the commander of the mountain corps, Eduard Dietl. He rose to the rank of colonel-general and, on 23 June 1944, was killed in an air crash in the Alps. The Arctic Front also brings to mind the commitment of the German–Austrian mountain troops and of the many other soldiers who served there and who, given the mercilessness of this theatre of war, had soon become as one with the mountain troops. Soldiers, airmen, and sailors, in addition to the men of the Waffen-SS and of the Reich Labour Service – indeed, all of the German and Finnish combatants who fought together on the farthest reaches of Europe – were of the same status. Their sacrifices and accomplishments are worthy of attention.

APPENDIX I

Composition of Mountain Corps Norway in the Second Half of 1941

Divisions

2nd Mountain Division (see Appendix 2 for its order of battle)
3rd Mountain Division (until 11 November)
6th Mountain Division (from 21 September, after its arrival)

Corps troops

Headquarters of Mountain Corps Norway with the 477th Motorised Map Reproduction Office
1st Battery of the 477th Heavy Artillery Battalion (four Norwegian 10.5cm guns) (from 1944, the 8th Battery of the 111th Mountain Artillery Regiment with four tractor-drawn leFH 18 light field howitzers)
463rd Corps Signal Battalion
477th Corps Supply Service (three light motor transport columns, one light motor transport column with fuel, one supply train)
477th Military Police Unit
231st Army Post Office

Troops subordinated to other units

Under the 214th Infantry Division (from 18 August)
388th Infantry Regiment with the 2nd Company of the 214th Pioneer Battalion and a cart section (later general headquarters troops – 388th Grenadier Brigade)

I Battalion of the 214th Artillery Regiment (leFH 18 light field howitzers, until 21 November)
Under the 199th Infantry Division
233rd Bicycle Battalion (25 July until 19 November)
Under the Luftwaffe
Flight of Lieutenant Hauschild of the 1st High-Wing Monoplane Squadron of the 32nd Reconnaissance Group
I Battalion of the 5th Flak Regiment (until mid-December)
II Battalion of the 46th Flak Regiment (until mid-December)
203rd Reserve Flak Battalion (from 26 November)
332nd Reserve Flak Battalion (from December)

General headquarters troops

4th Machine-Gun Battalion (10 July until 23 October)
14th Machine-Gun Battalion (from 26 July)
1st Company of the 40th Panzer Battalion for special purpose utilisation (until 30 September)
730th Heavy Artillery Battalion (10.5cm Skoda M.35 guns)
Headquarters of the 498th Army Coastal Artillery Battalion (until 11 December)
Headquarters of the 504th Army Coastal Artillery Battalion
543rd Army Coastal Battery (German 21cm howitzers)
546th Army Coastal Battery (Polish 10.5cm guns)
548th Army Coastal Battery (French 15cm guns)
558th, 562nd, 580th, and 585th Army Coastal Batteries (all with French 10.5cm guns)
869th Army Coastal Battery (German 21cm howitzers)
999th Army Coastal Battery (field guns, probably Norwegian)
503rd Meteorological and Direction-Finding Platoon
405th Construction Pioneer Battalion
55th Mountain Carrier Battalion (from October)
504th Heavy Motor Transport Column (from 24 July)
21st and 22nd Pack Trains (from 1 August)
477th Local Military Administrative Headquarters (Kirkenes)

Waffen-SS

9th SS Infantry Regiment (14 August until 14 October, belonging to SS Battle Group North, later the 6th SS Mountain Division North) with the 1st Anti-Tank Company and the 1st Battery (Norwegian 7.5cm mountain guns)

Reich Labour Service (RAD)

Headquarters of the 27th Section of the RAD
Group K 363 of the RAD with the units K 3/360, K 1/361, K 2/362, K 4/363, K 5/363, and K 6/363
Group K 376 of the RAD with the units K 1/371, K 3/373, K 4/376, K 5/376, K6/376, and one other unit

National Socialist Motor Corps

From the end of October, elements of Transport Group Speer of the National Socialist Motor Corps (approximately the strength of a battalion headquarters) with a motor maintenance repair shop platoon and four transport companies (transport capacity of approximately 150 tonnes)

Finnish forces

Ivalo Border Guard Battalion (commanded by Major Pennanen)
1st Border Guard Company Petsamo (Captain Tiitola)
2nd Border Guard Company Petsamo (Captain Turi) (formed in mid-July)
Petsamo Border Guard Battery (Captain Tähtelä, later Captain Granfeld) (Russian 7.62cm guns)
14th Infantry Regiment without the III Battalion (11 July until 13 September, home guard from the Åland Islands)
Civil road construction battalion of Savolainen Engineering (approximately 1,000 men, beginning of July until the beginning of September)

Total ration strength of Mountain Corps Norway

June 1941	approximately 65,000 men and 9,000 horses
compared with June 1944	approximately 110,000 men and 12,000 horses

APPENDIX 2

Notes on the Order of Battle of the 2nd Mountain Division

1. The order of battle of the 3rd Mountain Division is substantially analogous to that of the 2nd Mountain Division. It too had no more than seven batteries. The 6th Mountain Division had the usual III Artillery Battalion (tractor-drawn sFH heavy field howitzers), the 112th Mountain Reconnaissance Battalion (formerly of the 3rd Mountain Division) instead of a bicycle battalion, and a replacement training battalion. The light mountain infantry column was fully motorised.
2. Some of the mountain infantry battalions of the three mountain divisions still had heavy mountain infantry companies equipped with six medium mortars. In this case, the four heavy machine guns were assigned to the headquarters company as a third platoon.
3. The light mountain infantry columns of the 2nd and 3rd Mountain Divisions were mountain supply columns, each with a truck platoon.
4. The 1st, 2nd, 4th, and 5th Batteries of the 111th Mountain Artillery Regiment, just like four batteries of the 3rd Mountain Division, had Skoda M.15 mountain guns. The 3rd and 6th Batteries of the same regiment had been activated in 1940 with Skoda M.16 mountain howitzers, as had the 3rd and 6th Batteries of the 112th Mountain Artillery Regiment.
5. The III Battalion of the 111th Mountain Artillery Regiment had been released in 1940, as had the III Battalion of the 112th Mountain Artillery Regiment. The 9th Battery of the 111th Mountain Artillery Regiment and the 7th Battery of the 112th Mountain Artillery

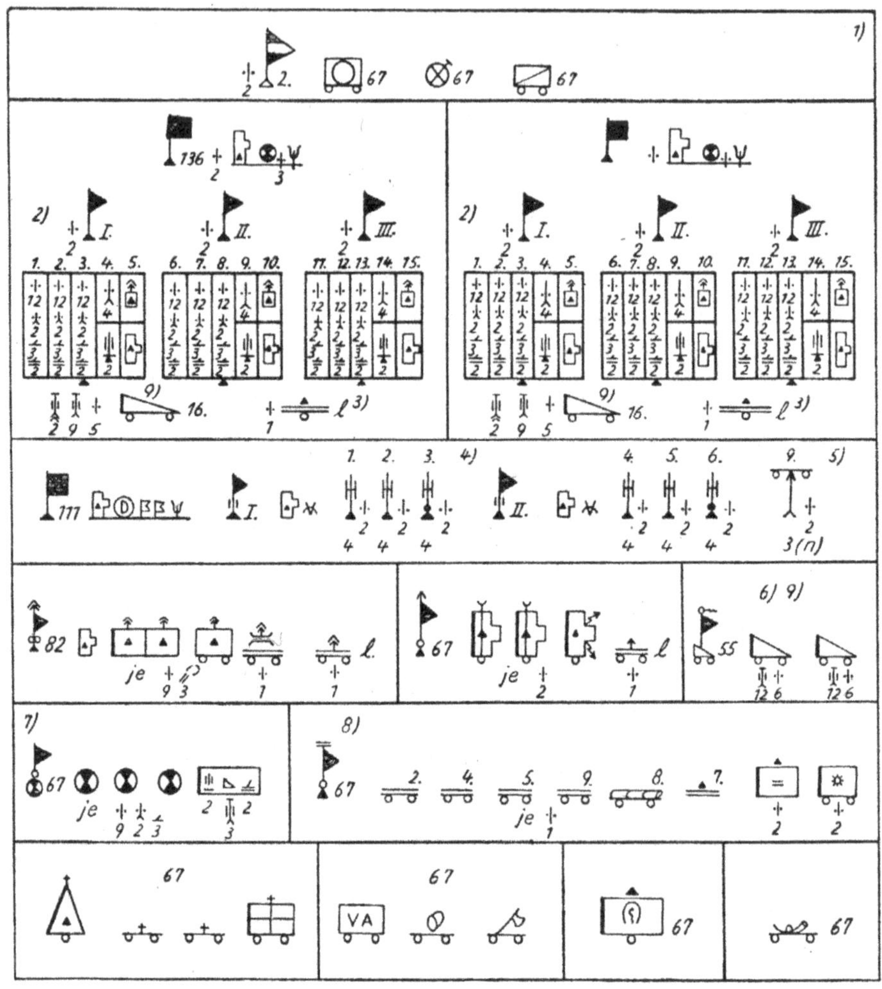

Kriegsgliederung der 2. Geb. Div.
(15. 9. 1941)

Order of battle of the 2nd Mountain Division, 15 September 1941

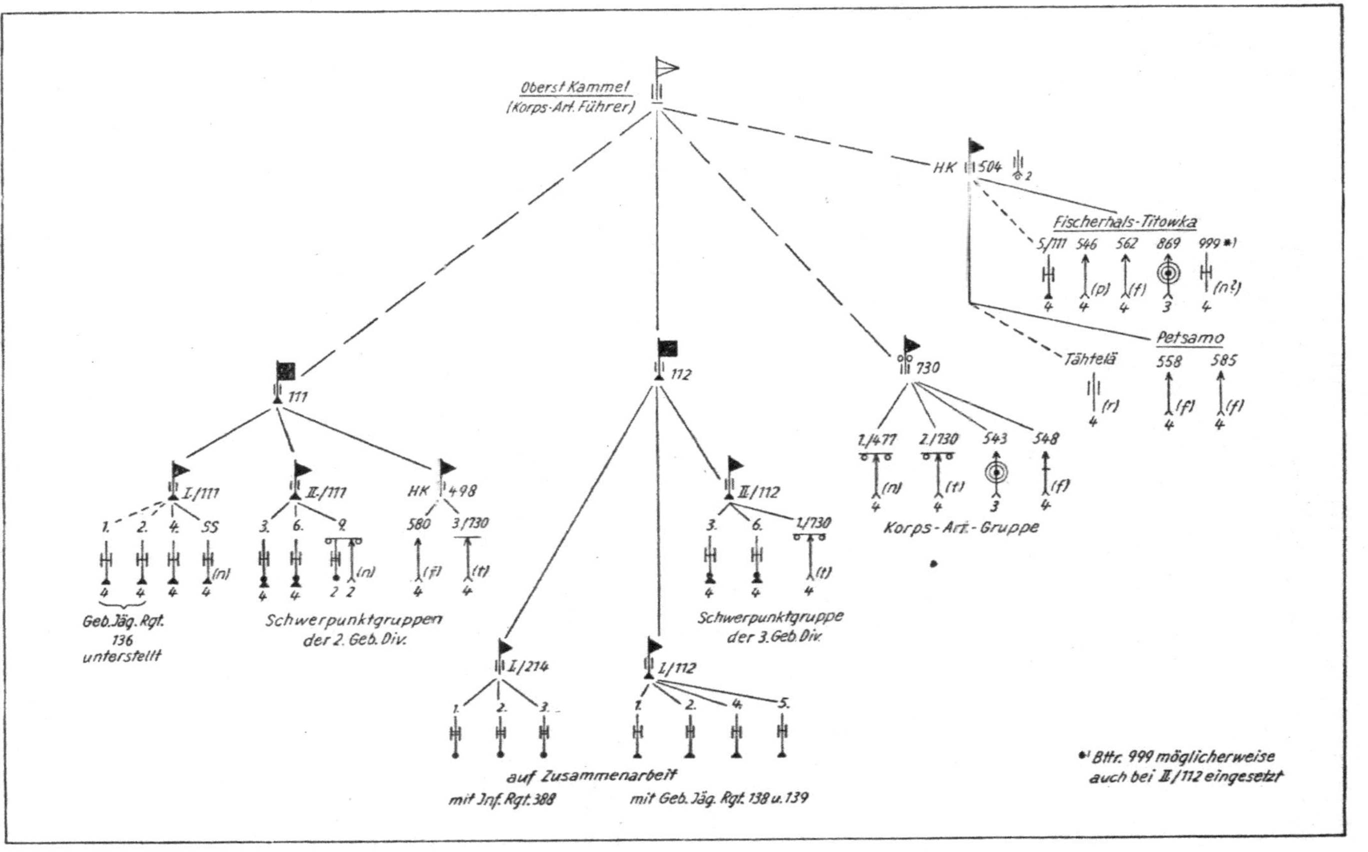

Organisation of the artillery units of Mountain Corps Norway

Regiment were newly activated units, each temporarily equipped with three tractor-drawn Norwegian 10.5cm guns. The latter unit only had those guns for a short time, while the former received motorised leFH 18 light field howitzers in September.

6. In the place of the 47th Anti-Tank Battalion, which had been transferred to the 6th Mountain Division in 1940. It possibly had a small signal communication platoon.
7. Newly activated in Norway at the beginning of 1941 to replace the 111th Reconnaissance Battalion, which had been partially released in 1940.
8. The 1st, 3rd, and 6th Light Motor Transport Columns of the 67th Divisional Supply Service had been released in 1940. The 4th and 5th Mountain Supply Columns had replaced the light mountain infantry column in 1940. They had been activated in Norway as motorised columns along with the 9th Light Motor Transport Column of the 67th Divisional Supply Service. By the second year of the war, the supply troops of the mountain divisions were no longer organised in a uniform manner. They had fought in different theatres and had adapted and been reorganised in different ways. The mountain carrier battalions had already been withdrawn after the Polish campaign. The 100th Mountain Supply Column Battalion of the mountain corps had been disbanded in the summer of 1940. Its elements had then been used for replacements or for new units, especially for the initially missing batteries of the 2nd and 3rd Mountain Divisions.
9. Each platoon of the company of the 47th Anti-Tank Battalion and each half platoon of the 16th Companies of the 141st and 143rd Mountain Infantry Regiments were available on 26 November and were equipped with 5cm anti-tank guns from the beginning of December 1941. All of these units belonged to the 6th Mountain Division.

APPENDIX 3

Headquarters staff in Scandinavia

Army

Headquarters of Army Norway, Commander in Chief: Colonel-General von Falkenhorst

Chief of Staff: Major-General Buschenhagen

Senior Quartermaster: Lieutenant-Colonel on the General Staff Kühl

Army Intendant: Senior Field Intendant Dr Stehling

Wehrmacht Transport Officer: Major on the General Staff Steltzer

33rd Military Geology Unit: Wehrmacht Administrative Officer Dr von Gärtner

Headquarters of Army Norway, Command Post Finland, Ia: Major on the General Staff Müller (Christian)

1st Quartermaster: Captain on the General Staff Freiherr Grote

463rd Army Supply Service Chief: Major Steinmetz

High Command of North Norway, Commander: Lieutenant-General Nagy

Ia: Major on the General Staff Müller (Werner)

Staff Officer for Artillery: Colonel Krappmann

Finnish Liaison Officer at Mountain Corps Norway: Captain Tollander

Navy

Naval Region Norway, Commander in Chief: General-Admiral Boehm

Chief of Staff: Captain Machens

Naval District Polar Norway, Commander: Commodore Schenk
Chief of Staff: Lieutenant-Commander Töttcher
Coastal Command Kirkenes, Commander: Commander Hesse
Deputising in August and September 1941: Captain Ruhfus
Harbour Master Kirkenes: Lieutenant-Commander Kolbe
Coastal Command T, later U-Boat Command Group, Commander: Captain von der Forst
6th Destroyer Flotilla, Commander: Commander Schulze-Hinrichs
Naval Liaison Officer at Mountain Corps Norway
Summer 1941: Lieutenant-Commander Schmidt (Wilhelm)
End of 1941: Commander Busch
Naval Region North Sea (from December 1941), Commander: Vice-Admiral Schmundt
Chief of Staff: Commander Schulze-Hinrichs
8th Destroyer Flotilla, Commander: Commander Pönitz

Luftwaffe

Fifth Air Fleet, Commander in Chief: Colonel-General Stumpf
Chief of Staff (command group for special use): Lieutenant-Colonel on the General Staff Nielsen
Air District North Norway, Commander: Lieutenant-General Bruch
Ia: Major on the General Staff Wiebel
Luftwaffe Liaison Officer at Mountain Corps Norway: First Lieutenant Seegers, First Lieutenant Bodenberger
Air Base Area Command Kirkenes, Commander: Colonel Müller
Air Base Command Luostari, Commander: Major May

Wehrmacht

Supply and Transport Office of the Wehrmacht in Scandinavia: Major on the General Staff Berling, Lieutenant-Colonel von Loebell, Captain Hegner

APPENDIX 4

Commanders on the Arctic Front

Headquarters of Mountain Corps Norway

Commander: General of Mountain Troops Dietl
Chief of Staff: Lieutenant-Colonel on the General Staff von Le Suire
Ia: Captain on the General Staff Busch
Quartermaster: Major on the General Staff Heß
Ic: Captain on the General Staff Müller
IIa: Major Herrmann
III: Judge Advocate Dr Kisser
IVa: Corps Intendant Andersch
IVb: Colonel (Med.) Dr Litz
IVc: Lieutenant-Colonel (Vet.) Dr Brodinger
Weapons and Equipment Department: Captain (Weapons) Kürschner
Corps Engineer: Major (Engineering) Graduate Engineer Kolck
Staff Officer for Combat Engineers: Colonel Kranyak

Finnish Liaison Officer: Captain Tollander

Finnish Units

14th Infantry Regiment: Colonel Hannelius
Ivalo Border Guard Battalion: Major Pennanen
1st Border Guard Company Petsamo: Captain Tiitola
2nd Border Guard Company Petsamo: Captain Turi
Petsamo Border Guard Battery: Captain Tähtelä

Corps and Army Troops, Anti-Aircraft Units, Waffen-SS Units, and Units of the Reich Labour Service

9th SS Infantry Regiment: SS-Lieutenant-Colonel Deutsch
388th Infantry Regiment: Colonel Daser, Lieutenant-Colonel von Ledebur
4th Machine-Gun Battalion: Lieutenant-Colonel Braun
14th Machine-Gun Battalion: Lieutenant-Colonel Saul
1st Company of the 40th Panzer Battalion for special purpose utilisation: Major von Burstin
233rd Bicycle Battalion
730th Heavy Artillery Battalion: Captain Schlögl
1st Battery of the 477th Heavy Artillery Battalion: First Lieutenant Daxer
Headquarters of the 498th Army Coastal Artillery Battalion: Captain Bromm
Headquarters of the 504th Army Coastal Artillery Battalion: Captain Müller
503rd Meteorological and Direction-Finding Platoon: Second Lieutenant Dr Reitz
I Battalion of the 5th Flak Regiment: Major Quodbach
II Battalion of the 46th Flak Regiment: Major Hohmann
302nd Reserve Flak Battalion: Major Heymer
405th Construction Pioneer Battalion: Major Bäder
463rd Corps Signal Battalion: Major Fuhrmann
477th Corps Supply Service: Major Dr Schmitt
Supply Headquarters North: Captain Clima
55th Mountain Carrier Battalion: Major Burckel
Transport Control Station of Mountain Corps Norway: Captain Habel
Supply Control Station of Mountain Corps Norway: Captain Hausmann, Captain Rzeczizky
Wehrmacht Transloading Headquarters in Kirkenes: Major van der Upvich
231st Army Post Office: Army Postmaster Drescher
Convalescent Battalion: Major Pirker

477th Local Military Administrative Headquarters (Kirkenes): Major Steinacker
Headquarters of the 27th Section of the Reich Labour Service: RAD-Lieutenant-Colonel Welser
Reich Labour Service Group K 363: RAD-Major Baulig
Reich Labour Service Group K 376: RAD-Major Liebig

2nd Mountain Division

Commander: Major-General Schlemmer
Ia: Major on the General Staff Zorn
Ib: Major on the General Staff Fussenegger
Ic: First Lieutenant Horsetzky-Hornthal
IIa: Captain Stute
IVa: Divisional Intendant Schramm
IVb: Lieutenant-Colonel (Med.) Dr Langendörfer
IVc: Major (Vet.) Dr Lamatsch
Weapons and Equipment Department: First Lieutenant (Weapons) Schmidt
Divisional Engineer: Captain (Engineering) Graduate Engineer Bastian
136th Mountain Infantry Regiment: Colonel Nake, Lieutenant-Colonel Hofmeister
I Battalion: Major Hauck
II Battalion: Lieutenant-Colonel Oertl, Captain Putzker
III Battalion: Lieutenant-Colonel Heinzle
137th Mountain Infantry Regiment: Lieutenant-Colonel Ritter von Hengl
I Battalion: Major Fuschelberger, Major Ruf
II Battalion: Major Vielwerth, Captain Hesselbarth
III Battalion: Lieutenant-Colonel Kräutler, First Lieutenant Waleser
111th Mountain Artillery Regiment: Colonel Kammel[51]
I Battalion: Captain Laurin
II Battalion: Captain Bargehr

82nd Mountain Pioneer Battalion: Major Drück
67th Mountain Signal Battalion: Major Friedrich
67th Bicycle Battalion: Major Lindinger
55th Anti-Tank Battalion: Captain von Seebach
67th Divisional Supply Service: Major Haack

3rd Mountain Division

Commander: Major-General Kreysing
Ia: Major on the General Staff Michael
Ib: Captain on the General Staff Mitlacher
Ic: Cavalry Captain von Ahlefeld
IIa: Major Lindemann
IVa: Divisional Intendant Harder
IVb: Lieutenant-Colonel (Med.) Dr Lottner
IVc: Major (Vet.) Dr Gaggermeier
Weapons and Equipment Department: Captain (Weapons) Schreiner
Divisional Engineer: Captain (Engineering) Graduate Engineer Wratschko
138th Mountain Infantry Regiment: Colonel Weiß, Lieutenant-Colonel Klatt
I Battalion: Major Brandl
II Battalion: Major Ritter von Pranckh
III Battalion: Major Schratz
139th Mountain Infantry Regiment: Colonel Windisch
I Battalion: Major Guder
II Battalion: Major Haussels
III Battalion: Major Holzinger
112th Mountain Artillery Regiment: Colonel Mönch
I Battalion: Lieutenant-Colonel Ritter von Mehlem, Captain Goriany
II Battalion: Major Blümel, Captain Lepez
83rd Mountain Pioneer Battalion: Lieutenant-Colonel Klatt
68th Mountain Signal Battalion: Major Till
68th Bicycle Battalion: Major Fleischauer

48th Anti-Tank Battalion: Lieutenant-Colonel Klinge
68th Divisional Supply Service: Major Ludwig

6th Mountain Division

Commander: Major-General Schörner
Ia: Major on the General Staff Gartmayr
Ib: Captain on the General Staff Vogel
Ic: Captain Rath
141st Mountain Infantry Regiment: Colonel Jais
143rd Mountain Infantry Regiment: Colonel Radziej
118th Mountain Artillery Regiment: Colonel Schricker
91st Replacement Training Battalion: Captain Merxmüller

APPENDIX 5

Organisation of Furlough Traffic from December 1941

Map 20

Once the 2nd Mountain Division had been relieved by the 6th Mountain Division and the fighting had subsided, General Dietl sought to arrange leave for his troops. Despite the approval of Army Norway and of the OKW, his efforts could only gradually bear fruit due to the significant demands on the entire transport system in the area of the mountain corps. Most of the troops had not been home for as many as 15–18 months. It was for this reason that, from December 1941, steps were taken for the long-term organisation of furlough traffic. This process can only be understood in the context of previous developments in North Norway, for there had already been troops who had gone on leave in the winter of 1940–41, albeit on a smaller scale.

The Lapland Route (I) ran via the Finnish harbour in Hanko (Hangö), which had already been given to the 42nd Forward Directing Centre for Personnel in Transit in 1942 along with the local stations in Turku (Åbo) and Rovaniemi. The men from the Arctic Front who were on leave would be brought by motorbus from their assembly point in Salmijärvi to Rovaniemi in approximately 12 hours. The motorbuses of the troops were used at first; later on, it was the vehicles of the 558th and Finland Motorbus Columns of the 463rd Army Supply Service that were employed for the task. From there, the men travelled an average of 36 hours on the Finnish railway to Hanko. In the summer, Route I continued from Hanko by ship over the Baltic Sea to Stettin or Danzig, a journey which took approximately 40 hours. The men would then travel south or west through Germany by rail. In winter, Route I would go by ship from Hanko over the Gulf of Finland to Paldiski and then from there by rail through the Baltic states (Riga and Kovno) and through Warsaw to Vienna and so on. For those men from the central or western parts of Germany, Riga or Kovno offered a direct connection to Berlin via Königsberg.

The limited furlough traffic that had opened in Norway in 1940 started from Kirkenes and went by sea to Narvik via multiple harbours. This journey could last two to four days, depending on the weather and the availability of escort vessels. From Narvik, the Swedish railway would take the men on leave to Trelleborg via Kiruna, Gällivare, and Östersund, or, later on, to Copenhagen and Warnemünde via Helsingør. The roughly 2,000-kilometre trip through Sweden took approximately 48 hours. After the seven-hour crossing from Trelleborg to Sassnitz with the train ferry, the men could continue their journey into the Reich via Berlin. This Route II for traffic from Troms and West Finnmark remained in existence for the rest of the war.

The use of Route I was considerably delayed due to the burden on the railways in South Finland, the slow organisation of a forward directing centre for personnel in transit, and, above all, the halt in shipping over the Gulf of Finland which had been brought about for several months by the build-up of ice in the particularly cold winter. Fortunately, Route II to Trelleborg could be used in the interim. The Tornio–Haparanda–Boden stretch was covered by road and the Boden–Trelleborg stretch by rail.

In parallel with the establishment of Route I through Lapland, measures were taken to organise rest camps for the troops. Operated by helpers from the German Red Cross, they were opened one at a time in Kirkenes, Liinahamari, Salmijärvi, Ivalo, Sodankylä, and Rovaniemi. A large motor inn was also built in Vuotso, roughly in the middle of the Arctic Ocean Highway. Provisions for German and Finnish hospitals were organised in Ivalo. Later in the war, the 10th Army Personnel Support Battalion gradually took over the most important locations between Petsamo and Hanko.

From the summer of 1942, soldiers who went on leave would usually be able to make the 5,000-kilometre journey from Petsamo to Graz in about seven days. Another day could generally be added at either end to account for the journey from the front to Petsamo and from Graz to one's home. The period of time at home allowed for German soldiers, including those of a higher rank, was 24 days per year. This meant that a soldier on leave would be away from the Arctic Front for about 33 days before he had to return. The annual furlough period was eventually set at a maximum 10 per cent.

Endnotes

1. R. Drinkuth, 'Wir fuhren gen Norden', p. 5.
2. A noteworthy example was the 139th Mountain Infantry Brigade, which came from the 3rd Mountain Division and was incorporated into Divisional Group Kräutler in 1944. It consisted of the 139th Mountain Infantry Regiment with three battalions (the 1st to the 15th Companies), the 16th Anti-Tank Company, the 17th Pioneer Company, and the 124th Mountain Artillery Battalion (formerly the I Battalion of the 112th Mountain Artillery Regiment) with three batteries of 7.5cm mountain guns.
3. Dietl & Herrmann, *General Dietl*, p. 183.
4. W. Hubatsch, *Die deutsche Besetzung von Dänemark und Norwegen 1940*, p. 255.
5. P. Herrmann, *7 vorbei und 8 verweht*, p. 406.
6. The Lapps are also called the Sami. The corresponding adjectives are Lappish and Sami. Samland, in East Prussia, may have taken its name from these people or may have had something to do with them in the distant past.
7. A vivid description of the Lapps and their reindeer are given in the books by Estrid Ott: *Doktors Frieda* and *Ravnas glückliche Zeit* (Albert Müller Verlag, Zürich). See also *Lux-Lesebogen* issues 92 ('Herden unter der Mitternachtssonne') and 130 ('Suomi') (Sebastian Lux Verlag, Murnau).
8. Personal notes of the author from 1941.
9. Hurtigruten is a coastal shipping route for passengers that sails between Trondheim and Kirkenes, a journey which lasts five days.
10. Nasjonal Samling was a Norwegian political party, led by Quisling, which was moulded in the style of National Socialism.
11. The BBC is the British Broadcasting Corporation.
12. Dietl & Herrmann, *General Dietl*, p. 216.
13. Translator's note: *Russia's Grip on Northern Europe*.
14. Translator's note: 'The Red Offensive Position along the Arctic Ocean'.
15. Dietl & Hermann, *General Dietl*, p. 219.
16. Dietl & Herrmann, *General Dietl*, p. 221; personal notes of the author. See also B. von Loßberg, *Im Wehrmachtführungsstab*, pp. 113, 166.
17. On the nature of the Murman Railway, see the pamphlet by Kaarlo Hildén, 'Die Murmanbahn', published in Helsinki in 1942. Dietl & Herrmann, *General Dietl*, pp 223–224, also refer to this pamphlet.

18. W. Erfurth, *Der finnische Krieg 1941–1944*, pp. 17–37; G. Mannerheim, *Erinnerungen*, pp. 425–42.
19. W. Erfurth, *Der finnische Krieg 1941–1944*, p. 39.
20. A Lapp trail is a path used by the native Lapps for movement with toboggans and reindeer. Such paths can lead over hills and even, mainly in winter, over lakes. Marked by stacked stones at regular intervals, they are nothing like roads, and can only be traversed on foot during the summer. For the troops, these trails represented nothing more than lines along which they could move.
21. Every light mountain infantry column had a platoon of 15 Austro-Daimler or Steyr half-track vehicles that had been used by the former Austrian Army. The caterpillar tracks were too narrow and too weak for the terrain here.
22. General von Le Suire, unpublished war diary, 29 June 1941.
23. Hitler's chief military adjutant, Lieutenant-Colonel on the General Staff Rudolf Schmundt, briefly visited the commander of the mountain corps on 6 July. When asked about the details of the reported plans for an English landing, Schmundt said that there were no particular signs of such plans. It had much more to do with Hitler's assumption that the British could exploit the situation in the Arctic to inflict some damage at little cost. With such an action, British support for the Soviet Union would get underway (General von Le Suire, unpublished war diary, 6 July 1941, 7:20 am). On 12 July, General Dietl addressed a memorandum to the commander of Army Norway, Colonel-General von Falkenhorst, referring to the remarks of the Norwegian ambassador in Lisbon and providing his assessment of the possibility of an English landing in North Norway or on the Murman coast. See also Loßberg, *Im Wehrmachtführungsstab*, p. 74.
24. On 5 July 1941, the security group in Petsamo comprised the 68th Bicycle Battalion, one platoon of the 55th Anti-Tank Battalion, the headquarters and two batteries of the 504th Army Coastal Artillery Battalion, the Finnish Tiitola Border Guard Company, the Finnish Turi Border Guard Company (in the process of being activated at that time), and the Finnish Tähtelä Battery.
25. In contrast to what is described in Erfurth, *Der finnische Krieg 1941–1944*, p. 49, there could be no relief for the mountain corps in this situation. Enemy reinforcements and our own heavy losses counteracted the arrival of both battalions of the Finnish 14th Infantry Regiment.
26. From the personal notes of the author in 1941.
27. On 10 July, the 2nd Mountain Division formed a branch headquarters under the second orderly officer, Captain Clima, to take care of the supply of the distant front at the neck of Rybachy Peninsula and in the area of the mouth of the Titovka River. This would lighten the load of the divisional quartermaster unit, which was extremely busy with the supply of the main front. The performance of this branch headquarters was outstanding. It was soon placed directly under the command of the mountain corps and was designated the Supply Headquarters North. Its location was approximately 4 kilometres north-west of Titovka, on the road to Kutovaya.

28. Group Braun was composed of the 4th Machine-Gun Battalion (until 30 August), the I Battalion of the 137th Mountain Infantry Regiment (until 10 August), the 68th Bicycle Battalion, the Finnish Tiitola Company, the 4th Battery of the 111th Mountain Artillery Regiment, and the 1st Battery of the 112th Mountain Artillery Regiment. From 30 August, all that remained in the Duchy under what had become Group Fleischauer were the 68th Bicycle Battalion and the Tiitola Company.
29. See Hildén, 'Die Murmanbahn', p. 8. The seizure by the Finns of the southern section of the Murman Railway between Lakes Ladoga and Onega did nothing to sever the connection between Murmansk and the interior of the Soviet Union. In fact, this connection remained intact throughout the entire war.
30. An advance officer is a general staff officer sent ahead of his unit with a small task force.
31. Before the war, Lieutenant-General Konrad had been the commander of the 100th Mountain Infantry Regiment (of the 1st Mountain Division) and then the chief of staff of the XVIII Mountain Corps (at that time based in Salzburg, with the 2nd and 3rd Mountain Divisions under its command).
32. The 35-kilometre path that led from Nautsi to Talvikylä, partly a cart road, was converted into a proper road for motor vehicles during the summer and autumn of 1941. It was fully open to traffic on 4 December.
33. By 15 September, the civil road-construction unit of Savolainen Engineering was for the most part no longer in the area of the mountain corps.
34. Note in the unpublished war diary of General von Le Suire, 5 September 1941.
35. Dietl & Herrmann, *General Dietl*, p. 231.
36. Dietl & Herrmann, *General Dietl*, p. 252.
37. Erfurth, *Der finnische Krieg 1941–1944*, p. 72. See also Erfurth, 'Das Problem der Murmanbahn', *Wehrwissenschaftliche Rundschau*, no. 6 (1952), pp. 293–96, especially with regard to the plan to head towards Soroka and the problem of a combined effort on the Finnish front.
38. Dietl & Herrmann, *General Dietl*, p. 233.
39. Speer Bridge and the connecting road there were only completed in the summer of 1942.
40. This had no perceptible effect.
41. General Dietl had obtained authorisation from the OKW to make the ration quantities of the prisoners of war in the area of Army Lapland higher than was usually the case in the Reich or on other fronts. These better ration quantities were maintained in Scandinavia to the north of the Arctic Circle until the end of the war. As a result, the work of the prisoners was outstanding. In Norway in 1945, approximately 75,000 prisoners had been used by Organisation Todt for the construction of a railway line from Mo i Rana to Fauske (heading towards Narvik).
42. The Supply and Transport Office of the Wehrmacht in Scandinavia had been created at the beginning of the Norwegian campaign in 1940. When it was also

entrusted with the transportation of goods to Africa in 1942, it was renamed the Supply and Transport Office of the Wehrmacht Overseas.

43. The senior quartermaster effectively had the authority of the quartermaster general when it came to the outlying post of the OKH in Scandinavia. He was authorised to act independently in determining what armaments were needed and in deciding what equipment should be issued to the troops of newly activated units. He was also in control of the army supply troops, of adapting general supply practices in accordance with conditions in Scandinavia, and of ensuring the constant flow of supplies to the Arctic Front.
44. A bill of lading is a document given to a ship captain after he has received the goods to be transported which obliges him to hand over the cargo to the correct recipient at the end of the journey. This is the international convention which was agreed to in Brussels on 25 August 1924. A copy of the bill of lading is also posted to the recipient.
45. Large ships that arrived in Kemi could only be unloaded in the roadstead, as the harbour had gradually become too shallow with the geological rise of the coast.
46. Each of the three German corps in Lapland had a special truck and trailer, procured from Sweden, with washing troughs, centrifuges, drying drums, and water heaters (trailer). This meant that the undergarments of as many as 600–800 men (i.e. a battalion) could be washed and cleaned in one day.
47. For example, see Erfurth, *Der finnische Krieg 1941–1944*, pp. 115, 285, 289, 308, 312.
48. Work commenced on the construction of two batteries of 15cm guns, two batteries of 21cm guns, and one battery of 21cm howitzers on 21 October 1941. This work was completed in 1942. Meanwhile, the navy installed a heavy naval coastal battery (Battery Sensenhauer) on Numeroniemi (Cape Romanov).
49. The enemy naval unit was made up of between two and four light cruisers, approximately seven destroyers, two merchantmen, and several small ships. Landings took place in Moskenesøya, Værøy, and Røst. Communication stations were destroyed and coastal security installations were damaged, but fishing facilities remained untouched. On 29 December at 1315 hours, a naval formation consisting of one battleship, two cruisers, eight destroyers, two torpedo boats, and 10 merchantmen was sighted 200 kilometres to the west of Lofoten. This was not at all a convoy with supply ships. What would 10 transports be doing in a standby position off the coast?
50. This route was always muddy. The subsoil was composed of the same type of wet silt as that of the terrace that had slid down the Petsamonjoki Valley. The men, with their pack animals, chose to wade through the shallow water along the sandbanks of the fjord rather than run the risk of sinking into the mud.
51. Kammel replaced the missing corps artillery commander from 22 July 1941. His replacement was Lieutenant-Colonel Ritter von Mehlem (from the I Battalion of the 112th Mountain Artillery Regiment).

Bibliography

Unpublished resources

Pages from the unpublished war diaries of:

Colonel-General Dietl (war diary memoranda, diary)

General of Mountain Troops von Le Suire (war diary text without appendices, 19 June to 31 December 1941)

Personal information, notes, and maps from:

General of Mountain Troops (ret.) Feurstein (commander of the 2nd Mountain Division)

Major-General (ret.) Herrmann (IIa of Mountain Corps Norway)

Captain (ret.) Schulze-Hinrichs (6th Destroyer Flotilla)

Colonel on the General Staff (ret.) Gartmayr (Ia of the 6th Mountain Division)

Colonel on the General Staff (ret.) Heß (quartermaster of Mountain Corps Norway)

Lieutenant-Colonel on the General Staff (ret.) Fussenegger (Ib of the 2nd Mountain Division)

Major (ret.) Fichtl (111th Mountain Artillery Regiment)

Major (ret.) Dr Enzinger (112th Mountain Artillery Regiment)

Published resources

137th Mountain Infantry Regiment, *Der Kampf des Gebirgsjägerregiments im Feldzug gegen Rußland 1941*, internally published account for regimental members, 1943.

Bessel-Lorck. *Kampf an der Liza*. Reval: Revaler Verlags- und Druckerei-Gesellschaft mbH., 1942.

Buchner, Alex. *Gebirgsjäger an allen Fronten*. Hannover: Sponholtz Verlag, 1954.

Buchner, Alex. 'Angriff in der Tundra'. *Wehrkunde*, no. 12 (1955).

Dietl, Gerda-Luise & Herrmann, Kurt. *General Dietl*. Munich: Münchner Buchverlag, 1951.

Drinkuth, Rudolf. 'Wir fuhren gen Norden'. Reprint in the annual *Der Wagen*. Lübeck: G. H. Rathgens Verlag, 1940.

Erfurth, Dr Waldemar. *Der finnische Krieg 1941–1944*. Wiesbaden: Limes-Verlag, 1950.

Erfurth, Dr Waldemar. 'Das Problem der Murmanbahn'. *Wehrwissenschaftliche Rundschau*, nos 6 & 7 (1952).
Heß, Wilhelm. 'Kriegsschauplatz Lappland'. In the book published by the OKH Inspectorate of Transport Troops, *Fahrplan Lappland*. Höchstadt an der Aisch: Mens-Verlag, 1943.
High Command of the Twentieth Mountain Army. *Bilder aus Lappland*. Rovaniemi, 1942.
Hildén, Kaarlo. 'Die Murmanbahn'. Pamphlet. Helsinki: Suomen Kirja, 1942.
Hölter, Hermann. *Armee in der Arktis*. Bad Nauheim: Podzun Verlag, 1953.
Hubatsch, Dr Walther. *Die deutsche Besetzung von Dänemark und Norwegen 1940*. Göttingen: Musterschmidt Verlag, 1952.
Kranz, Kurt. *Winteralltag im Urwald Lapplands*. Berlin: Wilhelm Limpert Verlag, 1944.
Loßberg, Bernard von. *Im Wehrmachtführungsstab*. Hamburg: H. H. Nölke Verlag, 1949.
Mannerheim, Gustaf. *Erinnerungen*. Zürich & Freiburg: Atlantis-Verlag, 1952.
Maurach, Dr Bruno. 'Die militärische Bedeutung der Sowjet-Arktis'. *Wehrkunde*, no. 8 (1955).
Pantenburg, Vitalis. *Rußlands Griff um Nordeuropa*. Leipzig: Schwarzhaupter-Verlag, 1938.
Pruck, Erich. 'Der Drang zum Pol'. *Wehrwissenschaftliche Rundschau*, no. 9 (1955).
Ruppert, Dr. *Front am Polarkreis*. Berlin: Wilhelm Limpert Verlag, 1943.
Ruppert, Dr. *Wir vom linken Flügel*. Rovaniemi: 640th Propaganda Company, 1943.
Wehrmacht propaganda officer at the Wehrmacht Command in Norway. *Unser Kampf im Norden: Rückschau auf das Jahr 1941*. Oslo: Aas & Wahl, 1942.
Weinberger, Andreas. *Das narrende Licht*. Kameraden im Kampf series, vol. 5. Munich: Schild-Verlag, 1952.

Pages from the following newspapers were referred to:

Die Gebirgstruppe, newsletter of the Kameradenkreis der deutschen Gebirgstruppe, Munich, from 1952.
Lappland-Kurier, publication of Army Lapland for German soldiers in North Finland 1942–44, Rovaniemi.
Wacht im Norden, publication of Army Norway for German soldiers in Norway 1940–45, Oslo.

The author would like to express his most profound thanks for the comradely support and help that he has received.

Index